CU00852990

Words and Deeds

An Introduction to the Thought of Ludwig Wittgenstein

Stephen Loxton

2018

Words and Deeds

Published by New Generation Publishing in 2018

The cover photograph is of the Sogne Fjiord in Norway where Wittgenstein's hut was built in 1914.

First Edition

www.newgeneration-publishing.com

New Generation Publishing

Words and Deeds

For Moreblessing

'All philosophy is a "critique of language".' (T 4.0031)

'In philosophy the winner of the race is the one who can run most slowly. Or: the one who gets to the winning post last.' (CV p. 40)

'Language is a labyrinth of paths. You approach from one side and know your way about; you approach the same place from another side and no longer know your way about.' (PI I 203)

'Our talk gets its meaning from the rest of our proceedings.' (Z 229)

'Ethics so far as it springs from the desire to say something about the ultimate meaning of life, the absolute good, the absolute valuable, can be no science. What it says does not add to our knowledge in any sense. But it is a document of a tendency of the human mind which I personally cannot help respecting deeply and I would not for my life ridicule it'. (PO p. 44)

Contents

Forward

This book is, as the subtitle says, an introduction to the thought of Ludwig Wittgenstein (1889-1951), arguably the most significant philosopher of modern times. As such, it is written for anyone interested in philosophy, the history of thought, or in the life and thought of Wittgenstein. The aim is to provide a guide to some of the most central concerns Wittgenstein had and to explore the issues that arise from these. It is introductory in character, in that no prior knowledge of philosophy is required. Consistent with this, issues and other thinkers discussed will be given the background explanation that is required. Insofar as these explanations relate to some wider points on the philosophical agenda, this book also serves as a kind of introduction to philosophy. This links back to the study of Wittgenstein, in the sense that as we study a great thinker in the philosophical tradition, we cannot avoid being drawn into the study of philosophy.

The title of the book, 'Words are Deeds', serves a dual-purpose. As a philosopher, Wittgenstein has a sustained interest in language, in the logic that he thought to underpin language, and in the problem of how language works to communicate valid meaning. Here he operates as the embodiment of a true philosopher, in that he is concerned with matters that most people take wholly for granted. Whereas we ordinarily assume that language works and that we can just get on and communicate in our exchanges, Wittgenstein asks, how does language work? How is meaningful communication possible? His concern is with the issues of how we know truth from error in the statements we read, hear or make, and with the matter of how we make valid statements: how are we able to say what is real, and distinguish it from what is nonsense? And

1

how is it that we can understand expressions and phrases that we have never heard before?

Wittgenstein has a lot to say about these matters. In one phase of his career he took the view that words (and so language) worked, and so had meaning, through a picturing or modelling relation between a name and an object. On this view, a word stands for and, via a form of modelling, points to the object that it names. This is rather like what happens in everyday speech when someone holds up a pen and says, 'This is my pen.' Gradually, Wittgenstein widened this view, and moved towards the idea that the real significance of words (and so language) was that it reflected the pattern of human activity, so that the meaning of word, and in a related sense, of human intention, was best understood as an act or deed within that flow of activity. On this view, the meaning of a word was shown through the way it was used. If someone is asked, for example, as they return from their working day, how the day went, they might say 'Fine', but what this means depends on how it is said, on the intonation, stress, and emphasis and on the body-language signals, that might, in point of fact, mean the reverse of the common meaning of 'fine'.

As well as looking at the views Wittgenstein developed on language, this book will also consider some of his ideas that arise from his thinking on some other matters. In particular, we will consider his views about the point and purpose of philosophy, for Wittgenstein had distinctive ideas here that are a considerable contrast with much in the philosophic tradition. We will also look at his ideas in the areas of ethics and religion, areas which mattered to him, again, in a quite significant manner. In making our review we will be citing a good deal of what Wittgenstein wrote. There are some of his ideas that we will look at on several occasions as we tease out their implications in different contexts. For all this, there is, however, much else that Wittgenstein wrote on, such as the philosophy of mathematics, philosophical psychology and the philosophy of mind, that go beyond what this study will consider. Finally, in an earlier book, *Religious Language*[1], I briefly covered some of Wittgenstein's ideas about language in connection with the issues and concerns arising in the philosophy of religion; within this book, I have recast and extended this material.

---

[1] Loxton, S. (2013) *Religious Language* PushMe Press, Wells.

A note on Wittgenstein's writings

From early in his adult life until almost the end, Ludwig Wittgenstein had a working habit which was to think with great intensity about the problems he was interested in. As they emerged, his ideas were then, as a rule, written down, almost always in German, as a series of remarks in notebooks, dozens of which were left at the time of his death. From time to time, however, Wittgenstein would select a series of his remarks to revise, elaborate and rewrite. He would often cut and paste remarks from other notebooks into the revision. If the revision reached a point that seemed right to him, he would send it to be typed. But it seems that invariably, by the time the typescript returned, his mind was moving on, and so the manuscript might be filed in a shoe-box or sometimes a box-file, the means by which Wittgenstein stored his work. Alternatively, the manuscript might then be the basis for another round of revision, re-thinking, and re-writing. Wittgenstein published only one philosophical book in his lifetime – *Tractatus Logico-Philosophicus* (1922)[2]. Since his death, including the *Philosophical Investigations* (1953), well over a dozen other texts of his writings have appeared It is the case with Wittgenstein, more than with any other thinker, that his method of composition was subordinate to his routine of work. This gave his literary executors a mighty task after his death in working out how to deal with the mass of manuscripts and notebooks he left.

A consequence of Wittgenstein's method of writing is that his works are made up from a sequence of often quite brief

---

[2] Originally the text was published in 1921 in a German periodical. The first English translation was published in 1922 and another in 1961. The work is invariably referred to as the *Tractatus*.

remarks. These are written in a wide range of ways, sometimes as open reflections, sometimes as questions, sometimes as criticism of another view, sometimes as assertions of a view Wittgenstein currently favours and often as one of a series of developmental points, and so on. Due to this, it is often tempting, but potentially quite misleading, to selectively quote Wittgenstein. The danger is that if we do, we can in this way 'interpret' Wittgenstein in a way that suits us, rather than him. In what follows, the aim is to portray Wittgenstein's thinking on the topics we review by giving a good range of illustrative quotations, so the shape and direction of his thinking can be shown.

As indicated, there is now a long list of works attributed to Wittgenstein, and these are of two main types. Some of the works are particular manuscripts the literary executors selected and then translated for publication. Works such as *Philosophical Investigations*[3] and *Philosophical Remarks* (1975) are of this type. Others are made from selections from the notebooks on a particular theme and/or from a specific period of Wittgenstein's life – for example, *Culture and Value* (1977; 2nd edition 1994), *Philosophical Grammar* (1974), and *Zettel* (1969).

Wittgenstein's works are available in a number of editions, and those consulted in this work, and the abbreviations used, are indicated below. Some of the texts used are German/English editions with the German and then the English translation (e) on the facing page. Needless to say,

---

[3] As a text *Philosophical Investigations* is usually seen as being in two parts, the first of which contains 693 numbered sections. These are quoted after the abbreviation 'PI I'. Part II, as it is was known in the original translations, is more varied in character. In the 4th edition of the text, Part II is retitled *Philosophical Psychology – A Fragment*, and the text is in 24 sections with a sequence of 372 numbered sub-sections. Quotations from this section are abbreviated as 'PI PPF' and then the sub-section number.

when a passage is cited from these texts, it is from the English translation.

BB. (2003) *The Blue and the Brown Books*, *Preliminary Studies for the 'Philosophical Investigations*, Edited by R. Rhees, Blackwell, Oxford.

BT. (2013) *The Big Typescript: TS 213* Edited and translated by C. Grant Lockhart and M. A. E. Aue, Wiley-Blackwell, Chichester.

CV. (1994) *Culture and Value*, Revised Edition, Edited by G. H. von Wright and Heikki Nyman; translated by Peter Winch; text revised by Alios Pilcher, Blackwell, Oxford.

NB. (2004) *Notebooks 1914-1916* 2nd Edition, Edited by G. E. M. Anscombe and G. H. von Wright; translated by G. E. M. Anscombe, Blackwell, Oxford.

OC. (1972) *On Certainty*, Edited by G. E. M. Anscombe and G. H. von Wright; translated by D. Paul and G. E. M. Anscombe, Harper and Row, N.Y. PG.

PG. (1990) *Philosophical Grammar* Edited by R. Rhees; translated by A. Kenny, Blackwell, Oxford.

PO. (1993) *Philosophical Occasions 1912-1951*, Edited by J. Klagge and A. Nordmann, Hackett, Indianapolis.

PI. (2009) *Philosophical Investigations,* Revised 4th Edition, Translated by G. E. M. Anscombe, P. S. M. Hacker and J. Shulte, Wiley-Blackwell, Oxford.

PR. (1998) *Philosophical Remarks* Edited by R. Rhees; translated by R. Hargeaves and R. White.

T. (1978) *Tractatus Logico-Philosophicus* Translated by D. F. Pears and B. F. McGuiness, RKP, London.

Z. *Zettel* (2007) Edited by G. E. M. Anscombe and G. H. von Wright; translated by G. E. M. Anscombe, University of California Press, Berkley and L.A.

Words and Deeds

1. Introduction

In Trinity College Chapel in Cambridge, there is a memorial tablet to Ludwig Wittgenstein as a Fellow of the College. The inscription is in Latin, but the translation[4] reads as follows:

'Ludwig Wittgenstein, Fellow of this College, Professor of Philosophy in the University for eight years, showed to many a new way of philosophizing, and perceived and taught by examples that reasoning should be freed from the shackles of language, thus yielding an even profounder knowledge of the nature of reality. There was a singular integrity to his devotion to the pursuit of truth. He died in 1951 in his 63rd year.'

The aim of what follows is to explore the 'new way of philosophizing' that Wittgenstein promoted, as well as the sense in which he sought to free reason from 'the shackles of language'. Above that, what we will also find much evidence of is Wittgenstein's 'singular integrity' in his 'devotion to the pursuit of truth', which is really as fine as any definition of the point and purpose of philosophy.

To set the scene for this, in any history of twentieth-century philosophy, a major focus would be on the tradition associated initially with G. E. Moore (1873-1958) and Bertrand Russell (1872-1970). In 1903, Russell published *The Principles of Mathematics* and Moore *Principia Ethica*, and these and other briefer writings, as well as their lecturing and method of argument, moved philosophical thought towards what is generally considered an 'analytical' approach. The major influence that came through Russell in particular, was itself in part

---

[4] This translation comes from McGuinness (2012) p. 480

derived from the methods and concerns of some continental mathematicians, notably the German thinker Gottlob Frege (1848-1925). But within British philosophy, the general influence of Moore and Russell led philosophers to abandon the approach which assumed that philosophical reflection could express fundamental truths about life, the universe, and everything. Instead, they put the focus on making an analysis of epistemological problems, that is to say, problems of what we can, with reasonable justification, say that we know about the nature of reality, and of related questions of meaning and truth. And this style of philosophical analysis operated with an emphasis on the nature and workings of both language and logic. There are related problems here: the epistemological problems of 'how I know what I claim to know' and of 'what can be known', are seen as being closely allied to the question of how, in a reasoned and logical manner, we will know the truth of a statement or proposition that is found in a linguistic form. This is because of the convention that, since what I claim to know is expressed in the form of a claim in sentences that make truth-statements: for most philosophers, such sentences as usually termed 'propositions'.

The connection of logical and epistemological issues here is reflected in the work of Wittgenstein in that one of his great concerns was to focus on the logical issues that enabled language to work, to make sense, and to convey meaning. It would be fair to say that insofar as Wittgenstein puts his focus here, he also thought that many of the other preoccupations of philosophers with the problem of knowledge, as well as with other areas of conventional philosophical interest, were unnecessary and to no benefit.

It is worth exploring the idea that it is by means of propositions that language has communicative sense. To illustrate, the statement 'My keys are on the window-sill in the bathroom' has a propositional character. It makes four truth claims – 'I have some keys', 'There is a bathroom', 'My keys are in the bathroom' and 'The keys are on the window-sill in the bathroom.' The proposition, 'My keys are on the window-sill in the bathroom' makes sense; we could say that it is not, on the face of it, meaningless or nonsensical. But we do not know from the proposition as an assertion that it is true that my keys are really in the bathroom (and on the window-sill). Thus, the proposition is not true by definition: to establish the truth of the proposition, 'My keys are on the window-sill in the bathroom' we would have to investigate the bathroom. If we can confirm the truth of the proposition we can say it is meaningful (and true), and if we fail to confirm the truth-claim of the proposition (say, we found the keys in the kitchen), then the proposition is still meaningful (because we know it to be false). Either way, the proposition has a *synthetic* character; meaning and truth are established by our investigation into the state and condition of the bathroom. This type of proposition may be contrasted with one such as the proposition that 'a triangle is a plane figure where the sum of the lengths of any two sides is equal to or greater than the length of the third side'. This definitional truth would be an *analytic* truth, true in virtue of the meaning of the terms used.

One line of thought puts great emphasis on these ways of calibrating questions of meaning and truth: this is the tradition of thought known as *logical positivism*, as in the form associated with the group of thinkers at the University of Vienna in the 1920s and 1930s known as the 'Vienna Circle' and with the British philosopher A. J. Ayer[5] (1910-1989): according to the logical positivists, a proposition can be meaningful if, but only if, it can be verified *analytically* as being true by definition, or verified

---

[5] See Ayer (1990) especially pp. 16-24 and pp. 171-185

by *synthetic*, i.e. experimental verification. Propositions which fail this test are by default meaningless. We will come across the logical positivists again later in this study.

The broader analytic tradition in modern philosophy also owes much to Wittgenstein, who is distinctive for producing what can be seen as two influential, challenging and partly competitive philosophies. As noted above, the first is embodied in the only philosophical book he published in his lifetime, *Tractatus Logico-Philosophicus* – a work usually referred to as the *Tractatus*. Wittgenstein first published this text in 1921 in a German periodical; it was published in English a year later. His second philosophy began to emerge in his work from about 1929 and is associated particularly with the *Philosophical Investigations*, a text he worked on for some years before his death and which appeared in 1953. As suggested, one view of Wittgenstein's work is that in effect he had first one, and then another rather different philosophical outlook. This view is grounded in the fact that Wittgenstein's *Tractatus* and later the *Philosophical Investigations* were, for several years after the publication of the latter, the two writings of Wittgenstein's in print and between them there were some clear points of contrast. In due course, a substantial body of Wittgenstein's work from the period 1929-1951 was published, and with this emerged a revised view, that, despite the distinct contrasts that can be drawn between the earlier and later phases, Wittgenstein's philosophical activity is more rather a continuum of developing reflection: thus, the later work is really best seen as an outcome and as a corrective development of the earlier. This developmental view, as taken in this study, where what changes are matters of emphasis and orientation, is consistent with the main strands of scholarship within contemporary studies of Wittgenstein, and it is linked to the consistent view that

Wittgenstein sustains throughout his writing on the core matter of the nature and task of philosophy[6].

This study presents first a general review of the approaches Wittgenstein developed in the work leading to the *Tractatus* and then in the development leading up to and including the *Philosophical Investigations*. The next chapter provides a biographical sketch of Wittgenstein's career up until the time of the publication of the English edition of the *Tractatus* in 1922. Then we undertake an introductory review of the *Tractatus*, with a discussion of some of the criticisms the *Tractatus*' perspective faces. In Chapter 4 we trace the story of Wittgenstein's career through the 1920s, when he began a teaching career in his native Austria, through to his death in Cambridge at the age of sixty-two in 1951. Within this we examine aspects of the philosophy he worked on through this period. In the next chapter, we then look at some of the ideas presented in *Philosophical Investigations*, which Wittgenstein worked on for sixteen years at his own reckoning without ever feeling ready and able to publish in his lifetime. Then we move on to an examination of some criticisms of Wittgenstein's later philosophy. In the subsequent chapters of the book some reactions to Wittgenstein's work are reviewed, and we consider Wittgenstein's emergent ideas on religion, philosophy, and ethics.

Before we set out on the main route of this study, it is worth considering another line of thought that will, in fact, be of particular value in relation to the later study we make of Wittgenstein's approach to language as well as make a link to the ideas of analytic and synthetic considered above. This concerns what happens when we are asked to *define* something.

---

[6] For more on this see Kenny (2006)

Suppose I have three objects before me, and in a social group of, say six of my contemporaries, I hold each object up in turn and ask, 'What is this?'

If all six chorus 'cup' to the first object, 'saucer' to the second, and 'spoon' to the third, I may well be reassured that all six have a sound grasp of all their faculties, for indeed, the three objects are a cup, saucer and spoon. All have been correctly identified and differentiated, and this by means of one way of defining: when we use a name to identify an object, named 'cup' for a certain type of drinking vessel, for example, we are using *ostensive* definition. The idea here is that the name or term points to and stands for the object.

However, sometimes we have a word, such as the word 'pause', where quite obviously the term does not point to an object. We cannot define a word like 'pause' by ostensive definition. Instead, as a rule, we would define it *verbally*, by explaining it via a range of synonyms, words which carry a near to identical meaning within the common vocabulary of English. As the word 'pause' is used to refer to a temporary interruption in some process, action or speech, we might refer to other terms such as 'stop', 'hesitate', 'halt', 'cease', 'desist', 'delay', 'rest', 'wait', or 'interrupt'.

We are here in a pattern of thought shared by many philosophers, whereby the way in which verbal definition works gives support to the idea that some certain, indubitable truths can be derived from exact definitions: 'A spinster is an unmarried woman ' is thus true by definition, and so again, the truth here can be said to be *analytic*: the truth of the proposition is given via an analysis of the meaning of the words used. In contrast, when we consider what is entailed by such a statement as 'There are two dogs in my garden', we find that the proposition points to the truth claims that a) I have a garden and b) that in it are two dogs. Neither truth claim is true by definition: the truth (or error) in the claims will have to be verified by a test or check on circumstance – an investigation as to whether I have a garden and if so, whether there are two dogs in it. Again, truths here are said to be *synthetic*, they emerge from and through an investigation of the mix or synthesis of experience. And it might be guessed that, if it turns out that I have not got a garden or that I have but it is dog-less, the truth claim I made is false; but then we know it is false and so it is still meaningful. We can see from this that issues of definition links to epistemological questions about knowledge and the matter of how we ratify the claims we make about what we consider to be true[7].

As we will see, in one part of his career Wittgenstein is thought to work in such a manner as to reinforce a view that says that all linguistic meaning is checked by the criteria to those of analytic and synthetic reasoning; the ideas of the *Tractatus* were thought by some who read it to imply this.

There is, however, an additional way in which we might define a word, and that is by exploring the way it is used. Wittgenstein moves to this style of definition in a gradual way, but it is clear in the *Philosophical Investigations* where he remarks that 'the meaning of a word is its use in the language.' (PI I. 43) Suppose we take the word 'Yes'.

---

[7] Some philosophers, J. S. Mill (1806-1873) and W. Van Orman Quine (1908-2000) for example have argued that all truth is based on sense experience and on the inductive methods of natural science. On such views, the only truths are contingent as within systems. of understanding or relative to particular experimental parameters. See Mill (1967) and Quine (1953). In effect the position of Mill, and Quine in tends to reduce philosophy to an empirical science, something Wittgenstein, and many other philosophers would not accept.

In English, this word can work as a noun, a verb or an adverb. It can be used to signal agreement, to express assent, to give emphasis. It can be used to express a contrary view ('You can't ride a bike!' 'Yes, I can'). 'Yes' can be used interrogatively to express curiosity, hesitation or doubt; it can be used to express tacit agreement – 'Did you enjoy the film?' 'Yes' – which, depending on intonation, could quite easily mean 'No' or something between the two. Neither verbal nor ostensive definition help here, but definition via looking for the 'meaning in use' does. We shall see how this emerges as we work our way into Wittgenstein's thought.

2. Wittgenstein's Life and Career 1889-1922

Ludwig Wittgenstein was born in Vienna in 1889. He was the youngest of eight children and the family was amongst the richest in Austria. Wittgenstein's father, Karl Wittgenstein (1847-1913), had a varied early life including a period doing a range of jobs in America. He returned to Austria and moved into engineering. He was an intelligent, active and enterprising man, with a dominant personality, and he became highly successful in business, and accumulated a vast fortune as an industrialist with interests in iron and steel manufacture. The Wittgenstein family was of Jewish ancestry, but Karl Wittgenstein's father had converted to Protestantism and Ludwig's mother, Leopoldine, (d. 1926) was a Roman Catholic, into which faith Ludwig was baptised. Karl Wittgenstein's business success was such that he retired in his early fifties, devoting time to writing articles on liberal economics for the Austrian press. Wittgenstein's home was a centre for musical and cultural life in Vienna, and the home was the context for Wittgenstein's early education.

Through childhood Wittgenstein was influenced by his mother's devout Roman Catholicism and later, in adult life, he contemplated taking monastic vows on at least three occasions. He exhibited considerable talent in music; he became a good clarinettist and maintained an ability to learn musical scores by heart. He would then impress friends by whistling whole symphonies through, and all his life he enjoyed intense discussions with professional musicians over styles of interpretation. His brother Paul became a successful concert pianist; despite losing his right hand during the First World War he continued his career and Richard Strauss and Ravel later both wrote piano concertos for him to play with the left hand.

As a boy, Wittgenstein also displayed an interest in design, engineering, and physics. His sister Hermione wrote in a later memoir[8] that at the age of ten Ludwig constructed from wire and wood an operational sewing machine. He did this from an intensive study of the family sewing machine. Nevertheless, his educational ambitions were thwarted when at the age of fourteen his general attainment was so poor that he could not reach the entrance standard set for either the Gymnasium (the grammar school) or the Realschule (the secondary modern school) in Vienna. Accordingly, he was sent to a provincial Realschule in Linz. He was there from 1903-1906, where at the same time, his exact contemporary Adolph Hitler was a student. Although the boys were of the same age, Hitler's progress was so poor he was held back a year, and as Wittgenstein was advanced by one, they were two classes apart.

After school, Wittgenstein's grades were too poor to allow him to transfer to the university in Vienna where he had intended to read physics. He thus studied mechanical engineering at the Technische Hochschule in Berlin from 1906-1908. There he studied a conventional, that is to say, a thorough course, in mechanical and technical engineering, and this included a good deal of physics. By the end he had, through his reading and his natural capacity for critical reflection, started to think about philosophical problems and to write remarks and thoughts into a notebook, a habit that was to remain with him.

Biographical studies of Wittgenstein emphasise the emphatic culture of his home life and although it would seem that he was regarded as something of a below average performer on the academic front, Wittgenstein did not grow up in an intellectual vacuum. He read and knew a

---

[8] 'My Brother Ludwig' in Rhees (1984) p.1

lot of poetry and, as mentioned, was deeply aware of the musical, cultural and intellectual heritage that Vienna was especially rich in[9], as was Berlin, where Wittgenstein studied Engineering. Within this there was, in the late nineteenth and early twentieth century, a great deal of innovative thinking: for example, Sigmund Freud (1856-1939) was developing psychoanalytic theory, Adolf Loos (1870-1933), who the Wittgenstein's knew, was innovating in architecture, and Oswald Spengler (1880-1936) was working up the ideas on cultural history that led to his *Decline and Fall of the West* (1918-1922). Besides these, there are a number of particular influences on his developing mind that we can note.

Like many of his generation in Austria, Wittgenstein was influenced by the writings of Karl Kraus[10] (1874-1936). Kraus was a prolific and influential writer who was concerned to expose hypocrisy and concealment in social life. He was a passionate advocate of authenticity in personal and intellectual life, and his deep fear was that Viennese culture was falling into pettiness, superficiality, and artificiality. A wave of intellectual and moral degeneration was, he thought, arising, and so, using satire, he wrote polemical reviews and criticism to prompt a revival of more informed critical thought. His most notable work was a fortnightly review, *Die Frackel*, to which many other notable writers contributed. This review ran for over 900 issues between 1899 and 1936.[11] Kraus wrote with wit and purpose to defend above all 'artistic honesty and truth'[12], even if this meant writing severely about the ideas of friends. Wittgenstein may well have been

---

[9] On the impact of Viennese life and culture on Wittgenstein see especially Janik and Toulmin (1996)

[10] McGuiness (1988) notes that Kraus's works were in the libraries of the Wittgenstein family.

[11] See Janik and Toulmin (1996) pp. 67-91

[12] Janik and Toumin (1996) p. 69

introduced to Kraus by his elder sister Gretl, and, as we shall see, he certainly seems to imbibe from Kraus the virtue of the primacy of honesty in criticism.

Another thinker who Wittgenstein read was Otto Weininger (1880-1903) who was more or less equally famous and notorious for his 1903 book *Geschlecht und Charakter – Sex and Character*, and for his committing suicide soon after the publication of the book, on the grounds that he could not live up to the ideals expressed within it.

Weininger's ideas have been diagnosed as 'superficial and half-baked at times'[13], which is really something of an understatement. In a manner that aimed to fuse biological as well as psychological factors to an ill-grounded philosophical stance, Weininger presented males and females as exemplifying contrasting ideals, so that in real life, men could only operate with reason, while women would be slaves to emotion and to raw sexual passion. Despite being Jewish, Weininger was fiercely anti-Semitic. He argued that Jews were distinctive in being orientated to the female ideals, all of which were seen as negative. Due to the contrasts he made between genders, Weininger argued that true love would always be corrupted by sexuality, so in effect, all relationships between men and women were doomed. As death is preferable to a life consigned to failure, the logic of Weininger's suicide perhaps becomes clearer.

Wittgenstein does not seem to have bought into the views of Weininger, but he appreciated one strand in Weininger's book, which he hints at in a letter to G. E. Moore, written in 1931,. He says Weininger's work is 'fantastic' – meaning fanciful and so not reasoned or

---

[13] McGuinness (1988) p. 40

wholly plausible – but also '*great* fantastic'[14] . This was by the way in which the work expressed an 'important truth'. The aspect of Weininger's work that Wittgenstein liked was the way in which the ideals of honesty, value, goodness, beauty, and truth were held in tension with the everyday practice of life. Weininger had a distinctive variant of the idea of a categorical moral imperative[15] whereby absolute fidelity to honesty would be the only means by which a person could realise their own potential for creativity and genius. These ideas seem to have had an abiding impact on Wittgenstein, who felt and wrestled with the tensions here, and we will see evidence of this in his life and writing later on.

Wittgenstein also read a book, *Principles of Mechanics* by Henrich Hertz (1857-1896), a German physicist who had done original work on electro-magnetic waves. His work, as well as that of another scientist Wittgenstein read, the Austrian mathematical physicist Ludwig Boltzmann (1844-1906), gave the insight, that science gave 'a picture or model created by the mind, often with the utmost daring and freedom'.[16] Hertz favoured the ideas that problems could always be tackled fruitfully by thinking out new possible solutions, new models or pictures. That ideas, true ideas, can be presented via a 'picture' or a 'model' was to stick in Wittgenstein's mind.

---

[14] McGuinness (2012) p. 193

[15] The idea of the categorical imperative is associated with Kant's moral philosophy and entails the notion that a good act is done for its own sake and in line with the theoretical possibility of the act being universalisable, i.e., one that could be done again and again for like circumstances with equal integrity. Universalisability gives the *form* of the categorical imperative; its *content* is given by the idea that a person, as a centre of rational autonomy, must always be treated as an end, and never only as a means; the teleological *goal* of the good act is, finally, that is must be done as something that could be applied in the hypothetical 'kingdom of ends'. See Kant (1907) pp. 47ff

[16] McGuiness (1988) p. 39

Another focus for Wittgenstein's reading when a student was Schopenhauer's *World as Will and as Representation* (1818/1844), which famously portrays the immediate external world of sensation as a world of appearance or representation. For Schopenhauer (1788-1860), the only ultimate reality is that of the impersonal Will of which the individual's will is an instance, and a person's ethical will the best instance by means of which an ethic of compassion can ameliorate the impersonal suffering of the world. Interestingly, given Wittgenstein's preference for writing his philosophical thoughts in brief comments, something Schopenhauer also did sometimes, it is also thought[17] that Wittgenstein was familiar with the writings of G. C. Lichtenberg (1742-1799), an academic physicist who produced a long series of writing in an aphoristic style, as in the following examples:

'He swallowed a lot of knowledge, but it seemed as if most of it had gone down the wrong way.'

'He who is enamoured of himself will at least have the advantage of being inconvenienced by few rivals.'

'A handful of soldiers is always better than a mouthful of arguments.'

'The fly that does not want to be swatted is safest if it sits on the fly-swatter.'[18]

We see here the basic qualities of an aphorism, which is that each one provides a condensed and acute expression

---

[17] See Janik and Toulmin p. 176

[18] These are quoted from 'G. C. Lichtenberg: a "spy on humanity" by Roger Kimball, in 'The New Criterion', May 2002, online at www.newcriterion.com/issues/2002/5/g-c-lichtenberg-a-ldquospy-on-humanityrdquo

of an insight or experience which the reader has to think about to unpack and consider. This makes quite a demand on the reader, we may feel that we are doing the writer's work for him, for, of course, an aphorism is always something that is not literal, but, to some degree, metaphorical. As we should appreciate, Wittgenstein has much in his work in an aphoristic form that rivals all other users of this genre of expression. Here, as a slight spoiler, are some examples[19] from his writings:

'The world of the happy man is a different one from the unhappy man.' (T 6.4311)

'It is not *how* things are in the world that is mystical, but *that* it exists.' (T 6.44)

'If someone is merely ahead of his time, it will catch up with him one day.' (CV p. 11)

'One can mistrust one's own senses, but not one's own belief.' (PI I 91)

Wittgenstein was also influenced by the work of the journalist Fritz Mauthner (1846-1923). Mauthner was a creative writer, producing some novels and plays, but a large part of his time was spent as a theatre critic and social commentator. He read widely and developed several key approaches to inform his thinking. He was convinced that ideas and theories were all expressive of particular individual experiences. Even language, he thought, was primarily the operational expression of the individual; only in and through social interaction was social language developed. Mauthner also thought that humans had a fatal habit of thinking that their ideas and theories were real and true. Against this, Mauthner maintained a sceptical view

---

[19] There are some more examples of Wittgenstein's remarks as the frontispiece to this book.

and defended this by making what he termed 'a critique of language' to show the individualised origin of language and thought. In effect, Mauthner was proposing a psychological critique of language. This Wittgenstein seems aware of, but due to the cast of his mind and the way in which he later conceived philosophical problems, when he writes that philosophy is wholly a 'critique of language' (T 4.0031) he immediately adds that this is 'not in Mauthner's sense' but in the style that was exemplified by Russell. Wittgenstein was, in a manner much more in line with Russell, making a critique through an analysis of the logical rather than the psychological aspects of language.

Mixing Kraus, Mauthner, and Hertz with Weininger, Lichtenberg, and Schopenhauer you get the imperatives of intellectual honesty and of the ethical will, as well as a concern to live in the here and now rather than in relation to some kind of metaphysical reality. From these writers, you might also get regard for the breadth of life and suspicion of narrow areas of specialist expertise, as well as a sense of the way in which language could be abused unless it was critically refined. Writing with precision, economy and in an aphoristic rather than elaborate and esoteric manner would come through too. And reliance on your own ability, and your own capacity to picture or model truth, could also be held in a cumulative package of influence. The point is that Wittgenstein has, through his upbringing in Vienna, a stimulus to encourage, equip and inform philosophical investigation. It has been suggested[20] that, in effect, the outline for a critical examination of language by means of models, and with an ethical purpose, was all in place from the wider influences of Viennese culture, and this was in place before Wittgenstein began to employ the logical techniques gained from his more focussed contacts with Frege and Russell.

---

[20] Janik and Toulmin (1996) p. 168

In later life, in 1931, Wittgenstein wrote self-reflectingly on his career and paid a notably selfless tribute to what we just termed the 'package of influence':

'I think there is some truth in my idea that I am really only reproductive in my thinking. I think I have never *invented* a line of thinking but that it was always provided for me by someone else & I have done no more than passionately take it up for my work of clarification. This is how Boltzmann, Hertz, Schopenhauer, Frege, Russell, Kraus, Loos, Spengler, Sraffa have influenced me.' (CV p. 16)[21]

Nevertheless, whilst philosophical interests were present in Wittgenstein's emerging outlook and mind-set, on balance, in 1908 his main drive was to continue the study of engineering. Here the influence of, and his respect for his father were probably leading factors.

Alongside his wider reading and emerging interest in philosophical questions, Wittgenstein had developed an interest in the very new science of aeronautical engineering. Five years after the first heavier than air flight by the Wright brothers, there was only one place to go to study aeronautical engineering: to pursue this interest Wittgenstein moved in 1908, to Manchester, England. The University of Manchester, as it happened, was the only university that had established a section in its Engineering Department for aeronautical engineering. Wittgenstein did not arrive in Manchester as an undergraduate, for he possessed his Certificate in Engineering from Berlin. Due to this qualification, he was given a job as a research assistant. He was sent to the Upper Atmosphere Research Station near Glossop, in Derbyshire. The research work was on various wing configurations tested on experimental

---

[21] Wittgenstein met the economist Piero Sraffa (1898-1883) in Cambridge after returning there in 1929. See Chapter 4 below.

kites flown on cables to high altitudes from the Derbyshire peaks. Wittgenstein worked with another student, William Eccles (1875-1966). He and Eccles became friends, and the two remained in correspondence with for most of the rest of Wittgenstein's life. To develop his own work further Wittgenstein also registered as a research student at Manchester University (1908-1911), although he also spent much of his time in Austria. He worked up and patented ideas for a jet propulsion engine for aircraft, planning a combustion chamber that sent power through jet nozzles at the tips of a rotor blade, an idea applied later by various manufacturers in the nineteen fifties[22]. At the same time, however, Wittgenstein's philosophical interests were continuing. He was having trouble finding the right mathematical techniques for solving some of the problems arising from his designs and was reading Bertrand Russell's *The Principles of Mathematics* (1903). In this way, Wittgenstein was led to mathematical philosophy and to the work of both Frege (the famous German mathematician, who was known to the family) and, of course, to Bertrand Russell himself.

In reading Russell's work Wittgenstein became intrigued by some of the paradoxical issues that were raised. *The Principles of Mathematics* was written to develop the view that mathematics, in general, was in fact grounded on a relatively small number of logical principles. The relation of logical truth to mathematics and also to grammar and so to language was to be the focus of Wittgenstein's developing interest.

---

[22] There is a very informative paper explaining, illustrating and assessing Wittgenstein's designs: 'Wittgenstein's Combustion Chamber' by J. Cater and I. Lemco, Notes and Records of the Royal Society, (2009) **63** 95-104, published online 06/01/09 – rsnr.royalsocietypublishing.org/content/63/1/95

One famous aspect of Russell's work involved the concept of classes. The key idea here was that each particular instance of a concept could be said to belong thereby, to the class of such concepts. To take an everyday example, let us say that Sam, Mike, and Gary are instances of the concept 'Male' and so belong to the class of 'Males'. Michelle, Mary, and Mavis are all female and they all belong to the class of 'Females'. We could then say that all human males and females belong to the class of 'Humans'. Russell had detected a logical problem in this system of classes[23]. It seemed obvious that some classes would belong to themselves and that some would not. Russell then considered whether those classes which are not members of themselves are, as such, a class. It seemed that one could argue that the class of all classes was itself a class and it belonged to itself. On the other hand, the class of all males was not itself a male, and so is not a member of itself. Russell thought that one could then have a class of all classes that do not belong to themselves, but his concern was that this was a contradictory concept. Could the class of all classes that were not in membership with themselves constitute a class in which those classes making up the class have membership with themselves? It seemed that they could, but if, and only if, they were not – a contradiction.

The problem of resolving this, was Russell realised, a threat to the plan to show that mathematics rested on a coherent system of logical principles. And he then thought that he was grappling with a paradox akin to a classical Greek puzzle associated with Epimenides the Cretan, who is said to have asserted, 'All Cretans are liars'. The paradox is that if this statement is true, then as it is said by a Cretan it must be false. But if it is true and false it breaks the intellectual and logical principle of non-contradiction –

---

[23] He writes about this in his *Autobiography* – see Russell (1975a) p. 150f

the view that statement cannot be both true and false. Russell suggests that much the same point can be made by taking a piece of paper. On one side of it you write:

> The statement on the other side of this paper is false.

On the other side of the piece of paper you write as follows:

> The statement on the other side of this paper is true.

In *The Principles of Mathematics,* Russell suggested a working solution to the problem of paradox via his 'Theory of Types'. According to this theory, concepts or entities could be placed into distinct 'types' of classes. Everything could be placed into a class of a given type, or a type of classes, and, as no class is an individual, no class can ever be a member of itself; it would always be a 'type'. This means that the problem of those classes that are not members of themselves dissolves, for to be a member of itself would be disabled by the concepts of type, within which the key idea was that truth would be calibrated in assessing the relationship between a judgement and a fact.

In 1909 Wittgenstein wrote up some ideas on the problems he found in Russell's work. He posted these to the Cambridge mathematician Philip Jourdain (1879-1919)[24]. It is thought that Wittgenstein had come across Jourdain's name from an article in a journal he read in Manchester. Jourdain apparently discussed the ideas with Russell at this

---

[24] See Monk (1991) p. 33

point, and neither thought there was anything by way of a valid solution in the work. Wittgenstein continued his reflections, however, and by the time he went back to Austria in 1911 he had elaborated more ideas. He duly arranged to meet Frege in Jena and said later that Frege 'wiped the floor with him'[25] in the discussion. Whether he did or not, Frege did not think so ill of Wittgenstein's ideas or interest as to wholly deter him; he advised that when Wittgenstein went back to England he should go and meet Russell. Wittgenstein followed this advice.

Russell at this stage was thirty-nine, a lecturer at Trinity College, a prolific writer and perhaps the most famous philosopher and mathematician alive. Quite apart from the innovative work he had done himself, he had spent over a decade working intensely with A. N. Whitehead (1861-1947) on *Principia Mathematica*[26], a major three-volume work on mathematics viewed as a system of symbolic logic. As to the meeting with Wittgenstein, what happened was that in October 1911 Wittgenstein arrived, without prior notice, at Russell's room in Trinity, whilst Russell was engaged in discussion with a student, C. K. Ogden (1889-1957). Ironically, Ogden would, a decade later, be involved in the publication and translation of the *Tractatus*. In a letter to his lover, Lady Ottoline Morrell (1873-1938), Russell reports on the arrival of an 'unknown German... speaking very little English but refusing to speak German'.[27] Russell (failing yet to realise that Wittgenstein was Austrian) professed to be 'interested' in 'his German', noting his 'passion for philosophy'; he came

---

[25] Wittgenstein told this to his friend M. O'C Drury, see 'Conversations with Wittgenstein', in Rhees (1984) p. 110.

[26] The work was published 1910-1913. Russell describes the problems and costs of bring the work to publication in his *Autobiography*: Russell (1975) p. 155

[27] BR to OM 18-10-11. Russell's letters are reproduced variously in his *Autobiography* (Russell 1975a), in Monk (1991) pp. 38-39 and 80-82, and in Griffin, N. (2002a) pp. 385ff and pp. 404ff

to Russell's next lecture and thereafter, to tea, to discuss matters further. Russell then reported that 'my German friend threatens to become an affliction, he came back with me after my lecture & argued until dinner-time – obstinate & perverse, but not, I think stupid'.[28]

Russell certainly found Wittgenstein's questioning a challenge, but his view moved, from puzzlement to wonder, as he quickly began to appreciate Wittgenstein's penetrating intensity of mind. Russell noted that Wittgenstein possessed '*genius*', and that 'he gives passionate admiration with vehement and very intelligent dissent.'[29] Russell promoted Wittgenstein within the intellectual fraternity of Cambridge, getting him, in November 1912, membership of the elite group 'the Society', also known as 'the Apostles'. Needless to say, Wittgenstein rapidly tired of such a group.[30]

Much later, in his *Autobiography*, Russell wrote that Wittgenstein 'was perhaps the most perfect example I have ever known of genius as traditionally conceived, passionate, profound, intense and dominating'.[31] Russell writes that by the end of the first term of their work, Wittgenstein (by now, at last, noted to be Austrian) was unsure of his future, as to whether to pursue philosophy or return to aeronautical engineering. Russell suggested that Wittgenstein write something over the vacation, which Wittgenstein duly did. Russell says, with perhaps a touch of exaggeration, that as soon as he had read the first sentence 'I became persuaded that he was a man of

---

[28] BR to OM 19-10-11

[29] BR to OM 18-03-12. Russell was the first to note Wittgenstein's quality of mind; but throughout his life, right up to his last visits to Ireland and America in the later 1940s, he made this signal impression on his acquaintances.

[30] See McGuiness (1988) pp. 146-155

[31] Russell (1975a) p. 329

genius'.[32] In his letters at the time he explains that the work was 'much better than my English pupils do', and he adds that he will 'encourage' Wittgenstein, who will perhaps 'do great things'.[33] This encouragement of Wittgenstein had a very positive impact on him, doubtless because he had never had such clear praise, support, and encouragement, nor any from such a prominent source as Russell. Wittgenstein also made a strong impression on G. E. Moore, Cambridge's other leading philosopher of the younger generation.

Wittgenstein formally changed his academic allegiance from Manchester to Cambridge early in 1912, but in effect, for five terms, from 1911 to 1913 Wittgenstein became a student in philosophy: he was registered initially as an undergraduate of Cambridge and a student of Trinity College under Russell's supervision. During the May Term of 1912, he was re-registered as an advanced student. He attended some lectures given by Moore, but his main focus was work with Russell, and rapidly this work was undertaken more as between colleagues, rather than as a student-teacher relationship. This was a manifest testimony to the strength of Wittgenstein's mind and character at this time, and equally to Russell's openness to the deep potential that he saw in Wittgenstein. It is also fair to say that Wittgenstein was extremely impressed with much that he found in Russell, whose approach to certain problems were and remained something of a benchmark for him.

As an example of this, we can note that in his *Tractatus*,[34] as well as in his lectures at a later period of his life and work, in 1930[35], Wittgenstein refers to Russell's so-called

---

[32] Russell (1975a) p. 330
[33] BR to OM 23-1-12
[34] See T 4. 0031
[35] See Stern et al (2016) p. 76

'theory of descriptions', in a way suggestive of his seeing it as something that gives the right method and approach for philosophy, with the focus in the logical analysis of language. As the work that Russell and Wittgenstein did together derives in some respects from what Russell was doing when he developed this theory, it is worthwhile explaining it.

Russell first expounded his 'theory of descriptions' in a paper entitled 'On Denoting', which appeared in the journal *Mind* in 1905. He gave another presentation of this theory in his *Introduction to Mathematical Philosophy*, (1919), and there is a clear and more concise account in his *History of Western Philosophy* (1946)[36]

By a 'description', Russell means a phrase:

'... in which a person or thing is designated, not by name, but by some property which is supposed or known to be peculiar to him or it.'[37]

Russell's concern was with the knotty problem of the status of certain expressions, which seem to bear a meaning, even though they don't denote anything that is 'there' in any concrete sense. Let's take an example: in mathematics, '-4' is a valuable figure for certain calculations, but it doesn't refer to anything, yet it is not the same non-thing as zero, or 'nothing'. If we take some linguistic examples, a phrase like 'the present Prime Minister' has propositional meaning, as has the proposition 'the present King of France'; but here the proposition carries meaning even though there isn't 'a present King of France'.

Essentially, the kind of 'nothing' '-4' was, and the sort of meaning a non-existent 'King of France' has, troubled

---

[36] See Russell (1975a) pp. 783-789
[37] Russell (1975b) p. 785

Russell's logical sense of what might count as a legitimate expression of meaning and fuelled his desire for intellectual clarity.

One of the famous propositions that Russell examined in the exposition of his theory was:

'A golden mountain exists.'

This in comparison with the similar proposition:

'The golden mountain exists.'

Here, without using the later vocabulary of Wittgenstein, Russell is orientating philosophical analysis to a 'critique of language' (T 4.0031).

According to Russell, there are slippery dangers in ordinary language. Through the lens of the theory of descriptions, the sentence 'a golden mountain exists' means that there exists an entity, which we can notate as 'x' such that 'x is a golden mountain' is true. Such a sentence is meaningful, though false, as far as we can tell, since, to date, no golden mountain has been found.

The sentence 'the golden mountain exists' is rather different, Russell thinks, from the logical point of view. The word 'the' in this sentence makes it what Russell terms a 'denoting phrase', that it, one that appears to be referring to something, the golden mountain, which is disturbing, since there isn't one, so far as we know.

The problem here is often termed the problem *of negative existential propositions*, meaning, the problems of subjects (like a 'unicorn', or 'the golden mountain') that play a significant role in certain propositions but are subjects we deny exist.

If we take as another example the proposition, 'Elephants exist but unicorns don't exist', and then ask of this, 'What is it that doesn't exist?', the obvious answer is that 'Unicorns don't exist.' But again, this sort of answer seemed odd to Russell, since it appeared to give some sort of significance and status to those Unicorns that don't exist. At one level, this is suggestive of some other realm of 'non-being' or potential being in which unicorns, and various other non-existent entities that are 'different' though equally non-existent, subsist.

Russell's view in its most extensive form was that there had been a long history of error in philosophy and in common sense which tended to be manifest as the assumption that meaningful discourse was possible about seemingly non-existent things, states, or relations, because there was at some level something substantial for which the term employed stood. Russell thought that the theory of descriptions, as an example of clear philosophical syntax, could clarify what was actually going on and what was truly being said or meant. It could also provide some useful nails for the coffin of traditional theology and metaphysics.

If we follow Russell's thinking, based on the theory of descriptions, assertions about unicorns, the golden mountain and the like are defined as hypothetical constructs, and claims like 'a unicorn' or 'the golden mountain exist' into the role of synthetic judgments, open to empirical testing. The theory of descriptions also provides confirmation of the Kantian view that the grammatical function of 'exists' in relation to a predicate is misleading, for 'exists' has a more fundamental logical function[38]. The terms 'existence' and 'exists' operate as summary assertions, that there are objects, states, or

---

[38] See Kant (1978) pp. 504-507

relations in the world of experience to which the description in question refers. 'The' is similar. It denotes and therefore can be misused if we aren't precise in our meaning. 'The golden mountain doesn't exist' thus means, if we translate 'the golden mountain' into 'x', that 'There is no x such that x is the case is true that is both golden and a mountain...'

By way of further illustration, we can follow Hick's example[39]: the assertion 'cows exist' means 'There are x's such that x is a cow is true'. Thus, existence isn't a particular quality of cows, to be put alongside udders, horns, and the various other predicates of the subject-concept 'Cow'; it is the assertion that there are some things in reality to which the subject-concept 'cow', *and* its various qualities and predicates, actually applies.

To illustrate how Russell's theory of descriptions applies in everyday life, suppose that we take a statement from a news report that says, 'The President of the USA is seventy years old'. This statement has propositional meaning by Russell's criteria, because it is capable of being tested for its truth or falsity. If there is an individual (x) such as the one posited in the assertion, who is the President of the USA, who is seventy years old, then the assertion is true. But if one or the other of these claims is not met by the individual then it is false. If, however, we assert the very similar claim that 'The Queen of Germany is seventy years old', we acquire a problem over the meaningfulness of the assertion. The statement seems meaningful, but we don't know how to determine its truth or falsity: we feel that it can't be true because there isn't a Queen of Germany, but to say that 'the Queen of Germany is sixty-five years old' is false, seems to imply that the statement 'the Queen of Germany is not sixty-five years of

---

[39] See Hick (1990) p. 19

age' is true, and this, without the theory of descriptions, might cause us some anxiety.

With reference to the core problem of how language works the theory of descriptions has clear implications: it confirms that 'existence' is not a real predicate. Thus, when we describe something by its various qualities – a zebra, say – we say, for example, that it is equine, with black and white stripes, and so on, we are giving the attributes or predicates of the concept in question, 'zebra'. If we then say, 'Zebras exist', we are not adding to the definition of the concept 'zebra', we are claiming that the concept occurs, or has incidence. Going back to the ideas discussed at the start of this book, we could say that defining a zebra in terms of its qualities is an analytic process, and so what is said, if true, is true by definition; when we claim that 'Zebras exist' we are making a synthetic claim, this the truth-claim here is an affirmation that is open to testing. Thus, 'existence' is not a defining predicate, so we can't think or define things into being.

Russell's theory of descriptions entailed a stricter concern to lay bare the logical structure of language; a point that appealed to Wittgenstein, of course. Together, these aspects of Russell's work on the theory of descriptions, as well as the work he had done on mathematical philosophy, gave a clear agenda for the work he and Wittgenstein went on to do.

Through the period 1911-12 and on into 1913 Wittgenstein's work fused with Russell's and became focussed on mathematical philosophy, logic, and philosophical analysis. Wittgenstein worked with great intensity and concentration, displaying passion and dogmatism in argument as well as anxiety and extreme self-doubt about his philosophical ability and vocation. As a measure of the quality of thinking generated through this period, it is worth noting that in 1913, in consequence of Wittgenstein's criticisms, Russell abandoned a book he had half-written on the theory of knowledge

The problem arose because Russell had been engaged to lecture at Boston and Harvard in 1914. With this tour in mind, in May 1913, it seems that he planned a popular series of lectures for Boston and something more novel and challenging for Harvard. With the latter in mind, early in May 1913, he began to write a new work, to be called *Theory of Knowledge*. Within days of starting, Russell reported to Lady Ottoline Morrell that he felt 'as happy as a king' with the progress of the book and with its novelty[40]. But within a fortnight despair had set in. Wittgenstein had discussed the work with Russell on 20th May and had said that 'it could not work' and that 'it was all wrong'. Russell admitted that he couldn't see the fault and that Wittgenstein was 'very inarticulate'. But, and this is the significant admission, Russell wrote that 'I feel in my bones that he must be right, and that he has seen something that I have missed'.[41] Russell went on with the book, feeling that the enjoyment in the process had evaporated and that Wittgenstein would regard him as dishonest for carrying a piece of work when, at some level, he must know it was flawed. But worse was to follow for Russell, in the sense that on 11th June Wittgenstein 'paralysed' him with a precise formulation of his criticism, the burden of which was to do with the nature of logical analysis and the explanation of complex propositions.

This was a problem that in a way goes back to the problems of classes and paradox to which the theory of types was a provisional solution, as well as to the methods of logical analysis in the theory of descriptions. It is also akin to a debate Russell had engaged in with another

---

[40] Russell (1975a) p. 282: BR to OM 8.5.13.
[41] BR to OM 27.5.13; quoted in Monk (1991) pp. 81-82

philosopher, the idealist A. C. Bradley (1846-1924). In 1911 and mainly in the pages of the journal 'Mind', Russell had been defending the idea that the analysis of complex propositions into their constituent parts was a valid means of explaining the true nature of the proposition. Bradley favoured the view that the unity of a complex proposition was of significance, and that a unity was, in fact, no more than its constituent parts. From this, it followed that there was nothing more that logical deconstruction could disclose.[42] Russell defends his view, but notes that as regards the problem of unities, 'I do not pretend to have solved all its problems'.[43]

The snag for Russell was that when he wrote his way confidently into the draft of *Theory of Knowledge*, he still had unresolved problems of the kind he had discussed with Bradley. Specifically, as far as Wittgenstein was concerned, Russell wrote with the assumption that our true beliefs had a correspondence with the complexes that made up reality. He thought that false beliefs were thus those which had no such correspondence and that we had the capacity, through our understanding, to use judgement to differentiate true from false propositions. However, if our understanding of truth and error is cast by the understanding in propositional form, Wittgenstein's insight was that it was not clear from Russell's account as to how this capacity to employ propositions was fitted into his theory of judgement. Russell seemed to think that reality was what it was, in forms that were complex, and that by means of the understanding, we construct what we can judge to be true propositions about the world. Wittgenstein's thought on this was that for it to be operational, the logical possibility of propositional form being right for the task of portraying reality must be prior

---

[42] This debate is detailed in Monk (1997) pp. 198-199
[43] Quoted in Monk (1997) p. 199

to the understanding that we have, that true beliefs can be expressed propositionally.

Wittgenstein expressed his criticism to Russell in a letter written in June 1913, using some technical notation to make explicit the logical problem he saw:

'… I can now express my objection to your theory of judgement exactly. I believe that it is obvious that from the proposition "*A* judges that (say) *a* is in the relation *R* to *b*", if correctly analysed, the proposition "aRb.v. ~ aRb" must follow directly *without the use of any other premiss*. This condition is not me by your theory.'[44]

In his 'Notes on Logic'[45] written soon after, as well as outlining in his *Notebooks 1914-1916* a number of ideas that were to emerge later in the *Tractatus*, Wittgenstein made some more remarks that expressed his criticisms of Russell in more direct terms. First, he clarified that he was dissatisfied with the existing logical notation, another indication of his great confidence. The problem he saw is easy to explain. Suppose you have a proposition, a truth-claiming statement; let us call it 'p'. Logically, you then have the thought that 'p' can be infinitely distinct from all other propositions, 'not-not p, not-not-not p, etc' (NB p. 93). The extension in such a logical scheme to infinity seems to Wittgenstein horribly inexact. As a corrective Wittgenstein suggests that:

'Every proposition which seems to be about a complex can be analysed into a proposition about its constituents and about the proposition which describes the complex

[44] LW to BR June 1913 in NB p. 122. The logical proposition "a R b.v. ~ aRb" is in effect affirming the direct either/or possibilities of the truth or error of the proposition that '*a* is in the relation *R* to *b*'.
[45] The 'Notes on Logic' of 1913 are printed in NB pp. 93-107

perfectly; i.e., that proposition which is equivalent to saying the complex exists.'

On such a view, propositions are either names for complexes and their constituents, or names for 'a relation', a connection that is actual and expressible. The basis of this view is that at root, 'the meaning of a proposition is the fact which actually corresponds to it' (NB p. 94). With calm confidence Wittgenstein moves on to affirm that:

'In my theory, p has the same meaning as not-p, but opposite sense.' (NB p. 95)

Naming, says, Wittgenstein, 'is like pointing'; names 'are points, propositions arrows – they have *sense*. The sense of a proposition is determined by the two poles *true* or *false*' (NB pp. 101-102).

With this scheme in mind, Wittgenstein argues that:

'Whatever corresponds in reality to compound propositions must not be more than what corresponds to their several atomic propositions.' (NB p. 98)

From this, it follows that what it is that 'corresponds in reality to a proposition depends on whether it is true or false. But we must be able to understand a proposition without knowing whether it is true or false', for otherwise, to take a critical example, we would never be able to understand what we can and do understand, namely, 'propositions which we have never heard before.'[46]

All of this helps to get around the problem with Russell's 'laws of deduction', which can be used to make logical inferences, but which 'cannot justify the inferences' (NB

---

[46] See also T 4.02: '… we understand the sense of a propositional sign without its having been explained to us.'

p. 100). But now Wittgenstein has a more exact method of naming, in which, as he writes:

'Only facts can express sense, a class of names cannot.

This is easily shown:

'There is no thing which is the form of the proposition, and no name which is the name of a form. Accordingly we can also not say that a relation which in certain cases holds between things hold sometimes between forms and things. This goes against Russell's theory of judgement.' (NB p. 105)

What Russell's theory is short of is, in Wittgenstein's view, a means to avoid a slippage into nonsense:

'Every right theory of judgement must make it impossible for me to judge that this table penholders the book. Russell's theory does not satisfy this requirement.' (NB p. 103)

Later, in the *Tractatus*, the point is restated:

'The correct explanation of the form of the proposition, "*A* makes the judgement *p*", must show that it is impossible for a judgement to be a piece of nonsense. (Russell's theory does not satisfy this requirement.)' (T 5.5422)

Wittgenstein's drive to develop a more secure logical approach to the explanation of judgement was aimed at getting a secure and tighter system. This aspiration is implied by the remark at the opening of the *Notebooks 1914-1916* that:

'Logic must take care of itself.' (NB 2)[47]

---

[47] This becomes 'Logic must look after itself' in the *Tractatus* – 5.4731

The meaning here is that logic as such is self-contained and self-regulating and in effect, the presupposition for all that can be done with logical application, such as mathematics and grammar, for example.

The upshot of the discussions, arguments, and letters in 1913 was that Russell took the immense step of abandoning *Theory of Knowledge* as a book. With his lecture tour looming, Russell restarted a different line of thought and later gave the lectures in America, publishing *Our Knowledge of the External World* (1914) as their embodiment. He also published a series of articles in *The Monist* which are now established as the opening sections of the draft of *Theory of Knowledge*. It was not until 1984 that the remaining sections of the draft were published.[48]

In a letter written in 1916, Russell judged the episode 'an event of first-rate importance' in his life since he had seen that Wittgenstein was right and that he (Russell) 'could not hope ever again to do fundamental work in philosophy'.[49] Whilst this was perhaps rather unduly self-deprecating of Russell, it was nevertheless a prescient comment, in that over the next forty years and beyond Wittgenstein's philosophical influence eclipsed Russell's.

Meanwhile, in 1913, Wittgenstein spent some time in Vienna in June and July, and during this time he was in correspondence with a friend he had made in Cambridge over the previous year. This was David Pinsent (1891-1918). Pinsent was an excellent mathematician who had gained a first at Cambridge and then moved on to study Law. He became the first serious personal friend that Wittgenstein had in adulthood. Pinsent and Wittgenstein first met in 1912, when both were guests at one of

[48] See Russell (1992)
[49] BR to OM in Russell (1975) p282.

Russell's social gatherings. They found a common interest in music, and Pinsent helped Wittgenstein with some research he was doing in the still very new psychology department at Cambridge. Some the work going on there interested Wittgenstein as it was exploring the communicative role of music within different cultures. The idea that Wittgenstein seems to have been developing was that there was a kind of parallel between how a proposition could have logical sense and how in a musical phrase, the key theme or compositional idea was what gave the phrase meaning. We have an example of this in his *Notebooks 1914-1916*: Wittgenstein, within a set of notes that was primarily developing ideas on logic and language, also wrote (in February 1915), that:

'Musical themes are in a certain sense propositions. Knowledge of the nature of logic will for this reason lead to knowledge of the nature of music.' (NB p. 40)

A tune, he adds, 'is a kind of tautology, it is complete in itself; it satisfies itself'.

Pinsent much enjoyed Wittgenstein's company and made many references to him in his diary. One entry provides insight into the fastidious way in which Wittgenstein shopped for furniture for his rooms, always looking for utterly simple and minimalist pieces.[50] In another entry, from May 1912, Pinsent noted with amusement that Wittgenstein was doing some systematic reading in philosophy, and that 'he expressed the most naïve surprise that all the philosophers he once worshipped in ignorance are after all stupid and dishonest and make the most disgusting mistakes!'[51] The two men enjoyed a good deal of time in conversation, going to concerts and taking walks around Cambridge.

---

[50] See McGuiness (1988) pp. 131-132
[51] Pinsent's Diary for 30.05.12, as quoted in Monk (1991) p. 50

In September 1912, Pinsent joined Wittgenstein for a walking holiday in Iceland, and a year later they took another trip, this time to Norway. They stayed in a hotel in the town of Oystese and combined walking with work on Law (Pinsent) and Philosophy (Wittgenstein). Back in Cambridge for the new term, Wittgenstein met with Russell to discuss his latest ideas on logic. Russell was alert to the importance of this and arranged for a typist to be on hand to take down dictation. It is from this that we get the 'Notes on Logic', referred to earlier, which was a kind of summary of his thinking to that point.

Wittgenstein then resolved to go back to Norway where, he thought, he could find the peace to write with more focus than had he stayed in Cambridge. He left for Norway in October, and this time he stayed in the village of Skjolden, which was close by the Sogne fjord, to the north of Bergen. He lodged with the local postmaster and worked on logic till Christmas, which he spent in Vienna. After this duty visit, he returned to Norway and resumed work, writing up much of his thinking on logic and philosophy in the light of his time with Russell. By March 1914 he had put plans in motion to have a hut built for him and whilst this was in construction it was arranged that G. E. Moore would come to visit him, so as to gather notes and ideas on Wittgenstein's latest ideas. Moore duly arrived towards the end of March and then very selflessly took dictated notes from Wittgenstein[52]. Wittgenstein subsequently hoped the notes on *Logik*, as he called them, could be used as a submission as a thesis for the B.A. degree at Cambridge: Moore had to write to explain the notes were not in the formal style of organisation to make a valid submission and, rather characteristically, Wittgenstein was furious to learn of this. This led to a breach in relations

---

[52] Moore's notes are published as an appendix to Wittgenstein, (2004) pp. 108-119. Wittgenstein's 'Notes on Logic' are published in the same work, pp. 93-107

with Moore, an innocent party in all of this, that lasted till 1929.

At the outbreak of war in 1914, Wittgenstein, who had been thinking over the possibility of entering a monastery, returned home and joined the Austrian Army. He served as a mechanic in an artillery workshop till 1916, when he was commissioned as an officer. In a period of leave at this time, Wittgenstein met again the architect Adolf Loos in Vienna. When Loos realised that Wittgenstein was on his way to a new posting in Olmütz, a town in Moravia, now the Czech Republic, he suggested he look up a student of his, and thus Wittgenstein met Paul Engelmann (1891-1965). The two became friends and correspondents and late in his life, Engelmann wrote a valuable memoir of his memories and thoughts about Wittgenstein.[53] In the 1920s they had another point of contact, but that we will come to later.

Throughout 1917, Wittgenstein's duties involved artillery observation which meant climbing to a lookout post high in the mountains to help plot the trajectory for the Austrian artillery, so they could shell the Italians. In the summer of 1918, Wittgenstein had a period of leave due to illness. He worked hard as he recovered to re-work his philosophical ideas, but early in July 1918 he was deeply upset to learn that David Pinsent had been killed in a plane crash. Pinsent was testing aircraft and was investigating a problem with a particular machine. During a test flight, there was a catastrophic failure, and Pinsent was killed. Wittgenstein wrote a heartfelt letter of condolence to Pinsent's mother and explained that he would be dedicating his forthcoming book to Pinsent's memory. This he did. Wittgenstein returned to active service, but later in 1918, towards the end of hostilities, he was captured by the Italians. He remained a prisoner of war till early in 1919.

---

[53] See Engelmann (1967)

During the war, Wittgenstein carried, as mentioned, notebooks in which he continued to work on his philosophy as and when there was an opportunity. These, the *Notebooks 1914-1916*, from which we quoted above, show the development of ideas towards a draft of the *Tractatus* that Wittgenstein proceeded to write. This has also been published as the *Prototractatus*. By the end of the war after more re-writing, Wittgenstein had a further manuscript complete and ready for publication. In 1919 he sent the work, entitled *Logisch-philosophische Abhandlung*, meaning a 'Treatise of Logical Philosophy', to Frege and Russell. Russell had not heard from Wittgenstein during the war and had feared that he had been killed. When he learned, in March 1919, that Wittgenstein was alive; he was delighted and, given the news of Wittgenstein's work, he arranged to a meeting in December 1919, in The Hague. When they met, they spent a week discussing the text line by line, and Russell urged Wittgenstein to get the book published. Difficulties then arose over finding a publisher. Wittgenstein was an unknown author and the work was not an immediately attractive or accessible text to persuade an editor or publisher to take on. Eventually, and after a year or more of disappointments, in 1921 it was arranged to publish the book, under its original title, in instalments, in three successive editions of a German journal devoted to the philosophy of science. This did not bring any notable attention to the work, but the next year the book was accepted for publication in Britain, as one in a new series being produced by the publisher Kegan Paul, the boldly-named International Library of Psychology, Philosophy and Scientific Method[54]. C. K. Ogden was an editor to this series, and on the suggestion of G. E. Moore, the book was given the Latinate title *Tractatus Logico-Philosophicus* – and as noted, it is now generally known as the *Tractatus*.

---

[54] See Monk (1991) pp. 203ff

The *Tractatus* was translated for English publication, officially by, as noted earlier, C. K. Ogden, who was, apart from his editorial and translating work, on his way to a distinguished career in the fields of semantics and linguistics. But in fact, most of the work was done by another emerging star in Cambridge mathematics, F. P. Ramsey (1903-1930). In 1961 another translation was done by the Oxford philosophers David Pears (1921-2009) and Brian McGuiness (1927 -).

In the Preface to the *Tractatus,* Wittgenstein suggests a reason for his interest in the mechanics of language comes through the view that it is a misunderstanding of the logic of language that gives rise to the traditional problems of philosophy. The proper understanding of the logic of language is thus posited as the means to the end of solving these problems. It should be noted that by the logic of language, Wittgenstein means the real 'nature' of language, not the grammar of vernacular language. The consequence of this view is that in the *Tractatus* Wittgenstein rejects the traditional philosophical approach of reviewing the problems of philosophy through systematic examination; instead, he seeks to show that a limit to language can be demonstrated as can the real limits of reality. The limits - and they are said to be correlated - once disclosed, will show that many philosophical problems arise and are insoluble because they aim to pass beyond the limits of reality, thought and language. Thus, the *Tractatus'* message is that:

'What can be said at all can be said clearly, and what we cannot talk about we must pass over in silence.' (T p. 3)

Until 1919 Wittgenstein had lived with considerable means at his disposal in consequence of the allowance he derived from his family's wealth. But then he gave away most of his share of the fortune to the rest of his family. He did this because he felt that, as they were already so rich, further wealth could do them no harm. Thereafter, Wittgenstein's somewhat nomadic style of life continued with greater simplicity and frugality. This was reflected in his attire. Before the First World War, Wittgenstein had dressed in due deference to convention; he had worn a suit and had always worn a tie. After the war, his clothing was much more casual, and he almost never wore a tie. Those who knew him before the war as a smart and well-dressed young man found the much more casually attired person they encountered post-war something of a shock.

Wittgenstein considered that the *Tractatus* embodied definitive solutions to the problems of philosophy and thus, for a brief period, he saw no purpose to further concentrated work in philosophy. He again pondered entering a monastery, but he elected to train as a teacher and followed a one-year course, qualifying in 1920. Thus, as the *Tractatus* came, in phased publications, before the philosophical community in 1921 and 1922, its author had already seemingly retired from philosophy and was engaged in the daily routines of teaching in rural elementary schools in Austria.

3. Wittgenstein's Tractatus

i. The Style and Aim of the Tractatus

The *Tractatus* is generally considered to be a distinctive, profound and influential text within twentieth-century philosophy. Whilst controversy continues over the merits of Wittgenstein's later work, there is consensus over the value of the *Tractatus*, which is seen as a coherent and definitive statement of a particular blend of logical and analytical philosophy in a form and style that demonstrates influence from the logic of Frege and Russell. It is also viewed as a text that 'shows what cannot be said', and this centres on the ethical point that infuses the text.

More of this later: from the reader's point of view the text is first of interest in consequence of its curious method of presentation. It will be remembered that throughout his philosophical writings Wittgenstein prefers to present his thought in numbered sentences or paragraphs rather than in conventional prose. He may well have been influenced in this from his earlier reading of Schopenhauer, and from Nietzsche, whose book *The Anti-Christ* Wittgenstein read in 1914[55]. Both philosophers employed aphorisms in their writing. In the *Tractatus,* this approach is followed with particular formality. Apart from the preface, the brief text (74 pages in the English translations) is written around seven propositions or theses, numbered one to seven, and on all but the seventh Wittgenstein adds a series of comments, or comments on comments, numbered through a system of decimal notation.

---

[55] See Monk (1991) pp. 121-123

The seven propositions that give the *Tractatus'* basic structure are as follows:

1. The world is all that is the case.
2. What is the case—a fact—is the existence of states of affairs.
3. A logical picture of facts is a thought.
4. A thought is a proposition with a sense.
5. A proposition is a truth-function of elementary propositions.
   (An elementary proposition is a truth-function of itself.)
6. The general form of a truth-function is $[p, \xi, N(\xi)]$. This is the general form of a proposition.
7. What we cannot speak about we must pass over in silence.

The sixth proposition's notation is not really given in the text, but Russell's *Introduction* helps out the reader:

p 'stands for all atomic propositions'; ξ 'stands for any set of propositions'; $N(\xi)$ 'stands for the negation of all the propositions making up ξ'.[56]

This means, in effect, that all brief or exact 'atomic' propositions are intelligible within sets of propositions, so all sets of meaningful propositions are made from their constituent or atomic parts. This means that a meaningful proposition can be logically constructed and affirmed, or equally, it can be negated via logical deconstruction; this gives an account of the truth-function of genuine propositions, and the means by which they have a distinct meaning.

---

[56] See Russell's 'Introduction', in Wittgenstein (1978) p. xv. ξ, pronounced 'sai', is the 14th letter of the Greek alphabet, and is used by Wittgenstein to denote variable propositions. Here the Pears/McGuiness translation is used.

Before the main text of the *Tractatus*, Wittgenstein wrote a Preface[57] (T pp. 3-4) in which he set out some highly charged, enigmatic and controversial views which serve to frame the work that follows. He writes that the text 'deals with the problems of philosophy' and says that he can show that 'the reason why these problems are posed' is one whereby 'the logic of our language has been misunderstood.'

When Wittgenstein refers to the 'problems' of philosophy, one might think that his purpose is comprehensive and that he is going to consider the range of problems that are characteristic of philosophical endeavour. Typically, philosophers from classical times to the present have explored, variously, the questions of being, truth, meaning, value, and power. Thus, philosophers have examined the question of being (ontology), that is, the problem of what is fundamentally real or significant in reality; the problem of metaphysics, dealing with the question of the ultimate nature of reality; the problem of knowledge (epistemology) and truth, that is, the question of how we can know we have secure, reliable means to acquire and calibrate what we think we know, so that we can have reasoned criteria for truth. Philosophers have pursued the problems of value in personal and social life in examining moral claims and ethical principles; the problems of the state, rule, power, governance, and liberty are explored in political philosophy. Then, the philosophy of mind explores the problem of consciousness and the issues around the mind-body problem. The questions of what is sublime and beautiful and how these are important are examined in philosophical aesthetics.

If a reader is mindful of these connotations to the 'problems' of philosophy then the *Tractatus* will come as a

---

[57] Unless indicated otherwise, the quotations that follow are from these pages.

considerable disappointment: the book has no systematic review of the fields of investigation that are characteristic of philosophy as a discipline, and references to these fields are rare. In fact, the second part of Wittgenstein's statement in the Preface is much more significant as a guide to the orientation of the work. Wittgenstein is clear that 'philosophical problems', and he means all such problems, have a common-core problem: they abuse the 'logic of language', and the implication is that if we attend rightly to that logic, then 'what can be said at all can be said clearly, and what we cannot talk about we must pass over in silence.'

Wittgenstein pays respects to the influence of Frege and Russell in the Preface, and as we have already noted, later in the text he writes approvingly of Russell's logical work when he affirms that 'All philosophy is a "critique of language"...' (T 4.0031). If we consider this, and the remarks from the Preface, what emerges is that Wittgenstein – a veritable unknown to the philosophical fraternity at large at the time he writes – is making the large claim that philosophy has a true purpose via the focus on the 'critique of language' which, given what he has said about the 'logic of language', means all language, including that of philosophers who have habitually and erroneously written about what, in Wittgenstein's estimate, 'we cannot talk about.' The purpose of philosophy, in his view, does not have anything to do with the first-order conditions of life or of reality: instead, the focus is a second-order one, of a 'critique' of language. This is clear from the sense Wittgenstein has of the 'logic of language' and it must be stressed that he does not mean by this simply the grammatical logic of vernacular languages such as German, English, Mandarin or Arabic. He means the residual logic by means of which we think, and by which any, and all, communicative languages or codes are possible.

There is a very strong sense of ambition in Wittgenstein's Preface when he says that the 'aim of the book is to draw a limit to thought' but he qualifies this immediately: 'or rather – not to thought, but to the expression of thoughts.' This distinction is very important, as we shall see. Wittgenstein says that 'in order to be able to draw a limit to thought, we should have to find both sides of the limit thinkable (i.e. we should have to be able to think what cannot be thought).'

He concludes this series of comments with this observation:

'It will therefore only be in language that the limits can be drawn and what lies on the other side of the limit will simply be nonsense.'

It is wholly consistent with this thinking that Wittgenstein writes in a key phrase that:

'*The limits of my language* mean the limits of my world.' (T 5.6)

And it follows that as Wittgenstein links thinking to what we can express in language, that 'We cannot think what we cannot think; so what we cannot think we cannot say either' (T 5.61). We will be considering these remarks again later.

If we now look at the opening of the work, the *Tractatus* begins with the following propositions:

1.   The world is all that is the case.

1.1   The world is the totality of facts, not of things.

1.11 The world is determined by the facts, and by their being *all* the facts.

1.12 For the totality of facts determines what is the case, and also whatever is not the case.

1.13 The facts in logical space are the world.

1.2 The world divides into facts.

1.21 Each item can be the case or not the case while everything else remains the same.

2. What is the case—a fact—is the existence of states of affairs.

At first sight, these propositions, which are stated in a quite definite, abstract and doctrinaire manner, might appear enigmatic, alluring, bewildering or mysterious; they might equally seem obscure and perverse. What does Wittgenstein mean here? It is to be noted that Wittgenstein uses a very simple and everyday vocabulary – 'world', 'facts', and 'things', and that he uses a straightforward logical switch – between 'what is' and 'whatever is not' the case. But some points can be clarified. When Wittgenstein refers to 'the world' he is not writing of the geo-environmental earth. He is asserting a point that is in one sense, ontological and, it soon becomes clear, in another sense, epistemological: that is, he is making a statement about what is truly the case as a basis for being or existence, and for what we can know about it, and this latter point is soon to be clearly dependent on what we can legitimately say about it. Thus, the world is 'all that is the case', so the 'totality of facts' which 'in logical space are the world'.

As the text unfolds the reader gets a sense that the ideas have a kind of pattern, perhaps akin to how we might begin to solve a complex jigsaw, when the many pieces that have been laid out, start to form a picture that might fit together.

Wittgenstein's idea of the world is constituted by 'objects':

'Objects are simple.' (T 2.02)

'Objects make up the substance of the world.' (T 2.021)

'Objects are what is unalterable and subsistent.' (T 2.071)

But objects can be related and configured, and this configuration gives what was said in Tractatus 2: 'the existence of states of affairs'. Wittgenstein says that the states of affairs given through the 'configuration of objects' fit together 'like links in a chain' (T 2.03). As to how language should be viewed, Wittgenstein has the idea that 'objects' can be named: 'A name means an object. The object is its meaning' (T 3.203). It then follows that the 'configuration of objects' as a state of affairs or a 'situation' is reflected in a relation of correspondence to elementary propositions. From these come propositions that can depict the 'facts' that states of affairs give.

'Facts' are distinguished from 'things', as in the proposition that the 'world is the totality of facts, not of things' (T 1.1). In the *Tractatus,* the 'facts' – 'things' relationship is of crucial significance. For Wittgenstein, 'things' are invariably what we can 'see' or 'describe' (T 5.634). Things are 'possible constituents of states of affairs' (T 2.01). For a thing to be 'possible' is, for Wittgenstein, distinct from it's being necessary. So 'things' is the descriptor for the contingent objects that make up our experience – these chairs and this table, for example. 'Facts', for Wittgenstein, determine 'the world', which is 'the totality of facts', which includes the range of 'what is', and 'whatever is not the case' (T 1.1 – 1.2). Facts are identified with 'the existence of states of affairs', a dynamic notion which Wittgenstein does not give examples for. He means, it would seem, the types of events that can and might and do happen within the spectrum of possibilities within the world of experience. My typing, or not typing, to the end of this sentence… My going, or not going, to make coffee… A cricketer is asked to bowl; he is a wrist spinner, and as he prepares to run in to deliver the ball he has to decide whether to bowl a) a standard leg-spinner; b) a googly; c) a flipper; d) an arm ball… All of the *possibilities* here are 'facts' in 'logical space.'

As we mentioned, Wittgenstein claims to solve the problems of philosophy, yet he does not deal with the classical problems of philosophy in a detailed or systematic way. What we find as the text of the *Tractatus* unfolds is that we are taken through a sequence of ideas which touch on a range of topics: the nature of reality, thought, language, existence, and life; the scope and limits of what can be said; the role of logic, ethics, philosophy, good and evil, life and death, and the mystical. The classic problems of philosophy are not given anything like a conventional examination: what we do have are some passages of technical difficulty and only readers with a secure grasp of modern symbolic logic and advanced training in mathematics can follow such sections with confidence; equally there are passages of romantic, poetic and incantational wisdom, aphoristic wit and charm, and humane simplicity.

But Wittgenstein's method here is correlated with the general theory the *Tractatus* expounds. As we saw from the ideas set out in the Preface, and it is a common concern running throughout his philosophical work, Wittgenstein focuses on the phenomenon of language. The line we cited earlier, that the '*limits of my language* mean the limits of my world' (T 5.6) is something of a mantra for the text as a whole, and the point that a 'name means an object. The object is its meaning' (T 3.203) is another key to the view that emerges.

What we find through the text of the *Tractatus* is the palpable sense that Wittgenstein finds fascination in the way that language can function in such a way as to enable meaningful communication. The problem he is dealing with is that of the possibility of language: we can frame this as the question of *how is it that meaningful language possible?*

Whilst we are all conscious of the extent to which language can mislead or blur meaning, the presupposition of this consciousness is an awareness of the effective power of language to operate as a vehicle of meaning by means of which issues can be presented and resolved; issues from the mundane to the profound. Wittgenstein is interested in the basic fact that language is possible and that it has the potential to work to the extent that we are able, as in everyday conversations or activities, to grasp the sense and meaning of sentences and propositions that we have never heard or read before. His interest and effort are thus shaped to the end of establishing some method, and the appropriate criteria, for quantifying the basic nature and operations of language that enable the transmission of sense and meaning. The solution he reaches is what is generally known as Wittgenstein's 'picture' theory of language.

ii. *The Picture Theory of Language*

In the *Tractatus,* the proposal is that everyday language works for us because of a deeper relationship between the logical form and structure of language and the form and structure of reality. Basic to thought, and so to linguistic activity, Wittgenstein implies, is ostensive definition – naming – and thus the fundamental components of language stand for basic elements in reality, which they name. Thus, the possibility of language is grounded in the fact that true linguistic propositions, that is, statements that say something that we understand to be true (either actually true or possibly true), convey a picture of reality; a picture, or model, of the world as it is, or as it could be. Thus, the link between language and reality by means of which language conveys effective sense about reality is created through the *picturing operation* of language. In another key statement, Wittgenstein says that a picturing proposition '*shows* its sense' (T. 4.022) and, Wittgenstein thinks, an analysis of the elements of the picture reveals a correspondence with the elements of reality; the character and shape of reality can thus be derived from an analysis of language.

Wittgenstein is clear that this view may seem strange. A proposition printed on a page, he remarks, 'does not seem to be a picture of the reality with which it is concerned' (T 4.011). But he suggests that neither does musical notation appear at first sight to be 'a picture of a piece of music' nor does the alphabet seem to be 'a picture of our speech'. Wittgenstein's key point is that the correspondence, the picturing, is *logical*, not *photographic*; it is more a logical model than a literal mirror image. Here he is developing ideas from Russell, which involve seeing logic as having to do with the nature and the relationship between complexes and their 'form'. This gives the explanation of the way complexes are or can be constituted. This is expressed in the remark that 'Logic deals with every possibility and all possibilities are its facts' (T 2.0121), and Wittgenstein's view is that the potential in language to truthfully represent and communicate what is the case is based in a correspondence between the elements in the structure of the world and the basic components in language.

In the *Tractatus* Wittgenstein suggests that language involves 'logical constants' – such as 'not', 'and', 'or' and 'if' – which don't picture but which work in a fixed pattern of conventions to enable linguistic pictures – and a logical structure of 'propositions', 'elementary propositions' and 'names'. The idea is that propositions involve a complex of elementary propositions which in turn involve a complex of names. The world also has a structure. As is stated early in the *Tractatus*, the world is the 'totality of facts' (T 1.1), facts constitute 'states of affairs' (T 2), and states of affairs involve 'a combination of objects' (T 2.01). Wittgenstein's picture theory unfolds through a correlation between the levels in the structure of reality and the levels in the structure of language. 'Objects', which are 'simple' (T 2.02) and 'make up the substance of the world' (T 2.021) and give the world 'an unalterable form' (T 2.026), are the basic units of reality denoted linguistically by 'names'; names combine to form the more complex 'elementary propositions' which reflect the complex of objects in and as 'states of affairs'. Wittgenstein writes then as follows:

'An elementary proposition consists of names. It is a nexus, a concatenation, of names. (T 4.22)[58]

And

---

[58] The terms 'nexus' and 'concatenation' are used to signify that a proposition is an interconnection of names.

'It is only in the nexus of an elementary proposition that a name occurs in a proposition.' (T 4.23)

At a further level of correspondence, propositions *picture* facts. Thus, as we have seen, the picture theory of Wittgenstein's *Tractatus* is grounded in the view that names denote objects:

'A name means an object. The object is its meaning.' (T 3.203)

Combinations of names form elementary propositions which reflect the combinations of objects in and as states of affairs:

'The simplest kind of proposition, an elementary proposition, asserts the existence of a state of affairs.' (T 4.21)

Here the logical pattern of elementary propositions mirrors or reflects the arrangement of objects in and as states of affairs:

'The configuration of objects in a situation corresponds to the configuration of simple signs in the propositional sign.' (T 3.21)

Thereby, propositions picture facts, and thus language and reality correspond to enable meaningful language.

There can be little doubt that Wittgenstein's interest in engineering has quite an influence on this view of language: language models reality in a fashion akin to the scale model used by the engineer in relation to the thing he is working on. During his army service in the First World

War, Wittgenstein[59] read a law report about a case concerning a car-accident where a scale model of the accident was used in court. The model, with its scaled figures, vehicles and buildings, gave a direct representation of what was depicted, and the direct correspondence here seems to have helped him to clarify the view that propositions depict in as precise a manner the form of reality. It may well be that Wittgenstein also recalled his reading of Hertz on the role in our thinking of pictures and models, for a picture, Wittgenstein says in the *Tractatus*, 'is a model of reality' (T 2.12). And this section of the *Tractatus* continues as follows:

2.13   In a picture objects have the elements of the picture corresponding to them.

2.131   In a picture the elements of the picture are the representatives of objects.

2.14   What constitutes a picture is that its elements are related to one another in a determinate way.

2.141   A picture is a fact.

2.15   The fact that the elements of a picture are related to one another in a determinate way represents that things are related to one another in the same way.

The phrase 'in the same way' is the key point to this correspondence view.

Wittgenstein terms the connexion of the elements of a picture its 'structure' and the possibility of this structure 'the pictorial form of the picture'. 'Pictorial form' here 'is

---

[59] Wittgenstein told this story to G. H. von Wright and it is retold in most accounts of Wittgenstein's life. See, for example, Monk (1991) p. 118

the possibility that things are related to one another in the same way as the elements of the picture' (T 2.151).

Thus:

2.1511   *That* is how a picture is attached to reality; it reaches right out to it.

2.1512   It is laid against reality like a measure.

This standout feature of this form of analysis is the clear implication that there are clear criteria for truth in language use. The truth-value of a particular proposition will generally be dependent upon the truth-value of the elementary propositions, on their being true in relation to the state of affairs in question. Wittgenstein means that atomic primitives in language, names, point to simple and irreducible atomic facts, objects. Complex propositions are built up from arrangements of elementary propositions, and the totality of such propositions represents the totality of possible language, just as the totality of all the facts represents the totality of the world, (see T 4.26). It follows that the truth-function of a complex proposition is determined relative to the truth-value of the constituent parts and Wittgenstein's view is that this analysis thus provides the framework for what is and what is not the case, and what in consequence can and cannot be said:

'In order to tell whether a picture is true or false we must compare it with reality.' (T 2.223)

This is a powerful idea for Wittgenstein, and some years later, when he was working back at Cambridge, he retained the idea, even as he was developing other, new lines of thought, writing that 'since language only derives the way in which it means from its meaning, from the world, no language is conceivable which does not represent the world' (PR 47). As we saw earlier, it was also an idea that, as presented in the *Tractatus*, had about the same attraction for the thinkers of the Vienna Circle as a bright lamp has, at night, for a moth.

When, in the *Tractatus*, Wittgenstein affirms that the validity of a picture comes via a comparison with reality, he means that his comparison involves empirical analysis, but of course he sees such investigations as primarily a logical and linguistic activity, and thus there is a vital sense in which the limits of factual language are set by the limits of logic. Logic provides the skeleton around which the flesh of factual language hangs. Logic thus reveals the structure of language, and the structure of language discloses the structure of the world. Logic really reveals the structure of both. In practice this happens, Wittgenstein thinks, as logical tautologies and contradictions – the self-evident truths that operate within the structure of language and logic, (see T 4.4611ff), indicate the range of possible meaning, and complex propositions then picture what is the case, subject to empirical and logical checks.

Wittgenstein concedes in the *Tractatus*[60] that his thoughts may well have been anticipated by others and with this in mind it is important to note here the extent to which the doctrine of the *Tractatus* accords with aspects of the empiricism of David Hume (1711-1776) in the eighteenth century, and the logical positivists of the twentieth century, who thought they drew on both Hume and Wittgenstein. The claim in the *Tractatus* that empirical reality 'is limited by the totality of the objects. The limit also makes itself manifest in the totality of elementary propositions' (T 5.5561) articulates an analytical form of empiricism and within the *Tractatus* Wittgenstein takes, in conjunction with the analytic truths and tautologies of logic and maths, the language and approach of natural

---

[60] See the Preface, p3

science as being the determinative approach for the language that maps and depicts reality through pictures or models that can be compared with reality through checks and tests. To be fair, Wittgenstein's cast of mind gives logical reasoning a more emphatic role than does the empiricist Hume, and philosophy, according to the *Tractatus*, can thus set limits to what can be thought, and it does so 'by working outwards from what can be thought' (T 4.114). And the implication is that what can be thought is what is articulated through logic, and the natural sciences, all of which Wittgenstein trusts rather more than the sceptically-minded Hume.

The view emerging in the *Tractatus* is that for language to have the capacity for precise meaning that it exhibits in relation to the world, the world must have a structure that is reproduced in and as the structure of relations in the inner logic of language. Logic expresses the basic and possible nature of these relations.

Thus:

'What any picture... must have in common with reality, in order to be able to depict it – correctly or incorrectly – in any way at all, is logical form, i.e. the form of reality.' (T 2.18)

The following remarks offer points of consolidation:

'Reality is compared with propositions.' (T 4.05)

And:

'A proposition can be true or false only in virtue of being a picture of reality.' (T 4.06)

Also:

'The sense of a proposition is its agreement and disagreement with possibilities of existence and non-existence of states of affairs.' (T 4.2)

Wittgenstein considers that this view sets the limits and conditions for authentic language and so for the correlation of language to thought. His ongoing claim is, that to be set meaningfully within language, the subject of a proposition has to be set within reality as an actual or possible state of affairs. But if a statement fails to express a proposition, that is a model or a picture of something in (or claimed to be in) the world, then it fails to say anything that could be true, or false, and such a statement is nonsense. In the *Tractatus*, Wittgenstein suggests that most of the problems of philosophy are nonsensical in this manner because they aim to advance to a metaphysical statement about the nature of things as such and as a whole, but such a move entails a shift beyond the correlated limits of language and reality. Wittgenstein's point is made clear in a later comment, written in 1949, in the collection of his writings entitled *Culture and Value*:

'God's essence is supposed to guarantee his existence - what this really means is that what is here at issue is not the existence of something.' (CV p. 94)

Interestingly, this remark is akin to the insight in most classical theological reflections, wherein 'God' is by definition placed outside of and prior to the realm of existent things as the eternal, self-existent creator. In the *Tractatus*' vision, this means 'God' is not an object and, therefore, not something about which anything can be said. In the *Tractatus* Wittgenstein remarks that objects 'can only be named', meaning that talk about non-objects does not involve naming, and continues to say that the simple signs, the names, representative of objects, can only be spoken 'about'. Wittgenstein denies that he can 'put them into words':

'Propositions can only say how things are, not what they are.' (T 3.221)

Wittgenstein means that whilst it is possible to assert the link – the logical form – between the 'form of reality' and the 'form of representation', it is not possible to represent the form that is common to reality and representation:

'Propositions can represent the whole of reality, but they cannot represent what they must have in common with reality in order to be able to represent it – logical form.' (T 4.12)

Wittgenstein suggests that the possibility of representing logical form requires the ability to 'station ourselves with propositions somewhere outside logic, that is to say outside the world.' Logical form is 'mirrored' in propositions, but 'What finds reflection in language, language cannot represent. What expresses itself in language, we cannot express by means of language' (T 4.121). Propositions 'show the logical form of reality', and thus Wittgenstein advances one of the *Tractatus'* most important doctrines, that:

'What *can* be shown, *cannot* be said.' (T 4.1212)

The key idea here is given with an illustration Wittgenstein gave in a later remark when he said that:

'The chief trouble with our grammar is that we don't have a *birds-eye view* of it.' (PR 1)

The classical Philosopher's hope might have been that by some means we could have a metaphysical perspective by means of which to view the totality of meaning and truth. But as we have seen, Wittgenstein rejects this prospect with his view that 'Logic must take care of itself', and in another later phrase, he says that 'I cannot use language to get outside of language' (PR 6). Language, through the logical model of picturing, shows what is, and what is not, the case, where what is possible or actual as being the case is within 'the world' but there can be no picturing of what cannot be shown: language cannot get outside of the reality it models, so it must follow that by means of language, we cannot picture the way in which the picturing or modelling of reality happens: we can't 'picture' the 'picturing'.

Here we see the deeper sense that Wittgenstein wanted to make with his point that:

'*The limits of my language* mean the limits of my world.' (T 5.6)

This, however, opens another issue in his thinking in the *Tractatus*, the issue of solipsism.

It is worth noting that all that Wittgenstein says in the *Tractatus* on solipsism is prefigured in his wartime *Notebooks 1914-1916.*[61] We will be looking at the *Tractatus'* version later, but in the *Notebooks,* Wittgenstein has a passage[62] that in some respects gives an overview of what he is aiming to do with his references to solipsism. However, before we consider this, and what else Wittgenstein wants to say, we must do something that almost always he fails to provide when he references a philosophical theory, in this case, solipsism, and that is to explain it, at least in the customary usage.

---

[61] See NB p. 49; p. 82; pp 84-85
[62] See NB p. 85

Solipsism can be defined as 'the view that only oneself exists.'[63] Whilst a quick review of one's acquaintances may give rise to the thought that we know at least one solipsist, it is fair to say that solipsism is not often a position that anyone seriously argues for. It is rather a quite extreme variation on a 'what if...' line of experimental thinking. It can be illustrated with the following example.

Suppose we imagine having a dream scenario so vivid that in our dreaming state, we thought *it was reality*, and so *the whole of reality* is our dream: it is reality, we, in our dream, believe, and as it is our dream, *this reality is self-dependent*.

Normally, when we awake, we realise this was 'all a dream'. However, the conventional solipsist argument is to say: imagine all of this 'dream scenario' as we have described it, but imagine it is *not a dream*, it *is reality*.

The solipsist view assumes that there is good reason to suppose that the only knowable and so real existent is the individual self; therefore, the individual's view of reality *is what exists* and *is real*. Dreams apart, solipsism can be explained as having a basis in the sense we have of our own individual certainty: this can be seen as distinct from and as superior to all other types of knowledge that can seem doubtful, or in some other way, insecure. But if it is assumed that only the individual subject exists, then the subjective certainty of the individual is the centre for all that is and all that can be known: the central claim of solipsism is thus that all that can be said to exist is a matter of the knowledge of the subjective, certain self.

When Wittgenstein writes that the '*limits of my language* mean the limits of my world', we have only to emphasize

---

[63] Honderich (2005) p. 883

'my' to have, 'the limits of *my* language mean the limits of *my* world', to draw out hints of solipsistic thinking. Wittgenstein has argued that the correlation of logical form in language allows the correlation between the 'picture' and the reality 'it reaches right out to'; this underpins how the limits 'of my language' correlate to the 'limits of my world'. Here again, Wittgenstein's famed comments that logic must 'take care of itself' (NB 1) or 'look after itself' (T 5.473) have real application. The view is that logic 'pervades the world' but 'the limits of the world are also its limits' (T 5.61). The example Wittgenstein gives is to say that in logic 'we cannot say' that 'the world has this in it and this, but not that'. This is because to do that presupposes that we have the capacity to exclude 'certain possibilities'. But as we have seen, this is logically impossible, because it 'would require that logic should go beyond the world.' Thus, Wittgenstein concludes that the link between logic, reality and thought results in the view that we 'cannot think what we cannot think; so, what we cannot think we cannot say either.'

Wittgenstein thinks that this last remark gives 'the key to the problem' of 'how much truth there is in solipsism' (T 5.62). This is a comment to be careful of as it is clear that Wittgenstein means this more as a question than as an assertion; he is interested in what truth there might be in solipsistic thinking; again, he is not interested in the conventional view of solipsism, so he does not affirm it as a true doctrine. Instead, what he says is that there is something correct in what the solipsist '*means*', but this meaning 'cannot be *said*', but is made '*manifest*':

'The world is *my* world: this is manifest in the fact that the limits of *language* (of that language which I alone understand) mean the limits of my world.'

Wittgenstein wants to engage with the correct meaning to be found in solipsism because he wants to articulate a view of the self that does not conceive of the self as distinct from the realities of world and language[64]. If the self were conceived as distinct from language and world, then another line of explanation would be needed to account for the capacity of the self to conceive and speak of language and the world. But this is ruled out by the logic of ostensive picturing in Wittgenstein's correspondence theory. On the line of thought we saw earlier, something that 'cannot be said' but can be made 'manifest' is something that '*can* be shown' (T 4.1212).

Wittgenstein's point is then that 'the subject', meaning, the subject who 'thinks or entertains ideas' (T 5.631) 'does not belong to the world; rather, it is a limit of the world' (T 5.632). Wittgenstein illustrates his meaning with an analogy. The metaphysical subject is 'a limit of the world' in a way akin to 'the eye and the visual field', where of course, there is nothing in the visual field 'that allows you to infer that it is seen by an eye' (T 5.633). Again, this leads to the idea that the real meaning of solipsism that Wittgenstein takes as correct is that it shows that solipsism 'coincides with pure realism', for the self 'shrinks to a point without extension, and there remains the reality co-ordinated with it' (T 5.64).

Wittgenstein thinks that he has a kind of innovation in this, in that 'the self' can be given a philosophical, as opposed to psychological, treatment through the fact and sense of 'the world is my world' (T 5.641): here the self is not 'the human being' or 'human body', or 'the human soul', but the 'the metaphysical subject, the limit of the world – not a part of it.' Thus, what emerges from this is that Wittgenstein is, in a careful manner, being in no sense at all a solipsist in the conventional way we defined earlier.

---

[64] For an excellent review of this topic see McGuiness (1988) pp. 309ff

He is taking the notion and finding in it a true or, as he puts it, 'correct', meaning; this meaning is in accord with his own correlative understanding of the relation between thought and reality via the logical medium that 'pervades the world'. What can be made 'manifest' is the self as 'a metaphysical subject', which means that thereby, and yet within his strictures, Wittgenstein can provide an explanation as to how the project of the *Tractatus* is possible.

In this context the passage referred to, but not referenced earlier, from the *Notebooks 1914-1916* is relevant. The passage is autobiographical in character, and starts with Wittgenstein saying, 'this is the way I have travelled' (NB p. 85), meaning, over a passage of time in his thinking. He continues as follows:

'Idealism singles me out from the world as unique, solipsism singles me out alone, and at last I see that I too belong to the rest of the world, and so on the one hand *nothing* is left over, and on the other, as unique, *the world*. In this way idealism leads to realism if it is properly thought out.'

Idealism, the view that what is most real is what is known by the mind or by minds, is problematic because the claim that all reality is knowable by the mind assumes that mental reality has priority over and provides a complete explanation for matter. The problem is acute because the idealist is then aiming to make an explanation of the relation of mind to matter via language that will try to say what in fact can only be shown, and this, to Wittgenstein, results in nonsense. Solipsism is a distinctive, extreme variant on idealism, and has, as Wittgenstein says in the *Tractatus*, something correct in the *meaning* that is entailed. We see this in his comment we cited earlier, that 'the world is *my* world: this is manifest in the fact that the limits of *language* (of that language which I alone understand) mean the limits of my world' (T 5.62). It is this expression of the 'the subject', meaning, the subject who 'thinks or entertains ideas' (T 5.631) and who 'does not belong to the world; rather, it is a limit of the world.' (T 5.632). This allows the paradoxical, but to Wittgenstein, the irresistible, conclusion that idealism 'leads to realism.'

A final point to check in this aspect of the Tractatus is the comment Wittgenstein has in connection with his view that 'the world is *my* world'. This, he says, is 'manifest in the fact that the limits of *language*... mean the limits of my world.' (T 5.62). But in parenthesis, he says of the language, that is 'that language which I alone understand'. At face value, this takes us back a step or two to a position that echoes solipsism in the more conventional sense, for if I alone understand the language with the limits that correlates to the limits of '*my* world', it sounds as if I alone know *my* language, and so *my* world. Reading this literally, I am alone in my world of thought and language that is, thereby, the only world for me. To get to the point that Wittgenstein is almost certainly making here the better thought to recall is his view that the correct meaning of solipsism is the way which it helps to articulate the sense of the metaphysical self, so that when he is writing, as in the passage referring to 'that language which I alone understand', he does not mean his or any other person as an individual, but the metaphysical self who can alone understand the logical correlation between language and reality as set out in the other remarks we have been considering. Again, this is a radical switch from the conventional solipsist who would argue that all that is, is as part of her own existence and outlook. Wittgenstein's claim is that the metaphysical self is that which can be shown but not said as the limit of the world via the logic of a language at the limit: all this is distinct from what might be said, or not said, about this or that particular self.

iii. The Role of Philosophy

Wittgenstein intends that the *Tractatus* should be seen as the demonstration of the correct role for philosophy. His view is that the classical concern of the metaphysician, to construct, through rational speculation, a theory of the meaning and structure of existence, is illegitimate. We can only operate through language, and language works through particular relations to objects. Thus, we have no access to an external perspective through which it would be possible to understand the operation of all propositions in language and thus the totality of objects and the totality of the world. As we have seen, we cannot, on Wittgenstein's view, gain '*a birds-eye view*' of 'our grammar': that is why we cannot 'say', but rather 'show' what is '*manifest*' (T 6.522). The definitive insight Wittgenstein has is that, rightly understood, philosophy is not definitive; it is descriptive.

Consequently, the *Tractatus* redefines the scope of philosophy. We get evidence her of why Wittgenstein was said, as on the memorial in Trinity College, to have cultivated a 'new way'[65] for philosophical reflection, in terms of an *activity*, 'not a body of doctrine', and an 'activity' that aims at 'the logical clarification of thoughts'. Thus, a philosophical work 'consists essentially of elucidations' (T 4.112). Philosophy seeks to remove 'cloudy and indistinct' thought and establish clarity, and as in the picture theory of meaning and truth, it sets limits: 'It must set limits to what can be thought; and, in doing so, to what cannot be thought' (T 4.114). The method advanced in the *Tractatus* enables philosophy to bracket off the sphere of natural science, for the 'totality of true propositions is the whole of natural science' (T 4.11). Wittgenstein adds that in fact, philosophy can 'set limits to

---

[65] See the *Introduction* above.

73

the much-disputed sphere of natural science' (T 4.113). He says that 'All propositions are of equal value' (T 6.4). This means that all of the propositions of natural science are of equal status as descriptors of what is in the world. He thinks that everything in the world 'is as it is' (T 6.41). In contrast, the 'sense of the world must lie outside the world.' This 'sense of the world', it must be noted, is thus quite outside the scope of natural science, and, of course, in no way invalidated by science.

That natural sciences are to be so circumscribed escaped many who read the *Tractatus* in the 1920s and thought that Wittgenstein was fully endorsing the sphere of natural science as the means of grounding all valid truth. But for Wittgenstein, since true elementary propositions picture actual states of affairs, the sum total of true elementary propositions 'is a complete description of the world. The world is completely described by giving all elementary propositions, and adding which of them are true and which false' (T 4.26).

Accordingly, Wittgenstein thinks that in philosophy:

'The correct method... would really be... to say nothing except what can be said, i.e. propositions of natural science - i.e. something that has nothing to do with philosophy – and then, whenever someone else wanted to say something metaphysical, to demonstrate to him that he had failed to give a meaning to certain signs in his propositions. Although it would not be satisfying to the other person – he would not have the feeling we were teaching him philosophy – *this* method would be the only strictly correct one.' (T 6.53).

On the one hand, the analysis and conclusion here proves devastating for those who seek to elaborate a traditional philosophical rationale for ethical, aesthetic, scientific,

social, political and religious experiences. But, on the
other hand, there is a sense in which Wittgenstein's point
coincides with another everyday sense that he was ever
conscious of, that some things are inexpressible; that in
ethical or aesthetic experience, for example, language is
inadequate as a medium for communication.
Wittgenstein's teaching is that such experiences move out
of court, so to speak, as regards the range for legitimate
linguistic use. Sense and meaning depend on the relations
between names and objects, and value statements about the
nature and quality of experience, or of reality, transcend
the bounds of sense. But, as we shall see in a moment, in
the *Tractatus* and in his thinking about it, Wittgenstein
does not regard such experiences as insignificant.

The implication of the method and outlook of the
Tractatus is interestingly paradoxical, since Wittgenstein
maintains that the method of *showing* the truth, *that*
language is related to reality in the direct way indicated,
cannot be extended to the point of *saying how* language
relates to reality so as to picture it. That this is the case *can
be shown*, but how language is so related cannot be
explored, since no exploration is possible save through
language, as in the remark already quoted: 'What *can* be
shown, *cannot* be said' (T 4. 1212). Then, in the
penultimate paragraph, he suggests that his propositions
'serve as elucidations in the following way: anyone who
understands me eventually recognizes them as nonsensical,
when he has used them – as steps – to climb up beyond
them. (He must, so to speak, throw away the ladder after
he has climbed up it)' (T 6.54).

It is a common experience to reach the end of the
Tractatus and feel that the text has played a trick on the
reader. Once we get to the end of the patterns of reasoning
in the *Tractatus*, we realise that everything achieved is, in
a sense related to key matters being showable but not

sayable, and so to all intents and purposes a good deal of what we thought we might be able to say is, in fact, something superfluous, that we can throw away.

iv. The Tractatus and the Mystical

In the *Tractatus* Wittgenstein makes a number of references to the 'mystical', (e.g. T 6.44, 6.45, 6.522). It is clear that Wittgenstein does not mean by the 'mystical' anything akin to the usual religious meaning of a spiritual trans-personal identity or communion between the individual and the divine. But it is equally clear that in Wittgenstein's usage the term has something to do with what Kant described as those matters which human reason can neither resolve nor ignore. [66]

It is in this context that Wittgenstein says, 'It is not *how* things are in the world that is mystical, but *that* it exists' (T 6.44). The 'how' of reality is examined and described via natural science, and it is clear on the *Tractatus'* prescription, that the referent of theological discourse isn't a part of reality in this sense - in addition to the comment from *Culture and Value* noted earlier, we may consider this:

'How things are in the world is a matter of complete indifference for what is higher. God does not reveal himself in the world.' (T 6.432)

But the 'that it exists' of the world remains as a question or problem that confronts us as that which we cannot answer or even frame... We 'feel' the problem, the classical question of 'Why something and not nothing?', the 'problem of being' as the existentialists might put it[67].

---

[66] See Kant (1978) p. 7
[67] See for example, Heidegger (1973) p. 19 & pp. 21-35

Wittgenstein comments that 'Feeling the world as a limited whole - it is this that is mystical' (T 6.45). And this section of the *Tractatus* continues:

6.5   When the answer cannot be put into words, neither can the question be put into words.
        The riddle does not exist.
        If a question can be framed at all, it is also possible to answer it.

6.51   Scepticism is *not* irrefutable, but obviously nonsensical, when it tries to raise doubts where no questions can be asked.
        For doubt can exist only where a question exists, a question only where an answer exists, and an answer only where something *can be said*.

6.52   We feel that even when all *possible* scientific questions have been answered, the problems of life remain completely untouched. Of course there are then no questions left, and this itself is the answer.

6.521   The solution of the problem of life is seen in the vanishing of the problem.
        (Is not this the reason why those who have found after a long period of doubt that the sense of life became clear to them have been unable to say what constituted that sense?)

6.522   There are, indeed, things that cannot be put into words. *They make themselves manifest*.
        They are what is mystical.

These remarks suggest a religious concern and an ethical sense, but one that has an *apophatic*[68] character of extreme proportions. In this context, it is important to consider some comments of Wittgenstein's in a letter to Ludwig von Ficker (1880-1967). Ficker was a literary figure of some standing and an acquaintance of Wittgenstein's. He edited the journal *Der Bruner* and published a range of influential writers, including Krauss. Wittgenstein had a number of contacts with him, before writing to him in the hope that he would agree to publish the *Tractatus* in *Der Bruner*. Having sent a copy of the text to Ficker, Wittgenstein wrote again to give a clarification of the point of the book. Wittgenstein writes that the 'purpose' of the book was 'ethical':

'I once meant to include in the preface a sentence which is not in fact there now, but which I shall write out for you here, because it will perhaps be a key to the work for you. What I meant to write, then, was this: My work consists of two parts: the one presented here plus all that I have not written. And it is precisely this second part that is the important one. My book draws limits to the sphere of the ethical from the inside as it were, and I am convinced that this is the ONLY *rigorous* way of drawing those limits. In short, I believe that where *many* others today are just *gassing*, I have managed in my book to put everything firmly in its place.'[69]

This remark is typical of others Wittgenstein made to friends suggestive of a far from negative attitude to the ethical and religious dimensions of experience. But his point is really that the ethical is a condition of experience,

---

[68] In theological reflection for example, apophatic thought affirms via negation – so you might indicate what God is, by saying what he is not.
[69] LW to LF – the letter is cited in G. H. von Wright *Wittgenstein* (1982) and often quoted in Wittgenstein biographies – e.g. McGuiness (1988) p. 288

not something that exists objectively as a part of the world of experience. In fact, Wittgenstein evinces a view of the natural world, including that of the human condition, that rivals Schopenhauer for gloom – perhaps not too surprisingly, since Schopenhauer was one of the few classical past philosophers he had read. In another remark from late in his life (1948) he reflects on the saying 'the cussedness of things' and then says that the saying was:

'An unnecessary anthropomorphism. We might speak of the *malice* of the world; easily imagine the devil created the world or a part of it. And we need not imagine the demon intervening in particular situations; everything may happen "in accordance with the laws of nature": it is just that the whole plan is directed at evil from the start. But a human being exists in a world in which things break, slide about, cause every possible mischief. And of course he is one of those things. – The "malice" of the objects is a stupid anthropomorphism. For the truth is much graver than this fiction.' (CV pp. 81-82)

Returning to the *Tractatus*, it can be argued that we should see the 'mystical' in Wittgenstein's presentation as what is shown in the ineffable relation between language and the world, the way that the relation of language to the world cannot be explained via language. It is this that can be *shown*, but not *said* or explained – it must be 'passed over in silence'. But this seems a very partial reading of the *Tractatus*, within which there is a range of other 'transcendentals': for example, 'ethics' (T 6.421), 'the sense of the world' (T 6.41), 'the world of the happy... and... the unhappy' (T 6.43), the 'riddle of life', (T 6.4312) and God (T 6.432). Really it seems that it is the case that the *Tractatus* acknowledges the transcendental and, in a neo-Kantian fashion, seeks to engage in a critique of religious knowledge in order to make plain the nature and possibility of faith – a faith that is manifest – though this is not explicit in the *Tractatus* – through a certain style of commitment in life. This then has to do with the qualities central to Wittgenstein's outlook: decency, honesty to self and to others and to practical action in accordance with these virtues.

v. *Some Criticism of the Tractatus*

We can now consider some general criticisms of the *Tractatus*.

The first concerns the style of the book. There is a case for the view that Wittgenstein's style of concise and suggestive assertions logically syncopated into a distinctive whole is highly appropriate in relation to the perspective which the *Tractatus* delivers. Wittgenstein is, after all, putting forth a critique of much in the philosophical tradition, and the style and cast of the *Tractatus* contributes to the criticism of those who seek to 'say what cannot be said'. The text combines technical difficulty and almost poetic incantation to the end of articulating with considerable subtlety and intensity a strict and radical view. Wittgenstein composes in German, and it should be said that his German prose style is regarded as being of exemplary clarity and beauty. But whilst most of Wittgenstein's critics appreciate all of this, there is the view that if the contents of the text are of such importance, then it matters that we are given their grounds and justification. But the text militates against this, for Wittgenstein hardly refers to other scholars and does not enter into disputation. He maintains a dogmatic and assertive pattern throughout. The *Tractatus* is said to offer elucidation in relation to the problems of philosophy, but the text tends to operate deductively, through definitions and axioms which are stated, developed and refined – there are plenty of examples in the preceding discussion. Consequently, it seems that the *Tractatus* is itself in need of elucidation and commentary before it can be understood and assessed.

Wittgenstein is evasive and almost mischievous in his introductory remarks to the text:

'Perhaps this book will be understood only by someone who has himself already had the same thoughts that are expressed in it - or at least similar thoughts. - So it is not a textbook. - Its purpose would be achieved if it gave pleasure to one person who read it.' (T Preface p.3)

These remarks can be seen as unduly obscure, signalling a playful rather than a serious intention. And, given the range of themes that are so swiftly addressed along the lines of 'the mystical', the *Tractatus* as a whole thus can appear to be too romantic and poetic a work to be deserving of serious attention.

The point of this criticism can be seen, but it cannot be wholly accepted. Wittgenstein does not always write in such a way as to ease his reader's passage through the text, in large part because he does not write in a conventional philosophical style. But Wittgenstein, in a manner akin to Nietzsche, is manifestly not interested in pandering to academic conventions, and he is consistent in the style he does follow such that, the mathematical sections apart, it is not all that difficult to grasp the central themes of the *Tractatus*. And in this respect, it is the case that the philosophical community appears to have a clear notion of the sense and point of the *Tractatus*. Whether the outlook is accepted or rejected, Wittgenstein's opinions are not in serious doubt.

Wittgenstein remains true to this view of philosophic activity, and as a further illustration of this idea, we can note a later conversation that Wittgenstein had with Rush

Rhees (1905-1989). Rhees studied with Wittgenstein in the 1930s and in due course became one of his literary executors and translators. He writes of a conversation he had with Wittgenstein in 1945. Rhees explains that he was thinking of joining the Revolutionary Communist Party – a Trotskyist party. Wittgenstein asked why he wanted to do this, and Rhees explained it was because, on most issues, he felt in sympathy with the Party. Wittgenstein suggested that one could agree with a Party without joining it, but Rhees was keen to join, to show his commitment. Wittgenstein then insisted they talk about this more seriously. Rhees explained that Wittgenstein argued that if one became a Party member, loyalty to the Party, and to its views, would become a requirement. You 'cannot turn back on the party line if you now see something shaky in it'. This is contrasted with the position in philosophy where you 'have got to be ready constantly to change the direction in which you are moving. At some point you see that there must be something wrong with the whole way you have been tackling the difficulty. You have to be able to give up those central notions which seemed to be those which you must keep if you are to be able to think at all. Go back and start from scratch.' [70] Thus, the ideas of communism cannot be treated differently by one who is truly philosophical in his thinking. A philosopher has a distinct calling in Wittgenstein's view. The philosopher 'is not a citizen of any community of ideas. That is what makes him a philosopher' (Z 455). The philosopher is not being true to the purpose of philosophy if he is committed to an ideology, a school of thought, or to the customs of style. We may suggest that a jury would be likely to conclude that Wittgenstein had a fair point here.

A second and more serious line of criticism is that Wittgenstein fails to specify the sense in which his analysis of language and his consequent terminology of names, objects, elementary propositions, states of affairs, propositions and facts have application within ordinary language. Throughout the *Tractatus,* it seems clear that Wittgenstein is concerned to attend to the features of a logically pure language rather than to the workings of this or that conventional cultural language. But there seems a strong case for having a translation of the features of a logical language – not least because it would appear to be unlikely that individuals are going to leap to abandon the languages of conventional usage. But Wittgenstein does not offer a translation and leaves us uncertain of the sense in which one would proceed. Consider the example of the fact-asserting proposition 'the pen is in my hand'. This 'fact' can, in the terms suggested by the *Tractatus*, be envisaged as a state of affairs, an actual state of pen-grasping as experienced by me and as expounded through the appropriate 'elementary propositions'. This would seem to suggest that the pen and my hand are named objects. But this is clearly problematic since on the *Tractatus'* view, objects are simple, whilst the pen and my hand are both complexes capable of extensive further definition. How, and in what sense Wittgenstein's elucidation really applies, is not made clear in the *Tractatus*.

Next, we will recall that the purpose of the book was an 'ethical one'. If this is the case, then a problem is that the ethical theory implied, if not stated, in the *Tractatus* is extreme in its minimalism. If the purpose of an ethic is to provide a reasoned way to consistently solve the moral problems that arise in life, there is not much by way of a tangible ethic in the *Tractatus*. According to the *Tractatus*, questions of value are mystical, they have to do with that which transcends the limits of legitimate discourse. Ethical value can be shown, and ethical concern arises over our consciousness of the problem of the sense of the world. This is linked to the sense in which Wittgenstein sees the point of the *Tractatus* as 'an ethical one.' The difficulty is that Wittgenstein seems to paint himself into something of a corner by the way he maintains that the issue of the problematic sense of the world and which is ethical in character, could be seen as a real issue for those living in the world, and as some kind of solution. But Wittgenstein then thinks that the problems cannot be resolved from within the world. One might hope that the ethical purpose of the text ought to have more emphatic application to help resolve some of the problems over the sense of the world. But Wittgenstein reasons that about ethics we can say nothing and should remain silent. We can be ethical, but we cannot elaborate more on this.

Wittgenstein's point is that there is a resolution of anxiety over the sense and value of life when we see – via the perspective of the *Tractatus* – that there is no value in the world. There is what there is and thus there is none of what there isn't, and the true nature of ethics involves seeing what there is and thus what there isn't. This is all very well – and it could perhaps be seen as a suggestion towards some type of ethic, but, of course, Wittgenstein does not advance one. He clearly sees a practical ethic implicit in the theory of the *Tractatus*, but he does not think that he can develop any 'theory' or explanation of ethics. But it can be argued that this is too modest and embryonic a view: the critical arguments Wittgenstein uses to develop his view involve the idea that it can actually be *shown* that ethical matters are practical, active and of immediate concern. This suggests that the ethic of the *Tractatus* should thus be capable of descriptive elucidation. Further, if, as Wittgenstein suggests, the book's point 'is an ethical one', some kind of elucidation might be consistent as well as profitable.

In ongoing discussion within moral philosophy there is concern and debate over the nature and form of the good, the just, the true and so on: this suggests that the nature and form of the good and the like remain of vital interest and it is worth considering that something of more general help might be lurking in the doctrine of the *Tractatus*. The view of the *Tractatus* is that ethical debates arise through misuses of the logic of language; that may often be so, but the *Tractatus* is also clear about the importance of the ethical, though these ideas are not elaborated. One could, for example, pursue a link to say that the transcendental nature of the ethical could be seen as bound up with its forward-looking teleological nature: ethical thinking is orientated to the possibilities of what we can become. Also, there is the role of motive and moral consciousness in relation to responsibility – to which Wittgenstein is wedded in his personal life. These various dynamics of ethical and human experience are well-worth further consideration and we will give more attention to them later.

We now come to the most famous criticism of the *Tractatus* – famous since it stems from Wittgenstein himself. As Wittgenstein's actually quite gradual shift to the perspective of the *Philosophical Investigations* demonstrates, the *Tractatus* has a limitation in consequence of its greatest virtues. The virtues of clarity, economy and a sharp focus on a particular and formal analysis carries with it the penalty of oversimplification. The *Tractatus* is, in its own terms, clear and rigorous but its analysis, conducted with such assurance, can be seen nevertheless as misleading in relation to the phenomenon with which it deals primarily – language. The *Tractatus* suggests that all language has a common essence disclosed through its logical structure as elucidated through the *Tractatus*. The *Tractatus* proposes the view that via its presentation of the form and logical structure of language, the essence of *all* language is known – that which links and forms *all* language is revealed.

But in the later philosophy, Wittgenstein repudiates this view. In the *Philosophical Investigations,* he characterises the perspective of the *Tractatus* in a beautifully lucid passage: Wittgenstein has in mind a particular proposition in the *Tractatus*. This is the statement that:

'In fact, all the propositions of our everyday language, just as they stand, are in perfect logical order.-That utterly simple thing, which we have to formulate here, is not a likeness of the truth, but the truth itself in its entirety. (Our problems are not abstract, but perhaps the most concrete there are.)' (T 5.5563)

In the *Philosophical Investigations* Wittgenstein re-states this as follows:

'Thinking is surrounded by a nimbus. - Its essence, logic, presents an order, in fact, the a priori order of the world; that is, the order of *possibilities*, which the world and thinking must have in common. But this order, it seems, must be *utterly simple*. It is *prior* to all experience, must run through all experience; no empirical cloudiness or uncertainty may attach to it. - It must rather be of the purest crystal. But this crystal does not appear as an abstraction, but as something concrete, indeed, as the most concrete, as it were, the hardest thing there is.' (PI I 97)

He then says that this view contains an 'illusion' that is possible to somehow grasp 'the incomparable essence of language'. The newer view is that terms like 'language' or 'experience' or 'world' if they have a use, have one that is 'as humble' as those of such words as 'table', 'lamp' or 'door'.

An assertion that famously encapsulates the new insight is that 'words are deeds' (CV p. 53)[71]. Here we have the idea that the truth about language is that, as a phenomenon, it is composed of a diverse range of activities and functions which exhibit meaning, sense and value: and in those contexts, relative to use and circumstance, language discloses meaning, and relative to that, truth. The new ideas here is, in a very deep sense, found in the colloquial saying, that 'actions speak louder than words'. The point of difference between this and the earlier view, is that in the *Tractatus* naming, ostensive definition, is regarded as *the* basis of meaning in language. But in the later philosophy reliance on this as the sole explanatory model is rejected. The range and diversity of the functions of language are seen to extend beyond ostensive definition. Questioning, commanding, promising, obeying, and so on exhibit meaning and involve sense, but such functions do not name and do not picture facts and are not helpfully elucidated through the analysis prescribed by the *Tractatus*. Thus, whilst the *Tractatus* operates on the view that the world is full of complexes analysable into their constituent parts and simples - the objects - and language is thus a corresponding structure scaling down to names, Wittgenstein's later philosophy sees language and reality as a more fluid and dynamic phenomenon, with aspects and degrees of meaning relative to deeds, to actions, to use and to context. Thus, in *Philosophical Investigations*, whilst Wittgenstein specifically retains an interest in the same issues as he considers in the *Tractatus*, the later philosophy challenges the view that propositional or picturing modes of meaning are determinative of all linguistic sense, and the aspiration to prescribe the formal general theory of the essence of language as a whole. Wittgenstein thus becomes the critic of his earlier self. This leads to the view, popular in the mid to late twentieth century, that Wittgenstein was remarkable for having

---

[71] See also PI I 546

developed two contrasting philosophies of language. But our view, as indicated, is that the movement from the earlier to the later view is much more one of organic development. Here it is worth noting that within his early work, in both the *Notebooks* and the *Tractatus*, there are already hints of the later approach, hints that the early Wittgenstein does not really follow up on, as he was to do in later years.

To take one example, in the *Notebooks,* Wittgenstein comments on how the way in which language 'signifies is mirrored in its use' (N 82). Here is the core of the 'meaning comes through use' thesis of *Philosophical Investigations*. And in the *Tractatus* Wittgenstein offers the thought that in philosophy 'the question, "What do we actually use this word or this proposition for?" repeatedly leads to valuable insights' (T 6.211). We shall see more on this theme in Chapter 5.

4. Wittgenstein's Life and Career 1922-51

In 1919-20 Wittgenstein had followed a teacher-training course in Vienna. Having obtained the qualification, from 1920 to 1926 he taught in rural elementary schools in Austria. To the outward view, he had retired from philosophy and was living a quiet life of service to others.

As a teacher, Wittgenstein was a strict disciplinarian, and he was rather unpopular with some of his students. But others enjoyed his creative manner of questioning and his willingness to take the classes he taught on walks into the countryside to do natural history in a more practical way than just sitting in the classroom. Eventually, problems arose with colleagues, and some parents brought official complaints against him. Wittgenstein won the case, but also resigned and returned to Vienna. However, one success that he had in this phase of his career came in 1924. A problem arose over providing his students with a decent and affordable dictionary to help in their progression in speaking, reading and writing in German. Finding nothing that was available or affordable, he devised a system of writing words and their common definitions up on the board and getting the students to copy them into their vocabulary books. He then had these books sewn together to make a wordbook and dictionary. The idea grew into working this material into a book and getting it published, and in November 1924 he got in touch with a Viennese publisher and the book was accepted. It was eventually published in 1926. In the period between completing the book and it's being published, in the summer of 1925, Wittgenstein took a holiday in Britain, visiting Cambridge and Manchester, where he stayed with his old friend William Eccles.

Back in Vienna Wittgenstein gardened in a monastery and once more considered taking up a religious life, but, at first in partnership with his war-time acquaintance, the architect Paul Engelmann, and then more or less on his own, he undertook to design and oversee the building of a house in Vienna for one of his sisters. Wittgenstein, like Engelmann, was influenced on matters architectural by modernists such as Adolf Loos whose style of design emphasised clarity, simplicity, and an avoidance of decorative detail.

Wittgenstein worked on this task with great seriousness and interest. The resultant house was distinctive – austere and modern in design and constructed out of concrete, steel, and glass. It can be thought of as an architectural model of the philosophy articulated in the *Tractatus.* The house, rather re-modelled from its original layout, now serves as the cultural department for the Bulgarian Embassy[72].

During the time of his work as an architect, Wittgenstein met Marguerite Respinger (1904-2000), a Swiss girl who was an art student, and who was, initially, a friend of another member of the Wittgenstein family. Over the next few years, Wittgenstein spent a lot of time in her company and it is clear that they fell in love to the point of considering marriage, this being the only serious heterosexual relationship that we know of in Wittgenstein's life. The friendship remained very close until 1931 when Wittgenstein invited Marguerite to spend time with him in Norway. However, he did not win prizes as a romantic host, as he spent his time working in his hut

---

[72] There is good information on the house on the internet and the TripAdvisor site has some excellent photographs of the house:
https://www.tripadvisor.co.uk/Attraction_Review-g190454-d2054287-Reviews-haus_Wittgenstein_Bulgarisches_Kulturinstitut-Vienna.html

and put up Marguerite with another family. She came to the view that she and Wittgenstein could never really be what the other needed. Wittgenstein was deeply saddened at this, and what emerges is that in his relationships Wittgenstein seems to have a capacity to feel a much stronger love and need for a person than he can ever express or communicate. A key element in this is in all probability the fact Wittgenstein was, over the period since the early 1920s, coming to terms with his sexual orientation being what now we would term gay. It is possible that he had experimented with this in some casual friendships when in Vienna, but nothing much is known of this, and it was not until the 1930s, when he was back in Cambridge that he developed this aspect of his life. We must bear in mind that this was a time when it was illegal in Britain at least, to be gay. But subsequently, Wittgenstein had two close and loving relationships in the last third of his life: with Francis Skinner (1912-1941) in the 1930s, and, in the last five years of his life, with Ben Richards (1924-2000).[73]

Through the twenties, during his time as a teacher, and whilst engaged in architecture, Wittgenstein continued to think about philosophy and, as before, to write thoughts and comments in notebooks. He also had ongoing contact with professional philosophy. He had some conversations in 1923 and 1924 with the Cambridge mathematician and philosopher F. P. Ramsey over matters arising from the English translation of the *Tractatus*, and as mentioned, he visited Cambridge briefly in 1925. During his time as a teacher, Wittgenstein began reading some of Dostoevsky's novels – *The Brothers Karamazov* and *Crime and Punishment*. The ideas of the religious and ethical life in Dostoevsky (1821-1881) seem to have reminded Wittgenstein of his earlier inspiration, Tolstoy, and

---

[73] On Wittgenstein's homosexuality see Monk (1991), especially pp. 328-335, pp. 401-402, pp. 491-494 and pp. 581-586

reaffirmed the view that an ethical life, free from doctrine, ritual, and liturgy, was the purest ideal for life and gave the true sense of a religious life.

From 1927 Wittgenstein also had occasional conversations with members of the 'Vienna Circle', which we may recall developed and favoured the approach in philosophy that came to be called 'logical positivism'. The group was made from a group of empirical and analytical thinkers, philosophers, political theorists, and scientists, who met weekly under the chairmanship of Moritz Schlick (1882-1936), Professor of the History and Philosophy of Science at Vienna. Wittgenstein met particularly with the philosopher and mathematician Friedrich Waismann (1896–1959). Schlick, Waismann and their colleagues thought highly of the *Tractatus* as a work of influence in relation to their approach. As we remarked, they thought the *Tractatus* supported their own position, which championed the view that no meaning was acknowledged save via propositions that were empirically viable or through propositions that were true by definition, synthetic and analytic propositions, as they were termed. The *Tractatus* was indeed having a strong influence on the analytical tradition in philosophy in Britain and the Vienna Circle were operating with similar interests.

However, Wittgenstein was eventually unwilling to pursue contacts with the Vienna Circle. For one thing, this was because he began to appreciate that they had not understood the weight of significance he attached to the matters in his work such as the ethical and mystical, that could be 'shown and not said.' Also, for Wittgenstein, a core reason for the discord with the Vienna Circle was the fact that they took a strong view of the validity of scientific verification as a criterion for all truth, bar that which was purely logical. As we have seen in our review of the *Tractatus*, Wittgenstein had never thought or meant that. But that the *Tractatus* could be thought to imply this suggested to Wittgenstein that for him there really was some more serious philosophical work for him to do.

Wittgenstein thus began a more emphatic phase of further philosophical reflection. He was in effect, re-thinking his earlier view that all the problems of philosophy had been solved by the *Tractatus*. As ever, he worked to fill new notebooks with comments and, thereby, develop more ideas. Then a new opportunity opened up. Correspondence with his old friends at Cambridge led to the discovery that, given the time he had spent in Cambridge before the war, he could, with a further period of residence in Cambridge, register and work for a doctoral degree. Accordingly, late in 1929, he made plans to return. When Wittgenstein arrived in Cambridge in January 1930, J. M. Keynes, with whom he had been in contact, agreed to meet him at the station. Keynes later wrote playfully to his wife as follows:

'Well, God has arrived. I met him on the 5.15 train.'[74]

Wittgenstein was again registered as an advanced student of Trinity College. F. P. Ramsey was appointed as his supervisor. By the spring, Wittgenstein realised that in fact, due to his period of residence at Cambridge in 1911-1913, and given the work he had gone on to, he could submit the outcome of that work, the *Tractatus*, as his doctoral thesis. To this end, he was duly examined in June 1929, by his old associates, Moore and Russell. He was, by this time, reconciled with Moore, with whom he had fallen out in 1913. It seems that Moore and Russell were appointed as his examiners on the grounds that no one else would be able to understand the *Tractatus* – although Wittgenstein was not, it seems, at all convinced of that.[75] At this stage, the Ph.D. was a new degree at Cambridge,

[74] As quoted in Monk (1991) p. 255.
[75] See Monk (1991) p. 271

and it was far from popular with Russell, Moore, and others of their generation, who saw in it the unwelcome influence of American academic conventions. This perhaps shown by the tone of Moore's report to the Cambridge authorities on Wittgenstein's submission for the degree written after the viva:

'It is my personal opinion that Mr. Wittgenstein's thesis is a work of genius, but be that as it may, it is certainly well up to the standard required for the Cambridge degree of Doctor of Philosophy.' [76]

After a term at Cambridge, Wittgenstein returned to Vienna for the Christmas break. Over this holiday, he had more uneasy conversations with Schlick and Waismann. They remained enthusiastic about the *Tractatus,* which they still saw as endorsing the logical positivism that they had developed. But Wittgenstein now made it clear to them that he thought that the *Tractatus* gave a mistaken view of elementary propositions and logical inference:

'... at that time I thought that all inference was based on tautological form. At that time I had not seen that an inference can also have the form: This man is 2m tall, therefore he is not 3m tall.'

Wittgenstein goes on to say that his mistake was 'that I believed that the syntax of logical constants could be laid down without paying attention to the inner connection of propositions.' His developing idea was the rules pertaining to logical constants was in fact simply a part of 'a more comprehensive syntax about which I did not know anything at the time.'[77] In effect, Wittgenstein was rejecting the oversimplification of logical positivism.

---

[76] The details of the viva for Wittgenstein's PhD can be found in Wood (1957) p. 156 and in Monk (1991) pp. 271-272.

[77] McGuiness (1979) p. 64

Wittgenstein had obtained a research grant to work at Cambridge on his philosophical ideas, but this would be for a year or so at most, and so he soon applied for a five-year fellowship from Trinity College. To obtain this he had to submit evidence of his latest work and his proposals for further research. He submitted the notes he had been working on and gained the award on the basis of Russell's report on these. He continued to work on them until 1930 and the text, entitled *Philosophische Bemerkunden*, was in due course lodged with G E Moore who held it safe until after Wittgenstein's death in 1951. He then passed it to Rush Rhees, G. E. M. Anscombe and G. H. von Wright, Wittgenstein's literary executors. The text, edited by Rhees, was published in German in 1969 and English in 1975 as *Philosophical Remarks*.[78]

As well as working on these notes, from 1930 Wittgenstein ran groups and classes for small groups of advanced students. His course was listed as 'Philosophy'. This title was given because Wittgenstein was asked to offer a lecture course by the Moral Sciences Faculty. Richard (R. B.) Braithwaite (1900-1990), later a professor at Cambridge and a specialist in the philosophy of science, came to ask Wittgenstein about the lectures, and asked, in particular, what the title of the course would be. Apparently, there was a long pause, before Wittgenstein said:

'The subject of the lectures would be philosophy. What else can be the title of the lectures be but Philosophy.'[79]

---

[78] The book is divided into twenty-two sections but has a continuous sequence of numbered paragraphs; quotations will be by paragraph number.

[79] This comment is cited in a letter of 5.4.78, between two of Wittgenstein's students, S K Bose and John King, quoted in Monk (1991) p. 289

Wittgenstein worked under this broad title thereafter. His routine was to give one lecture and one discussion group each week. Each session lasted about two hours. There was room for about twenty students at most, and as time went on Wittgenstein refused to admit 'tourists', that is, students who came sometimes or people who just dropped in to see what was going on.

What was going on was soon rumoured to be a new approach to philosophy. In part, this was assumed to be Wittgenstein changing his mind about the views of the *Tractatus*, but in fact, it was as much a clarification of the right method for philosophy which was not really too far removed from the perspective given by the *Tractatus*. We have some insights into Wittgenstein's lectures from some of those who attended his lecture; from his students, some of whom who made detailed notes, which were later published[80], and from G. E. Moore, who attended most of Wittgenstein's lectures and classes from the Lent Term of 1930 through to the May Term of 1933. Moore made detailed notes of the lectures, filling six notebooks with his jottings. In due course, he wrote an account of the lectures from his notes and this was published in instalments in editions of the journal 'Mind' in 1954 and 1955, as well in other collections.[81] More recently Moore's notebooks have been transcribed and published, so we know that Moore was noting Wittgenstein's new approach to philosophy in lectures on October 13th and 21st 1930.[82]

Moore explains that within his lectures, Wittgenstein used a neat analogy for explaining how he wanted to pursue

---

[80] See Lee (1980) and Ambrose (2001)

[81] A slightly revised version of the article 'Wittgenstein's Lectures 1930-1933' was published later in Moore (1959) and the article is also reproduced in PO pp.46-114

[82] Stern et al (2016) pp. 67-73

philosophy. He compared alchemy with chemistry to make the point that, with chemistry, a far stronger and more skilful approach came to the fore, displacing alchemy. Similarly, Wittgenstein suggests, he has found a new and 'skilful' (PO p. 113) way of doing philosophy. Wittgenstein is, however, being quite playful with his imagery. The point of the analogy is not to suggest that philosophy is a kind of science. The implication is that philosophy has lost its 'nimbus'[83], the traditional concern with metaphysical explorations, and that in a sense philosophy really deals with 'trivial' things (PO p. 114): philosophy is dealing with trivia, because it does not deal with 'new facts'; that is the job of science. In contrast, philosophy 'is the synopsis of *many* trivialities.' It does not deal with building grand structures – it much more to do with the business of 'tidying up… a room where you have to move the same object several times before you can get the room really tidy.'

We noted how Wittgenstein developed considerable reservations about the contacts he had with members of the Vienna Circle, and over their reading of the *Tractatus*. Despite this, commentators have often suggested that, in the *Philosophical Remarks*, Wittgenstein presents a view that shows quite a definite orientation to an idea of verification of a type that is close to that of logical positivism[84]. This because in the text he quite often appears to set out variations on the maxim that the logical positivists employed, which can be stated as the view that, *the meaning of a proposition is given by its method of verification*: this works as a form of the so-called 'principle of verification'[85], on the basis of the assumption made by the logical positivists, that, to state it again, a

---

[83] Stern et al (2016) p.67
[84] See, for example, Ayer (1986) pp. 36-39; Grayling (1988) pp. 65-65; Kenny (2006) pp. 104-110
[85] See Ayer (1970) pp. 31f and pp. 35ff.

proposition is meaningful if, but only if, we know that it can either be verified analytically as a tautological definition, or as an empirical, synthetic claim that can be tested experimentally. Propositions of either sort can be known to be true or false, and thus are they cognitively significant and so meaningful.

Wittgenstein's remarks that can seem to align with the principle of verification include the comment that 'the meaning of a question is the method of answering it' (PR 27).

We can also cite the following comments:

'To understand the sense of a proposition means to know how the issues of its truth or falsity is to be decided.' (PR 43)

'Every proposition is the signpost for a verification.' (PR 150)

'A proposition has sense only if I know what is the case if it is false.' (RP 154)

'The verification is not *one* token of the truth, it is the *sense* of the proposition.' (PR 166)

If we consider the setting and context of these remarks with the template of what the logical positivists meant by the principle of verification, we find that things are very far from putting Wittgenstein into that mode of thought. In fact, as a rule, he always seems to be referring to the notion of verification in the context of a sequence of thought designed to show that a wider, and more flexible idea than that of verification is needed.

In the first instance, when Wittgenstein writes that 'the meaning of a question is the method of answering it', he uses it to set up a question, as to whether two men who use the word 'white' can be known to mean the same thing by it. He then remarks 'tell me *how* you are searching, and I will tell you *what* you are searching for' (PR 27). This is a basis for a review of the contrasts between following orders, considering expectations and so on. All this reveals the varying settings and outlooks that are linked to what we say, and these variations militate against a singular method of verification.

When Wittgenstein says that 'to understand the sense of a proposition means to know how the issues of its truth or falsity is to be decided', this comes in a sequence of points flowing from the view that 'for any question, there is always a corresponding *method* of answering it' (PR 43). This notion of there *always* being a corresponding method of answering a question means that when Wittgenstein says that 'to understand the sense of a proposition means to know how the issues of its truth or falsity is to be decided', his stress is on the appropriate, not a singular, method of deciding the 'truth or falsity' of the proposition. In this, as well as in the earlier discussion, Wittgenstein seems to be taking the notion of verification he had discussed with members of the Vienna Circle and using it to tease out its limitations.

If we now consider the comment that 'every proposition is the signpost for a verification' (PR 150), the key to this passage is that there needs to be a stress on the last part of the phrase – '*a* verification'. Wittgenstein makes this point in the context of a discussion of how the meaning of a proposition is given via a consideration how words are used, and in what manner, in terms of intention. Again, the discussion is not aligning to the reductive notion of *the* principle of verification.

The next comment, that 'a proposition has sense only if I know what is the case if it is false' (PR 154) comes in a discussion of the truth that can be known from mathematical propositions, such as definitional axioms, where it makes no sense to ask for a solution. Wittgenstein's point is that mathematical propositions sometimes entail questions or problems to where we cannot express a solution; in contrast, we can make sense of propositions where we identify error or contradiction. Here Wittgenstein seems to be echoing the eliminative reasoning that can be traced by back to Bacon[86], and anticipating the idea later cultivated by Popper[87] as his 'principle of falsification', the ideas that science actually progresses by eliminating errors and, so that in effect we learn most from our mistakes. Again, this is a view contesting the singularity of the view that truth comes via verification as proposed by the logical positivists.

Turning finally to the passage asserting that, 'the verification is not *one* token of the truth, it is the *sense* of the proposition' (PR 166), we should appreciate that this comment comes in a series of remarks which come to the point that 'how a proposition is verified is what it says'; and the example that Wittgenstein uses is the notion of generality, which is differently verified in arithmetic, as compared with how it is in 'genuine propositions'. The point we have here is, as in the others we have examined,

---

[86] See Francis Bacon (1561-1626) and his *Novam Organum* (1620) Anticipating Popper's notion of falsification by over 300 years, Bacon thought that if through experimental work we found contrary evidence that refuted a law previously established, then this could give us an even clearer lead than inductive reasoning towards the formulation of a truer hypothesis, and in due course, a more definitive explanatory law. Bacon thought that this eliminative element in his inductive method was a powerful innovation and he expressed it in the maxim *major est vis instantiae negativae* – 'in establishing any true axiom, the negative instance is the more powerful'. (*Novum Organum* 1 46.266).

[87] Sir Karl Popper (1902-1994). See Popper (1972)

putting the nature, setting, and type of the proposition as the basis for the *form of verification* that is appropriate. This is in effect a complete inversion of the logical positivist's view that all propositions of every type, mode or genre must be subordinate *the* 'principle of verification' as outlined above.

As Wittgenstein was giving lectures and discussion at the same time as writing the *Philosophical Remarks*, it is no surprise that he refers to verification in his classes. Here we can again consult G. E. Moore, who notes that when Wittgenstein discussed the issue of verification, and commented that 'you can determine the meaning of a proposition by asking how it is verified' (PO 59), he also said that this was simply a 'rule of thumb', meaning it was an approximate guide. This was because, in different settings, 'verification' can 'mean different things.' Indeed, sometimes the question of verification 'makes no sense', as in the statement 'I've got toothache'. Moore explains that Wittgenstein meant that if someone reports that they have toothache, 'it makes no sense to ask' the question of verification, such as 'How do you know that you have?'[88] Moore explains that in his lectures, Wittgenstein was developing his thinking. At one point he thought that propositions, as distinct from hypotheses, had 'a definite verification or falsification' (PO pp. 59-60). Moore says that Wittgenstein moved on to think that verification, even if it had some use, was never as relevant as all that. An example Moore recalls is that statements about the boat race in newspapers[89] could verify the 'hypothesis' that 'Cambridge had won the boat race'. But such comments do little to explain the meaning of 'boat race'. Again, the statement that 'the pavement is wet' seems to serve as

---

[88] See Stern et al (2016) pp. 285ff: the lecture notes for March 3rd 1933 gives the example of toothache.
[89] See Stern et al (2016) p. 311: the lecture notes for April 24th 1933 gives the example of the boat race.

verification for the proposition 'it has been raining'. But this does little to 'give the grammar of "it has been raining"' (PO p.60)[90] Moore notes that Wittgenstein moves on to make verification subordinate to 'grammar':

'Verification determines the meaning of a proposition only when it gives the grammar of the proposition in question.'

That matters of meaning become for Wittgenstein 'a matter of grammar' is a key aspect of the view he developed in the work of the 1930s, towards the eventual writing of the *Philosophical Investigations*.

Moving back to the earlier text of *Philosophical Remarks*, the work, as published carries the original forward Wittgenstein wrote in 1930, a part of which runs as follows:

'I would like to say "This book is written for the glory of God", but nowadays that would be chicanery, that is, it would not be rightly understood. It means the book is written in good will, and in so far as it is not so written, but out of vanity, etc., the author would wish to see it condemned. He cannot free it of these impurities further than he himself is free of them.' ('Forward' to PR)

Wittgenstein's consistent view of the importance of purpose in life is evident here, as well as of the ambiguity of being sincere and committed in one's work and endeavour. Just as the true point of the *Tractatus* was 'an ethical one', so the work in *Philosophical Remarks* was 'for the Glory of God'. Yet to set this out in any more deliberate way would seem, he thought, to be a confusing trick on the general readership who would not 'rightly understand' how the book had been written 'in good will'.

---

[90] See Stern et al (2016) pp 314f: the lecture notes for April 28th 1933 gives the example of the wet pavement.

What Wittgenstein means here is something we will explore more in a later chapter.

Soon after arriving back in Cambridge, Wittgenstein met Maurice O' Connor Drury (1907-1976). Drury was from Ireland and had studied moral sciences at Trinity College, Cambridge, and he went on to study theology with a view to entering the priesthood. Drury found Wittgenstein a challenging, but also a rewarding friend. Largely due to his influence, Drury moved away from theology and eventually, via a period of social work, retrained in medicine, (1933-1939), later becoming a specialist in psychiatry. Drury entertained Wittgenstein in Ireland in the 1930s and 1940s and his subsequent writings give some of the most important insights into Wittgenstein's character.

Another significant figure who Wittgenstein met was Norman Malcolm (1911-1990), who subsequently became a professor of philosophy at Cornell. Malcolm attended Wittgenstein's lectures in 1938 and he left some clear impressions of the experience of being taught by Wittgenstein. He recalls that the lectures were delivered 'without preparation and without notes'.[91] The lecture would begin with Wittgenstein giving a summary of the outcome or endpoint of the previous lecture; then he would move on by trying to develop a further line of thought. Wittgenstein 'spoke emphatically and with a distinctive intonation.'[92] He 'sat in a plain wooden chair at the centre of the room' and 'he carried on a visible struggle with his thoughts.'[93] Although billed as 'lectures', Malcolm suggests that the sessions were really meetings for 'original research', this because in them Wittgenstein could think about and explore problems 'in a way that he could have done if he had been alone.' The

---

[91] Malcolm (1984) p. 23
[92] Malcolm (1984) p. 24
[93] Malcolm (1984) p. 25

sessions were conversational but demanding and Wittgenstein could be 'impatient and easily angered'. But he was often highly self-critical, saying things like 'I'm a fool' or 'You have a dreadful teacher', or 'I'm just too stupid today!' Malcolm thought that Wittgenstein's severe manner was due to his 'passionate love of truth'[94] which meant that he had to seek 'a *complete* understanding' of the 'deepest philosophical problems'. Here again, we get a sense of the qualitative input Wittgenstein made to the study of philosophy, something the Trinity College memorial refers to.

The classes run by Wittgenstein were intensive and demanding, partly due to his character and disposition, and because of his use of the meetings for creative and exploratory thought. He thus infused many of his students with excitement as they felt themselves to be a part of a great endeavour of novelty. This gave an aura of secrecy about the work that Wittgenstein was now doing, but inevitably, the news gradually broke that the author of the, by then, famed *Tractatus*, was advancing new theories which were thought to be challenging the doctrines of the earlier work. All the while, between classes, Wittgenstein continued to think and write, and, as we noted earlier, it was his habit to store the notes he wrote either in notebooks, or on slips of paper that he clipped together and kept in shoe-boxes or box-files. As an example of this, one box-file was found after Wittgenstein's death with material that started in 1929. The material was for the most part concerned with ideas on issues in the philosophy of mind, and Wittgenstein kept the line of thinking going until about August 1948; when the collection was published in 1967 it was given the title *Zettel*, the German for 'splinters' or 'fragments'.

---

[94] Malcolm (1984) p. 26

As to the new shift in thought, we will recall that the *Tractatus* examined, amongst other things, the problem of how it is that language can convey meaning. The solution was a strict correspondence view: meaningful language is said to picture reality in a direct fashion – the logical structure of language corresponds to the structure of objects in the world. Thus, the only language that can convey meaning is fact-stating language. The upshot is a critique of much traditional philosophy – it is regarded as failing since it aims to say what cannot be said, whilst what cannot be said, says the *Tractatus*, must be 'passed over in silence' (T. 7). The general line of thought here is not unique, for as we have said, Hume argued the same sort of thing in the eighteenth century. But Wittgenstein's text involved the applications of modern logical notation and philosophical analysis as developed with Russell. However, in the classes and the writings of Wittgenstein's second period at Cambridge the perspective shifts. The approach developed and eventually presented in the *Philosophical Remarks* maintains the picture theory and, as we have seen, plays with the positivist doctrine of verification as part of a richer and broader theory of meaning, with the emergent notion that meaning is to be seen as being relative to grammar, use, context, and situation. At some points in the *Philosophical Remarks* Wittgenstein echoes the *Tractatus* with comments like 'since language only derives the way in which it means from its meaning, from the world, no language is conceivable which does not represent the world' (PR 47) and 'What belongs to the essence of the world cannot be expressed by language' (PR 54).

However, as we briefly noted earlier, the text also contains many hints of the thinking that was to open up towards the ideas of the *Philosophical Investigations*. There are, for example, a number of comments and reflections that anticipate the 'meaning given through use' theory that emerged most emphatically in the *Philosophical Investigations*. Wittgenstein considers, for example, the view we might be presented with that language expresses meanings via the range of nouns, verbs, and adjectives. This may be so, but the range of meaning here is so complex that 'it is necessary to distinguish between entirely different kinds of nouns, etc., since different grammatical rules hold for them' (PR 92). He adds that 'our language contains countless different parts of speech.' He also has the idea of making an analogy between language and how it works, and the role and function of the pieces in Chess. In *Philosophical Remarks*, Wittgenstein has the thought that the question 'What is a word?' is 'completely analogous' to the question 'What is a chessman?' (PR 18) This is a prelude to a much longer discussion of the role of the king in chess in *Philosophical Investigations* (see PI I: 31). And in a similar vein, in some early remarks in *Zettel*, Wittgenstein says that to discern 'meaning' requires 'a particular intelligible situation', or 'a context' (Z 17). Thus, 'meaning' cannot be presented as a purely 'mental activity' (Z 20).

In his lectures and classes, as attended and noted by Moore, which ran parallel with his writing of *Philosophical Remarks* and other works, Wittgenstein was rapidly introducing a range of new ideas. Whilst the first lecture (2oth January 1930) retained the *Tractatus*' notion that a proposition was a 'picture', a week later Wittgenstein is reflecting on the need for philosophy to focus on the 'clarification of thought' and on the problem of making sense of words that have multiple meaning.[95] By Lecture 7 (3rd March 1930) Wittgenstein is talking about 'rules of a game' and about 'rules of grammar' having to do with how 'words are used in particular ways in significant sentences.'[96] The development of new

---

[95] See Stern et al (2016) pp 5-9
[96] Stern et al (2016) p. 28

thinking carries on, so that by the end of the Lent Term 1931, Moore writes that Wittgenstein has said that the meaning of a word 'is no longer for us an object corresponding to it'.[97] He reinforces the point in Lecture 6 of the May Term (1st June 1931):

'The meaning of a word cannot depend on a fact... Meaning is fixed inside language... The meaning is the place of the word in a grammatical system. The meaning is not the thing to which I point in ostensive definition.'[98]

In developing these ideas, which go some way to lay to rest the picture theory of the *Tractatus*, Wittgenstein was influenced not only by conversations in his classes, but also by discussions he had with others in the Cambridge intellectual community. One of particular note was the Italian economist Piero Sraffa (1898-1983). Sraffa, who had studied at the London School of Economics in the early 1920s, had later become a professor in Italy. An opponent of Mussolini, he then fled Italy and thanks to the influence of Keynes, he came to Cambridge, where in due course he became a Fellow of Trinity College. He and Wittgenstein met regularly for discussion and it seems that it was due to one conversational moment that a certain insight was given to assist Wittgenstein in his move away from the strict view of logical grammar and of reliance on ostensive definition, as in the picture theory of the *Tractatus*. Norman Malcolm relates how Wittgenstein was apparently arguing the view that a given proposition, to have true meaning, must have some 'logical form' in common with that which it describes. Sraffa considered this, and responded with a gesture well-known to all Neapolitans, used to signal disgust or contempt: it involves brushing the underside of the chin 'with an outward sweep of the finger-tips of one hand'. Having performed the

---

[97] Stern et al (2016) p. 136
[98] Stern et al (2016) p. 151

gesture Sraffa asked Wittgenstein, 'What is the logical form of that?'[99] This response gave Wittgenstein the thought that a more open and fluid concept of meaning might be necessary, one that had a stronger basis in anthropology; and of course, as his thought developed, it was with this theme at the fore.

Through the period 1930-35 Wittgenstein continued to work and write prolifically. In 1933 he assembled and dictated notes based on his ideas produced since 1929. He produced a text entitled *Philosophische Grammatik*, eventually published in German in 1969 and English in 1974 as *Philosophical Grammar*.[100] Within this he wrote a note in the light of Sraffa's comment as just noted: '"I understand that gesture" – it says something' (PG p. 43). He also has a passage where it is almost like a diary of an evolving thought. He starts by saying that 'the place of a word in grammar is its meaning' (PG p. 59). But then he says, as if giving a corrective: 'But I might also say: the meaning of a word is what the explanation of its meaning explains'. But perhaps this too needs clarification, for he then says the 'explanation of the meaning explains the use of the word.' Here the idea of 'meaning through use' slips into use!

A whole body of dictated notes Wittgenstein dictated over this period gained the nickname 'The Big Typescript', TS 213 as it was numbered in the catalogue of manuscripts made after Wittgenstein's death by his literary executors. *The Big Typescript* became a repository of ideas that Wittgenstein drew on in subsequent years; it was eventually published in 2005.[101]

---

[99] Malcolm, N. (1984) p. 58
[100] This work is in two parts each with its own series of numbered paragraphs. Here quotations are by page number.
[101] A paperback edition was published in 2013.

In his teaching and discussions with his students, Wittgenstein operated as with something of a closed circle, in that he suspected that his thoughts would gain wider circulation and thereby, he feared, misrepresentation. This came to a head in 1933 when he discovered that R. B. Braithwaite had published an article in which he explained the impact on his own thinking that a variety of philosophers, including Wittgenstein, had made on him.[102] Wittgenstein wrote a letter to the journal Mind (edited by G. E. Moore) to distance himself from any views attributed to him by Braithwaite, and Braithwaite duly wrote an apology, to which he appended the slightly cryptic view that the extent to which he had misrepresented Wittgenstein would become clear only when the book that all were 'eagerly awaiting'[103] was published.

The book in question, *Philosophical Investigations*, was still some way off. But as a step in that direction Wittgenstein, he dictated more notes to students and circulated the notes in typescript as *The Blue Book*, (1933-34) the title deriving from the colour of the binding. Then, in 1934/35 Wittgenstein dictated another manuscript, *The Brown Book*. *The Blue Book* developed ideas from the first part of *Philosophical Grammar* and can be seen as an anticipation of the study Wittgenstein worked on intensively in his last years – *Philosophical Investigations*. *The Brown Book*[104] is, even more, a draft for *Philosophical Investigations* and in these texts from the mid-1930s, Wittgenstein writes against the use of a general explanatory theory of language and in favour of a notion of meaning relative to practical activity. He presents philosophy as a 'purely descriptive' activity (BB p. 19) and says that 'the use of a word in practice is its meaning' (BB p. 69). He develops the idea of 'language-games' (BB p. 79ff)

---

[102] See Monk (1991) p. 335
[103] Quoted in Monk (1991) p. 335
[104] *The Blue and Brown Books* were published in 1958 – 2nd edition 1969.

and, all-round, writes to give an account of relationships between styles of understanding, against the idea of such relations being grounded in a unifying logical structure. Against such relations of identity, Wittgenstein proposes a relation through similarity - and all this represents a move away from the doctrines of the *Tractatus* and is akin to the line of *Philosophical Investigations*.

As the period of his Fellowship drew to a close Wittgenstein devised a plan to travel to Russia – the USSR as it had become. He had formulated support for the ideals of the Soviet revolution, learning Russian in preparation for the trip. In 1935 he left Cambridge and went to the USSR. The realities of life in Russia did not prove attractive, however, and he returned before the end of the summer and spent the best part of the next year in his hut in Norway – which he had first to rebuild. He holidayed in Ireland and eventually returned to Cambridge in 1936 and resumed teaching and writing. In 1939 he was elected Professor of Philosophy in succession to Moore. War broke out before Wittgenstein could take up his duties. By this time, he was a British citizen, and in support of the war effort, he worked first as a porter in Guy's Hospital in London and then as a laboratory technician at the Royal Victoria Hospital Newcastle-upon-Tyne, which he did until 1944, when he returned to Cambridge and to teaching.

Although Wittgenstein took his teaching seriously, he found the role of professor increasingly absurd. He despised dining in college and the conversations that ebbed and flowed between dons. He resigned the chair in 1947 and retired to Ireland, spending time in Galway and later Dublin, to write. During his visit to Ireland, he met up with Drury, who recalled that Wittgenstein was working on ideas for the text that eventually became *Philosophical Investigations*. Wittgenstein was keen to publish this as he was growing concerned that his ideas were being developed or expressed in a way that was misleading by some of his former students from the 1930s. Wittgenstein was wondering what to call the book. He thought it might be called 'Philosophical Remarks', re-using the title he had given to now filed draft from the early 1930s. Drury asked, 'Why not just call it "Philosophy"'. Despite having used this as a title for his lectures, Wittgenstein was not pleased with this suggestion as the title for his book, saying that, given how much the word (Philosophy) had meant 'in the history of human thought', how could he call a book of his that? 'As if my work was anything more than just a small fragment of philosophy.'[105]

In 1949 Wittgenstein he travelled to the USA to visit his former student Norman Malcolm. He enjoyed the trip, and discussions with both Malcolm and others, including O. K. Bouwsma (1898-1978), who had also taught Malcolm and had encouraged him in going to Cambridge to study with Moore and Wittgenstein. Bouwsma's notes of his conversations with Wittgenstein were subsequently published[106] and offer many important insights into Wittgenstein's manner and method of philosophical discussion. As in his early meetings with Russell in 1911, his American hosts in 1949 found his philosophical company intense and very demanding.[107]

Whilst he was in America Wittgenstein's health was poor. He had been diagnosed with anaemia, but on his return to England, prostate cancer was diagnosed. Wittgenstein's life was not in immediate danger and he was able to go on with his work. A text of *Philosophical Investigations* had been almost complete in 1945, but Wittgenstein characteristically wanted to revise the work some more. He also developed new ideas which he worked on hard in

[105] Drury, 'Conversations with Wittgenstein' in Rhees (1984) p. 168
[106] Bouwsma, (1986)
[107] See Monk (1991) pp. 553f

the last period of better health he enjoyed. The notes provided material for a further volume, eventually to be published as in 1969 as *On Certainty*. As his conditioned gradually worsened Wittgenstein, who had a great fear of hospitals, returned to Cambridge and spent his last months living and working in the home of his doctor, Dr. Bevan. He completed a great deal of work in his final months, and before his final lapse into unconsciousness he said to Mrs. Bevan, 'Tell them I have had a wonderful life.'[108] When he died (on 28th April 1951) his friend Ben Richards, as well as Maurice Drury and Elizabeth Anscombe, were present, as was the local Catholic priest.

---

[108] Monk (1991) p. 579

5. Philosophy and Language in the Philosophical Investigations

i. Contrasts with the Tractatus

Wittgenstein's *Tractatus* presents the view that language operates through ostensive definition and via the provision of logical pictures of reality. Names denote objects, and thereby sense, meaning and truth in discourse are established relative to the correspondence between the linguistic structure and the structure of reality. Wittgenstein's later philosophy counters this view with the idea that language actually defies a singular explanatory model; language, he has come to realise, involves a diversity of logic; there is logic, and thus meaning, relative to the context of use and to the practical functions to which language is put. This means that the sense and meaning of language are to be examined in and through a description and analysis of practical language use. The contrast is that the sense of language is not given through the isolation of language from the context of use, nor through the application of some abstract or general criteria, but rather through the web of activities and concerns within and for which it comes to expression. As we examine this we will note that there is a focus on the role of language in the 'natural history' of humans (PI I 415), a matter we look at in the next section; that the meaning of a word is seen as being given by its 'use in a language' (PI I 43). That language use is so varied, but, invariably, in some way rule-governed, it is appropriate to speak of 'language-games' (PI I 7). This term is used to denote the total range of the many and varied 'language-games' which are said to reflect and arise from 'an activity or... a form of life' (PI I

23); and from all this words are no longer names for objects; words now are seen as 'deeds' (PI I 546).

In his later philosophy in general, and in *Philosophical Investigations* in particular, Wittgenstein holds on to the basic view of the *Tractatus* that philosophical concerns have their origin in errors in our understanding of the logic of language. The *Tractatus* has, as a solution, a specific view of the logic of all language which thus serves to dissolve philosophical difficulties. But the *Philosophical Investigations* suggests that the analysis and elucidation of language reveals that there is an error in seeking or generating a single logic for language – that such attempts manifest a serious misunderstanding of language – the error, we may say, involves looking for the meaning *of* language instead of at the meaning *in* language.

Accordingly, whereas the *Tractatus* views the task of philosophy as one of elucidation and clarification by means of the criteria drawn from the inner logic of ostensive definition as the operating system inherent in all language, the view in *Philosophical Investigations* is of philosophical problems being dissolved through a therapeutic approach:

'The philosopher treats a question; like an illness.' (PI I 255)

This is another aspect of how, in his work as a whole, Wittgenstein is a fruitful source of new approaches in philosophy. He has the memorable characterisation of the aim of philosophy being to 'show the fly the way out of the fly-bottle' (PI I 309).

This a catchy phrase, and a very helpful one, so long as we grasp the elements being used. By a 'fly-bottle' Wittgenstein means a fly-trap, a very useful addition to alfresco home dining during a hot summer. The fly-bottle represents the baffling puzzles set by language, that the fly – in other words, the ill-informed philosopher – is wrestling with, and finding no solutions for; there is no way out from the puzzles of language, when language is misunderstood, any more than the fly can escape the fly-bottle. However, whilst we probably do not want to release a fly from a fly-bottle, Wittgenstein's focus is on the philosopher, who, being typically akin to a trapped fly through being trapped by philosophical problems, is worthy of more redemptive aid.

To return to the view of the task of philosophy in *Philosophical Investigations*, Wittgenstein remarks that 'philosophical problems arise when language *goes on holiday*' (PI I 38), and confusions arise 'when language is, as it were, idling, not when it is doing work' (PI I 132) .

Here Wittgenstein develops an idea he used in *Philosophical Remarks* in which he noted that there was value in the 'recognition of which parts of our language are wheels turning idly' (PR 1).

For Wittgenstein, in the early 1930s, this notion of language as analogous to an engine, and to one that can be in or out of gear, harks back to his experiences in engineering. The idea represents a staging-post in Wittgenstein's move away from the particularism of ostensive definitions that was at the core of the view of language developed in the *Tractatus*. This process of movement is, as we have suggested, a steady transition towards the later position, and as the version of the comment in the *Philosophical Investigations* suggests, all round, the view that emerges is that language should be seen as something that we understand rightly when it is at work in the business of life, when it operates and behaves akin to an engine that runs effectively in gear. As the ideas develop, we will see that language in the *Philosophical*

Investigations is seen to consist of a multiplicity of language-games which can be defined and explained descriptively or phenomenologically rather than, as in the *Tractatus*, in an ostensive manner.

Wittgenstein's wider point is that problems and misunderstandings follow from a consideration of language when it is removed from its practical context of use, or when it is examined through some abstract criteria – as when we attempt to establish 'the order' of language against some 'preconceived idea to which reality must correspond'. Here the approach of the *Tractatus* is implicit. Such analysis and explanation lead to the 'dogmatism into which we fall so easily in doing philosophy' (PI I 131) and must be replaced by 'description' of the possible orders of language. Here the implication is that the *Tractatus* was too dogmatic and that now a more neutral descriptivism is to be adopted.

Thus philosophy:

'just puts everything before us, and neither explains nor deduces anything.' (PI I 126)

The problems of philosophy are solved:

'through an insight into the workings of our language, and that in such a way that these workings are recognized – despite an urge to misunderstand them.' (PI I 109)

'Misunderstanding' here would, of course, be the result of abstracting to a 'dogmatism', to a theory to which linguistic, and human activity must conform.

Wittgenstein had long been developing a reluctance to such approaches. When writing the *Philosophical Remarks*, at a time when he still used the picturing relation to explain meaning, Wittgenstein says, that that just as you can 'draw a plan from a description', you can 'translate a description into a plan' (PR 20). He adds that the same process is involved in translating 'from one verbal language into another.' His worry is that the process here can be undone if a 'wrong conception' of how languages operate is used. Here he takes the concept of 'intention' as an example and argues that the 'essential' role of intention is 'the picture: the picture of what is intended.' His fear is that some other prevalent theories risk using intention as some kind of 'uncheckable... metaphysical element'. Here he is thinking about the causal theory of intention that he found in Russell's *The Analysis of Mind*[109], as well as in the linguistic approach taken by C. K. Ogden and I. A. Richards in their book *The Meaning of Meaning*[110]. Wittgenstein suggests that the causal theory assumes three, rather than two aspects to the process whereby 'a thought is true, i.e. the thought and the fact'. Russell is said to have the thought, the fact and then a third element, 'recognition'. This, Wittgenstein, argues, changes intention from an 'internal' to an 'external' relation, but the 'external' aspect, 'recognition' in this case, is 'irrelevant to the essence of the theory.' Russell's position amounts to the view that 'if I give someone an order and I am happy with what he does, then he has carried out my order' (PR 22). The idea here is that intention is working to bring about a cause, so that the right word used in the right way is effective if it brings about the expected outcome.

The problem here is, Wittgenstein thinks, is that my being made happy 'by what happens... requires that something else should happen, which I cannot know in advance.'

---

[109] Russell (1921)
[110] Ogden and Richards published this text in 1923.

Wittgenstein has a memorable way of caricaturing the position he criticises:

'If I wanted to eat an apple, and someone punched me in the stomach, taking away my appetite, then it was this punch that I originally wanted.'

Wittgenstein denies that philosophical problems are solved through the provision of new 'external' information. The philosopher's task is to reflect on what is given through the phenomena of language, and then it involves an arrangement or rearrangement 'of what we have always known.' This means that essentially philosophy has a very simple task: it has the job of unravelling the problems we make for ourselves by the abuses of thought and language that lead to misunderstanding. Wittgenstein long fretted about this problem, writing somewhat rhetorically in *Philosophical Remarks*:

'Why is philosophy so complicated? It ought, after all, to be *completely* simple. – Philosophy unties the knots in our thinking, which we have tangled up in an absurd way; but to do that, it must make movements which are just as complicated as the knots. Although the result of philosophy is simple, its methods for arriving there cannot be so.' (PR 2)

He goes on the say that the 'complexity of philosophy is not in its matter, but in our tangled understanding.' In the *Philosophical Investigations*, these comments are given a slight twist in the evocative phrase that philosophy is 'a struggle against the bewitchment of our intelligence by the resources of our language' (PI I 109).

As a battle against this 'bewitchment', as a revised way of looking at the problems of philosophy, Wittgenstein suggests in *Philosophical Investigations* that the investigation is 'a grammatical one. (PI I 90). It seeks to remove those misunderstandings which arise through too great a focus on 'surface grammar', by which Wittgenstein means the style of meaning and the sense that we anticipate finding in expressions when we are 'bewitched' into thinking that all meanings operate in a particular way. In contrast, we should look for the 'depth grammar', the variety of sense and meaning that is disclosed in and through actual language.[111] That matters of meaning and truth become orientated to matters of grammar and usage is central to the outlook of *Philosophical Investigations.*

ii. From Logic to Anthropology: A Shift in the Sense of Meaning

Throughout his philosophical work, Wittgenstein maintains an interest in the problem of how language operates to the end of enabling the effective transmission of meaning. A concern with this issue runs through the *Tractatus* into the work leading up to the *Philosophical Investigations*. But by the time of the later work the emphasis changes. The *Tractatus* proposes a formal and totalistic theory of the logic and nature of the essence of all language. The meaning and sense of a proposition are determined relative to its significance as an expression of a state of affairs in reality. Thus, each genuine proposition permits a complete analysis through to its sense which will at root involve an actual or possible correlation between names and objects. But in the later philosophy this view is criticised through extension – Wittgenstein never wholly rejects the view that some modes of linguistic use operate through picturing and ostensive definition, but he no longer advances this mode of expression as *the* determinative criterion for all meaningful expression.

---

[111] See PI I 664

Instead, his view is a totalistic rejection of the possibility of a totalistic view of language.

In the *Tractatus* Wittgenstein has one remark which appears rather prophetic as an anticipation of the perspective that *Philosophical Investigations* cultivates:

'Everyday language is a part of the human organism and is no less complicated than it... The tacit conventions on which the understanding of everyday language depends are enormously complicated.' (T 4.002)

Whilst in the face of this complication the Wittgenstein of the *Tractatus* sees merit in subjecting the conventions of language to a specific and reductive theory, the Wittgenstein of *Philosophical Investigations* sees an error in seeking the essence of language through abstractions from the concrete uses words have.

Thus, in his *Philosophical Investigations* Wittgenstein moves towards a view of language in its human, social and cultural setting and towards a descriptive, situational, contextualist view of meaning, use and function. We may say that whilst the *Tractatus* subordinates anthropology to logic, the focus of the later philosophy is anthropocentric, rather than logical. We can see how the process of change here is one of transition. In the 1929-30 work *Philosophical Remarks*, Wittgenstein thinks that the '... the natural history of the use of a word can't be of any concern to logic' (PR 15). By the time we get to the *Philosophical Investigations* Wittgenstein, as we noted in the previous section, alters the emphasis:

'What we are supplying are really remarks on the natural history of human beings'. (PI I 415)

He provides a list of examples:

'Giving orders, asking questions, telling stories, having a chat, are as much a part of our natural history as walking, eating, drinking, playing.' (PI I 25)

These remarks are anticipated in *The Big Transcript*:

'Indeed, the rules of chess too could be taken as propositions that belong to the natural history of man. (As the games animals play are described in books of natural history).' (BT 87)

This view is also supported by a comment from *Zettel*, where Wittgenstein notes that the 'concept of a living being has the same indeterminacy as that of a language' (Z 326). Here the key term is 'indeterminacy', suggestive of the distinct, unique, and so variable character of individual life, and so, individualised and variable language-use.

Rather than the view that a single essence of linguistic logic runs through all legitimate language-use, Wittgenstein suggests a view of language as a complex and diverse structure set within human life; it contains many particular logics that operate relative to acts or deeds. Language does not simply point to things, it reflects the practical dynamics of life rather than a theoretical concept of meaning. In this spirit, he suggests in *Philosophical Investigations* that:

'For a *large* class of cases of the employment of the word "meaning" – though not for all – this word can be explained in this way: the meaning of a word is its use in the language.' (PI I 43)

And he thus advises that we should:

'Let the use of words teach... their meaning.' (PI PPF 303)

The 'meaning comes via use' notion is cultivated in the *Philosophical Remarks*, where Wittgenstein, in another engineering example, uses a mechanical analogy to develop a point about language. 'Words in a language', he says, are like 'handles in a control room', so words have meaning 'in the context of a proposition'. Thus, he says that we would say that, 'only in use is a rod a lever' (PR 13).

Developing this line of thought, Wittgenstein deploys another mechanical example, with the idea of a gearbox, to illustrate the point about meaning and use: if we imagine a gearbox with four positions we can imagine how, in use, the gear lever would move through the various positions, depending on the circumstances and road. The meaning, the point and the significance of the gears would thereby become clear. Even if the gearbox was damaged so the lever was stuck in one position we could still appreciate the complexity of the design and the range of possibilities for which it was intended. Wittgenstein says he would like to say something similar about language – that is a very complex phenomenon:

'What's the point of all these preparations: they only have a meaning if they are put to use.' (PR 15)

Let's take another example, to make clear Wittgenstein's idea. Suppose I have a coffee machine in my kitchen, one of those into which you place a coffee pod so that when you switch the machine on, so long as the detachable water jug is attached and full, you can make a coffee. The point Wittgenstein has in mind is that the coffee machine in a dormant state, sitting on a shelf, devoid of water, does not mean 'coffee machine' in the right or full sense. What a coffee machine means is what happens when it is operational, when it is making coffee. Suppose that I have a coffee machine and use it for many years until eventually, it breaks down irreparably. I will then be right to say, think and feel that, 'This coffee machine is no use anymore!'

In the *Philosophical Investigations* Wittgenstein extends his insight to the view that language as a whole is an extremely complex working phenomenon; it has too much legitimate flexibility and diversity in use to be determined as to its powers of meaningful expression by the specification of picturing set out in the *Tractatus*. A sequence of ideas to express this insight comes in one version in the notes that were eventually published as *Philosophical Grammar*, Wittgenstein used another workmanlike analogy, between language and the collection of tools you might find in a tool box:

'Language is like a collection of very various tools. In the tool box there is a hammer, a saw, a rule, a lead, a glue pot and glue. Many of the tools are akin to each other in form and in use, and the tools can roughly be divided into groups according to their relationships; but the boundaries between these groups will often be more or less arbitrary and there are various types of relationship that cut across one another.' (PG p. 67)

In *Philosophical Investigations* Wittgenstein re-employs this analogy to convey the new view:

'Think of the tools in a toolbox: there is a hammer, pliers, a saw, a screw-driver, a rule, a glue-pot, glue, nails, screws. - The functions of words are as diverse as the functions of these objects. (And in both cases, there are similarities).' (PI I 11)

The key insight in all of this is given in the view that the 'functions of words are as diverse as the functions of these objects'; this is a more variegated and diverse notion of understanding the communicative and representative functions of language. And at the heart of this is the mantra, quoted a moment ago, that we must let 'the use of words teach... their meaning' (PI PPF 303).

One early expression of Wittgenstein's developed approach to language and meaning is presented in a remark from his lectures as cited by G. E. Moore:

'The meaning of a word is no longer for us an object corresponding to it.' (PO p. 54)

This remark signals Wittgenstein's realisation of the limits of ostensive definition, naming, as a model that can serve to explain the functioning of all language. The whole process of development in his work is signalled in the Preface to *Philosophical Investigations*, where Wittgenstein writes that a reading of the *Tractatus* (about two years earlier) made him aware of 'grave mistakes' in his 'old way of thinking' (PI Preface, p. viii). The primary mistake of the *Tractatus* seen by Wittgenstein is, of course, the reliance on the picture theory of meaning which rests upon the ostensive correspondence posited between names and objects, a theory that, in retrospect, we can suspect that Wittgenstein sees as contributing to the misunderstandings and confusions to which *Philosophical Investigations* is the intended cure. But although Wittgenstein very clearly orientates many of his remarks in *Philosophical Investigations* to the end of presenting a thorough critique of the *Tractatus*, he doesn't assail it openly or directly. Instead, he begins with a discussion of a passage from Augustine's *Confessions* in which Augustine recalls how he learned the meaning of words and thus gained insight into the workings of language:

'When they (my elders) named some object, and accordingly moved towards something, I saw this and I grasped that the thing was called by the sound they uttered when they meant to point it out.'[112]

Wittgenstein comments that this recollection provides 'a particular picture of the essence of human language' (PI I 1), one that says that 'the words in language name objects - sentences are combinations of such names'. In discussing Augustine, Wittgenstein does not say that it this picture of the essence of human language is to all intents and purposes the theory of the *Tractatus*, but he says much about the same thing when he remarks that this picture of language provides the basis of the following idea: 'Every word has a meaning. This meaning is correlated with the word. It is the object for which the word stands.' This is clearly the theory of the *Tractatus*, but it is this theory that *Philosophical Investigations* attacks through a rejection of Augustine's testimony. It is only fair to Augustine to point out that in his *Confessions* he also moves away from a purely ostensive theory of linguistic meaning.

According to the *Philosophical Investigations*, the approach of Augustine exemplifies the quest to find an essence to language. But Wittgenstein sees the danger in such a quest, which is manifest as the drive to '*see right into* phenomena' (PI I 90). This involves the idea that somehow the essence of language 'lies open to view', that it becomes '*surveyable* through a process of ordering' (PI I 92).

The job in *Philosophical Investigations* nevertheless echoes the anti-metaphysical stance of the *Tractatus*, as when Wittgenstein remarks that his aim is to 'bring words back from their metaphysical to their everyday use' (PI I 116). What 'lies open to view' in *Philosophical Investigations* is the diversity of everyday language-use, and this diversity renders incoherent any attempt, even that

---

[112] *Confessions*, 1. 8., quoted in PI I 1

of the *Tractatus,* to frame a general theory of the nature and essence of language. Thus, with regard to the business of naming objects as in Augustine's recollection, Wittgenstein's point is that for the idea of names standing for objects to have sense for the young Augustine, it must have been already the case that the activity of naming was understood as being amongst those things that can be done within language. He remarks that 'much must be prepared in the language for mere naming to make sense' (PI I 257). The role of gesture, or pointing, what we might now call the role in communication of body-language, is really what Wittgenstein is incorporating into his theory. In *Zettel,* there is the comment that 'Pointing is itself only a sign, and in the language-game it may direct the application of the sentence, and so shew what is meant' (Z 24). Note the use here of the term 'language-game', a key notion of course, in *Philosophical Investigations.* The point for now, however, is that as Wittgenstein sees it, for a first-time learner of language, the ability to comprehend that my pointing to the window and uttering 'window' is an exercise in naming depends on the learner's having grasped that naming, 'pointing to', stands amongst the operations of language. (Think of all the things that my action might be taken to signify: a comment on the weather, on colour, sound, etc, on the function of the referent – or some other object perceived through the window, a command to leave, a question, and so on.) Wittgenstein's point is that other things can be done meaningfully within language and that even with regard to the so-called definitive relation of naming, there is authentic scope for diversity.

As illustrations of the matters at stake here, there are two comments about Socrates that Wittgenstein made. The first is recalled by his friend Maurice Drury from a conversation in about 1930:

'It has puzzled me why Socrates has been regarded as a great philosopher. Because when Socrates asks for the meaning of a word and people give him examples of how that word is used, he isn't satisfied and wants a unique definition. Now if someone shows me how a word is used and its different meanings, that is just the sort of answer that I want.'[113]

The second comment, which dates from 1937, refers to the difficulty faced by Socrates when he seeks the definition of concepts:

'Again and again a use of the word emerges that seems not to be compatible with the concept that other uses have led us to form. We say: but that *isn't* how it is! - it *is* like that though! - & all we can do is keep repeating these antitheses.' (CV p. 35)

Another example comes from the comments Wittgenstein makes on the word 'slab'. He refers to this first in *The Brown Book*[114] and then in *Philosophical Investigations* (I 2), where he assumes for the sake of argument the truth of the Augustinian view, ostensive definition – also the view of the *Tractatus*. He uses the example of a builder and his assistant.

On this view if, during the construction of a building, the builder (A) has an assistant (B), it might be B's job to pass to A the materials he needs. Words like 'block', 'pillar', 'slab' and 'beam' might be used. If A called out 'Bring me a such-and-such', and used a given word, B would bring the correct stone. In section 19 of *Philosophical Investigations* Wittgenstein returns to this example and points out that the grammatical meaning of the word 'slab' is not the same as the call, as in the utterance of command,

[113] 'Conversations with Wittgenstein', in Rhees (1984), p. 115.
[114] See BB pp. 79-80

'Bring me a slab'. And of course, A might just call in a certain tone of voice 'Slab!' and this 'Slab!' could mean 'Bring me a slab'.

Wittgenstein elaborates a number of thoughts in this example to suggest that in and through the variables of usage, language contains a range of possibilities for meaning and truth. A person has to have a natural mastery of the language, to '*know* this language' (PI I 20), to engage in this complex of usages. Another complex (PI I 21) comes if we compare what we mean by 'Five slabs'. 'Five Slabs' can be the content of report given by B to A: here the meaning might be that there are five slabs left. 'Five slabs!' can be A's insistent command that B get five more slabs. Here, whether the phrase is a report or a command, and what the tone of voice is, will vary the meaning, and so the truth, of the phrase.

Wittgenstein often writes about other genres of communication, such as music and poetry, and in *Zettel*, he has the point that both music and poetry can be seen as communicative but not in the everyday or factual manner. He says that a poem may be composed 'in the language of information' but it is not using the 'language game of giving information' (Z 160). Wittgenstein then suggests a thought experiment: imagine a person has never heard the music of Chopin but is then taken to a recital where he hears 'a reflective piece of Chopin' played. Won't the person think that what he is listening to is 'a language', one that 'people merely want to keep the meaning secret' from him? This leads to the point that there is a 'musical element in verbal language'. Wittgenstein gives some examples – a 'sigh, the intonation of voice in a question, in an announcement, in longing; all the innumerable gestures made with the voice' (Z 161). Another remark confirms this: if we understand a musical phrase this 'may also be called understanding a *language*' (Z 172).

Wittgenstein certainly gives plenty of comments to confirm the idea that music works as a communicative language, as in his remark, 'The *strength of the musical thinking* in Brahms' (CV. p. 27). And in general, the view that characterises his later thought is that 'Only in the stream of life and thought do words have meaning' (Z 173).

We can take another example to develop Wittgenstein's point with regard to how music has significance. Suppose I have a copy of the music for Beethoven's Piano Sonata No. 29, the 'Hammerklavier', Op. 106. What 'Beethoven's Piano Sonata No. 29' is and means is, in some respects given by the musical score. For a musicologist, the analysis of the score will bring many insights to bear on the form and structure of the composition. But is this what the work actually or wholly means? A concert pianist, or a lover of the piano repertoire, might think that the score alone is not really the most vital expression of, or for, this work. What is more significant is another possibility for use, namely, playing or hearing the work in performance. In the activity and realisation of the work in an idiomatic performance, the meaning, and 'the musical argument' of the work, for the performer and audience may be experienced.

A great deal of the work that Wittgenstein produced through the period of his later philosophy is termed 'philosophical psychology' in consequence of the attention he pays to the psychological processes of understanding linguistic expressions. This concern is reflected in *Philosophical Investigations* in terms of the criticism of views – such as that of the *Tractatus* – which suggest that the process of understanding involves crucially a mental process. Experience suggests that we simply cannot rely on the associations we have before the mind when we hear or speak a word or expression to know the actual meaning of the word or expression in and for the application in question. The understanding of a word or expression that we have heard that we grasp 'in a flash' mentally is one thing – dependent upon the various associations that we might have for it on the basis of earlier experiences of use – but the meaning of the word or expression that fits the case in the application to hand is another. The meaning, Wittgenstein thinks, cannot be given through the understanding if, as he believes:

'the meaning is the *use* we make of the word.' (PI I 138)

His view is that:

'What is essential now is to see that the same thing may be in our minds when we hear the word and yet the application still be different. Has it the *same* meaning both times? I think we would deny that.' (PI I 140)

Wittgenstein illustrates the inadequacy of working on the assumption that an inner mental process of understanding provides the means to the end of understanding the meaning of expressions through a consideration of the word 'cube'. (See PI I 139/40) Having the concept and mental picture of a cube before the mind does, Wittgenstein thinks, elucidate the sense and meaning of the term in use. We might have in association with the concept 'cube' a number of images – ice, sugar, and the like, but the meaning of a given expression is determined through a consideration of the context of use. In use, we will see which of the possible images of the term or expression hold and in what sense it applies, and we may find, through some kind of development, a novelty of usage.

Wittgenstein has another example in *Zettel* which helps clarify the new perspective and the contrast with the restrictive idea of ostensive definitions where names 'picture' facts. Taking 'thinking' as a concept Wittgenstein comments it 'comprises many manifestations of life' and says that 'the *phenomena* of thinking are widely scattered' (Z 110). And it is not right to consider that 'thinking' has a fit with reality: such a view is now thought 'naïve', and what we get if we pursue this, if we revert in effect to the theory of the *Tractatus*, would be 'a false picture'. Thinking, says Wittgenstein, 'does not correspond to reality at all'. We in vain look for a correspondence theory to give us a 'smooth contour' but what we have is more 'ragged' (Z 111). We might have thought that the concept 'thinking' had 'unified employment', but 'we should rather expect the opposite' (Z 112). If we are to learn to understand the word 'think' properly we must, therefore, learn 'under certain circumstances' (Z 114).

These comments reveal something of the difference between a systematic philosophy, like that of Plato (or of Wittgenstein to a degree with the singular theory advanced in the *Tractatus*), and the descriptive method adopted in the *Philosophical Investigations,* which maintains that understanding meaning is a more open and dynamic affair involving grasping the sense of the term or expression in question through looking at the practical context of active, human and social engagement. Accordingly, naming and ostensive definition is neither the true nor the only game that can be played within language – and here we meet a central notion in Wittgenstein's *Philosophical Investigations*.

iii. On 'Games' (and Language-Games)

In *Philosophical Investigations* Wittgenstein advances the view that language-use is actually so diverse that it is a serious error to engage in the reductionism, the 'assimilation of expression' and over-simplification of theories like that of the *Tractatus*. We noted earlier

Wittgenstein's observations of the tools in a tool-box, and he concludes the remark in *Philosophical Investigations* with the comment that:

'what confuses us is the uniform appearance of words when we hear them in speech, or see them written or in. For their *use* is not that obvious. Especially when we are doing philosophy!' (PI I 11)

His next remark provides a good illustration of the point – so long as we are aware of the usual arrangements of the interior of the driver's cab in a steam locomotive:

'It is like looking into the cabin of a locomotive. There are handles there, all looking more or less alike. (This stands to reason, since they are all supposed to be handled.) But one is the handle of a crank which can be moved continuously (it regulates the opening of a valve); another is the handle of a switch, which has only two operative positions; it is either off or on; a third is the handle of a brake-lever, the harder one pulls on it, the harder it brakes; a fourth, the handle of a pump: it has an effect only so long as it moves to and fro.' (PI I 12)

Wittgenstein means that when we trot out the view that 'every word in a language signifies something', the fact of the matter is that we have said nothing until we have 'explained exactly what distinction we wish to make'. As in our observations of the cab of the locomotive – all the handles have a job – but really this generality is less significant than knowing the actual use-value of each switch in relation to its function.

Perhaps the best-known image Wittgenstein employs to articulate this perspective is the term 'language-game' which he develops in various writings in the 1930s and introduces and defines in a rather diffuse manner early in *Philosophical*

Investigations. He suggests that the 'games' through which we learn our native language – pointing, repeating, naming – are language-games, as is the primitive language that enables such other games to signify.

But he also calls 'the whole, consisting of language and the activities into which it is woven, a "language-game"' (PI I 7).

Perhaps a more helpful sense of the key meaning here derives from a passage a little later in the text:

'... the term "language-*game*" is meant to emphasize the fact that the *speaking* of a language is part of an activity, or of a form of life.' (PI I 23)

Wittgenstein then invites us to consider the multiplicity of 'language-games' in the following examples:

'Giving orders and acting on them -
Describing the appearance of an object, or by its measurements -
Constructing an object from a description (a drawing) -
Reporting an event -
Speculating about an event -
Forming and testing a hypothesis -
Presenting the results of an experiment in tables and diagrams -
Making up a story; and reading one -
Acting in a play -
Singing rounds -
Guessing riddles -
Making a joke; telling one -
Solving a problem in applied arithmetic -
Translating from one language into another -
Requesting, thanking, cursing, greeting, praying.'

Ostensive definition is 'a language-game on its own' (PI I 27), but there is within language (and life) a great variety of language-games. Consider what can be done with exclamations – Wittgenstein offers another list:

'Water!
Away!
Ow!
Help!
Splendid!
No!'

He then asks rhetorically, 'Are you still inclined to call these word "names of objects"?'

And of the various language-games that can be observed Wittgenstein comments, with due self-reference:

'It is interesting to compare the diversity of the tools of language and of the ways they are used, the diversity of kinds of word and sentence, with what logicians have said about the structure of language. (This includes the author of the *Tractatus Logico-Philosophicus*)' (PI I 23).

By the 'multiplicity' of tools and uses for those tools in language, what Wittgenstein means is that there are distinct conventions or rules for usage within the language game. Here we can note a comment from the second part of *Philosophical Investigations* – the part which consists of various notes on matters in the area of philosophical psychology that Wittgenstein probably intended to integrate into the first part of the text, where we have the following remark:

'We don't notice the enormous variety of all the everyday language-games, because the clothing of our language makes them all alike' (PI PPF 335).

Wittgenstein's judgement is that the 'clothing of language' must not be viewed apart from the body of life, from the dynamics of action from which the sense of language emerges. Words can be regarded as a 'signal', Wittgenstein suggests, but we evaluate the sense of the signal and 'whether it was rightly applied' by what the language-user 'goes on to do' (PI I 180).

In general terms, Wittgenstein's view is that understanding language-use thus involves description, 'noting a language game', and looking at what happens, rather than seeking explanation through some prefabricated criteria. (See PI I 654/5). The fundamental realisation must be – to cite again the phrase alluded to in the title of this study – that 'Words are... deeds' (PI I 546 and CV p. 53).

Understanding language is thus dependent, not upon a theoretical or conceptual insight, on a state of mind, so to speak, but upon our having 'mastered a technique' (PI I 199). He notes, with masterly understatement in *Zettel*, that, 'A language-game comprises the use of *several* words' (Z 644). So we must get away from the notion of word naming objects, and simple representational views of meaning via correspondence. We must instead appreciate the variety, complexity, and multiplicity of language-games, and employing this appreciation we can then identify and discriminate between the various uses to which words may be put: and Wittgenstein does not push the notion of 'meaning as use' exclusively; he writes of the 'functions', the 'purpose', and the 'aim', of words, and of expressions in language 'performing their office' (see PI I 5, 6, 8, 11, 17, 402) so as to convey the flavour of the diversity and flexibility of roles, sense and employments within language-games and forms of life. The critical point is that we are to avoid reliance upon one particular language-game, and thus Wittgenstein opposes the elevation of scientific thought and discourse, 'technical reason', to use Tillich's[115] phrase, that the *Tractatus* set such store by.

There are some helpful illustrations of the way Wittgenstein employs the notion of language-games in *Culture and Value* (pp. 27-28). Suppose we are comparing the eyes of two people and say that one person's eyes have 'a more beautiful expression' than the others; we 'do not mean by the word beautiful what is common to everything that we call "beautiful".' What we are doing is 'playing a game with this word that has quite narrow bands.' And the game here would be distinct from the game in use when we speak of 'the beauty in the shape of a nose.' The suggestion is that in use the rules for the meaning of a term – 'beauty' in this case, and the 'particular grammar' of the term will be 'apparent' and explicable. In a later remark, Wittgenstein says that the 'origin & the primitive form of the language game is a reaction' from which 'more complicated forms grow' (CV p. 36). He adds that language should be seen as a 'refinement, in the beginning was the deed.'

Wittgenstein draws attention (PI I 65) to a criticism that the theory of language-games faces. The criticism is that the explanation so-called of language through the notion of language-games ducks the question as to the essence of language-games and thus of language. The use of the term 'language-games' suggests that there must be some common feature that defines an activity of a particular sort as a language-game, but Wittgenstein's exposition appears to run against such an analysis: he affirms the virtues of noting and describing language-games, but analysis and explanation are vetoed. Wittgenstein accepts that he is denying that there is 'something common to all that we call language' and affirms that his perspective has what may be termed a relational and dynamic notion of

---

[115] See Tillich 1968 pp. 80ff.

language. The phenomena of language, Wittgenstein says, 'have no one thing in common in virtue of which we use the same word for all', rather, the phenomena of language are related to one another in a variety of ways and it is this system of inter-related meanings and language-games that constitutes language.

A key problem with this emerges if we take the example of the word 'biscuit'. Suppose that, as is the case, there are a great many types and varieties of biscuit, and so there is a very large range of possible language-games that could be played relative the wide range of biscuits available relative to many possible 'forms of life'. However, if we think about 'biscuit', we would be able to formulate a generic explanation of what it is for a biscuit to 'be a biscuit'. In like manner, if we acknowledge 'complicated forms' of language-games, and 'the prodigious diversity of all the everyday language-games', are we not able to formulate a generic explanation of what is for a language-game to 'be a language game'? Won't all language-games share something in common?

However plausible this sounds, Wittgenstein's antipathy to theory means that he does not want to entertain the notion of seeking and then setting out an explanation of what all language-games have 'in common.'

What he does is to launch into a discussion of the 'proceedings' we call 'games' (PI I 66/7). We can think of card-games, ball-games, Olympic games and as many of the other games people play as we like. Wittgenstein seems to think that our assumption that all games must, in virtue of being called a game, have something in common is a dangerous distraction, it is an example, perhaps, of our intelligence being bewitched by language. He says, 'don't think, but look!' (PI I 66) Rather than thinking about things, and reactively looking to find the truth, we should *look* at the cases of the use of 'games' to the end of seeing what there is, if anything, that is in common to them all. Wittgenstein's own view is that we won't find anything like this. What we do find is are 'similarities, relationships, and a whole series of them at that.' His affirmation that we should not 'think but look' is a brief but typical assault on the temptation to rely on theory, but by looking and through the description of use, we will see the 'multifarious relationships' of board-games, and when we pass to consider card-games we will notice that whilst some of these features remain, some drop out of view and that others come into play. The same sort of thing happens when we look at ball-games. And some games are 'amusing', whilst some are serious. Snap and bridge are card-games of very different function, for example. Some games are competitive, but some are relaxing and purely recreational. Some games can be either, depending on who you play with. For example, if you play cricket for the 'Kings Arms XI', it is likely to be for fun; but if you play for the county or the country, the business of the game becomes much more serious. Some games involve more luck than others, and games involve different degrees of skill and energy, and so on.

The outcome of such a review, Wittgenstein concludes, is that 'we see a complicated network of similarities overlapping and criss-crossing: similarities in the large and the small.' We thus see patterns and relationships rather than a common essence. Wittgenstein then uses the idea of 'family resemblances' (PI I 67) to characterize the point: the similarities of features and manners and temperament in members of a family 'overlap and criss-cross in the same way'. It is like a thread which we spin from many fibres and then twist together to form the whole. The 'strength of the thread resides not in the fact that some one fibre runs through its whole length, but in the overlapping of many fibres.'

Wittgenstein then makes a remark of particular importance given our consideration of whether we can have a 'theory' of language-games: he considers whether the view he has presented amounts to a theory of the common essence of language that amounts to 'the disjunction of all their common properties'. Wittgenstein's reaction is dismissive: this is merely 'playing' with words and here he develops the point we cited a moment ago, suggesting that one might just as well say that 'Something... runs through the whole thread – namely, the continuous overlapping of those fibres' (PI I 67).

The important point here is that whilst Wittgenstein might have scored well against the semantics of the view that he has presented a theory of the common essence of language, it is less clear that he has avoided the presentation of a general theory of language and meaning. For in presenting the idea of the language-game, Wittgenstein surely manifests a characterization, amounting to a theory, of linguistic activity as a whole. Moreover, in and through his discussion of games and language-games he draws upon one special feature that games all appear to exhibit to some degree and which language also shares in a significant fashion. This is the *rule-governed* nature of games and of course, of language-games, and in so far as it is held to be significant it appears to constitute the shape or core of a general theory of the nature, function, style, and character of all language-games, and thus of language.

iv. Rules and the Social Dimension of Meaning

From Wittgenstein's discussion of games and language-games, we can see that his theory of meaning is social in character. All games, and all language-games, have rules and conventions, and the key point, reflecting the anthropological orientation of Wittgenstein's perspective, is that rules and conventions are fixed through the activity of playing the games in question and they are revised and altered in the same way, as are the meanings and uses of language in general. The rules that are manifest through experience for language-use, the character of the language-game, are set through agreements, customs, traditions, and conventions. The rules for language-use that accrue within and for this or that socio-cultural setting may be represented in theoretical systems, but they arise through practical use and are modified and implemented in that context, in and through situational, dynamic and relational exchanges. Theory is therefore always secondary: Wittgenstein's point is that it would be artificial to attempt to fit and fix into a theoretical template or scheme onto something active and dynamic. The significant points of reference for meaning in language are thus public and social, not private and analytical, and there cannot be any objective and external point of reference for meaning and truth as a whole, so no external justification for our linguistic activity as a whole.

In his last writings Wittgenstein remarks that giving grounds or justifications for our linguistic practices – a language-game of a sort, of course – meets an end in 'our *acting...* which lies at the bottom of the language-game' (OC 204). The rules we learn through the practical dynamics of life are grounded upon existing applications and customs and in developing this notion, Wittgenstein thinks that it follows that there can be no sense whatever to the idea of the possibility of a logically private form of rule-following and language-use. This gives rise to the so-called 'private language' argument in Wittgenstein's later philosophy about which something should now be said.

By a 'private language' Wittgenstein means 'a language in which a person could write down or give voice to his inner experiences' so that what was in evidence was 'private' and represented the person's 'immediate private sensations' which no other person could understand (PI I 243). Here we have a discussion that is reminiscent of the consideration of solipsism in the *Tractatus*.

The idea that language could be a purely private matter is rooted in the tradition of empirical thinking that goes back to the work of John Locke (1632-1794) as in his *Essay Concerning Human Understanding* (1690). Locke's book sets out to show the implausibility of the view that human reasoning was based on 'certain *innate principles*'[116]. This view, also associated with traditional rationalism, assumes that the principles by which the mind reasons, orders, sorts and determines are somehow 'stamped upon the mind' and brought 'into the world with it'. The contrasting view, that Locke favours, is famously expressed in his notion that the mind is better viewed as 'white paper, void of all characters, without any ideas.'[117] Locke thus argues[118] that through the senses, varied experiences of perception bring before the mind the qualities we assume to be of 'objects'. Locke's example is that we employ such terms as '*yellow, white, heat, cold, soft, hard, bitter, sweet*' to describe the 'sensible qualities' we have perceived. Locke also assumes that the mind has a residual capacity, of which we are aware, to organise 'another set of ideas' such as '*perception, thinking, doubting, believing, reasoning, knowing, willing*'.[119] This 'source of ideas' is distinct from the perception of 'external objects', and Locke calls it the 'internal sense' of 'reflection'. Working with this theory, Locke then suggests that we use words as '*the signs*' of

---

[116] Locke (2004) 1.II. 2. Locke's *Essay* is divided into books, chapters and sections and it is the convention to make citations in this way.
[117] Locke (2004) 2. I. 2.
[118] Locke (2004) 2. I, 3 & 4.
[119] Locke (2004) 2. I. 4.

our 'ideas'.[120] This is not a 'natural connexion', says Locke, or else there would be 'but one language amongst all men.' Instead, we each use words 'by a voluntary imposition, whereby… a word is made arbitrarily the mark of such an idea.' The upshot of this view Locke states with great conviction: words, as these 'marks' are, 'in their primary or immediate signification, stand for nothing, but the ideas in the mind of him that uses them.'[121] This line of thinking can be seen as suggesting the possibility of a personal and private language.

Locke's empiricism can now be seen to be unwittingly assuming a false view of the generic capacities of the mind. In effect, Locke thinks that all individual minds are blank receptors that accumulate and then, somehow, organise the matters of experience. But more modern thinking sees the human individual as always being embedded in a socio-linguistic culture[122] and as possessing inherent capacities to rationally and linguistically order thought and structure language-use. Consistent with this, Wittgenstein's developed view of the nature of language emphasises its public and social nature. He sees language as conveying meaning and sense through its relation to a social, and rule-based, contexts of use and application. This entails the view that the human world, and all the elements of language, operate so that a wholly private human language is impossible. Any private code, any secret language, could only work if it was encoded from a public language, so no language invented by and meaningful for a single individual can be wholly and logically private. Language, in contrast to Locke's view, is acquired and worked up by the active capacities of the mind, as well as through social and interpersonal bonds of meaning, and this context of order and convention is

[120] Locke (2004) 3. II. 1
[121] Locke (2004) 3. II. 2.
[122] On this see Pinker (2008)

necessarily located within the structures of a community of shared meaning.[123]

Wittgenstein's idea of language as social activity and thus as rule-orientated, is not intended as an exhaustive description. He does not suggest for a moment that there is a sum total of rules for the consequent sum of language-games. On the contrary, he sees (PI I 68 & 83) that due to the social basis for the activities that generate linguistic systems, structures of rules are open to development and alteration within broad and indeterminate constraints.

To illustrate, we may say that he thinks of rules for language-use and thus meaning as being akin to the convention that holds in cricket that bowlers have a run-up before they bowl. There is no set rule as to the length of the run-up, it can range from one pace to thirty yards or more – although there are clear and generally-accepted conventions for bowlers of each of the main types. The broad context is set, however, by the boundary markers on the field of play, since the bowler cannot begin his run-up from beyond the boundary. To take another example, and not one that Wittgenstein would like, Wittgenstein's notion of the rules for language use is akin to the sense in which we offer and expect to have to offer justifications, as in morality, where we have to be able to give account of our decisions and actions since we are held responsible for them. Moral conventions are not fixed, the conventions and norms alter, as we could trace in and through the history of ethical thought on matters of moral conduct. But for morality and for language-use there is a context and an arena within and before which justifications are necessary. This precludes the combination of legitimacy and privacy in actual language-use just as in the moral sphere. In life, if someone acts with regard to nothing but an assumed

---

[123] Wittgenstein has an extended discussion of this issue in PI 1 243-304. Kenny (2006) pp. 141-159 has an excellent analysis of this debate.

private moral sense, he or she is sooner or later diagnosed as psychotic, and his or her actions are said to be 'inhuman.'

Wittgenstein devotes a great deal of attention to this issue in *Philosophical Investigations* since the points articulate the central thrust of his criticism of much of the philosophical tradition since Descartes (1596-1650). Wittgenstein's later philosophy is opposed particularly to the view that the basis for knowledge and understanding is the subjectivity of individual self-consciousness, the individual's consciousness of his own mental awareness. Descartes' rationalism[124] employs the individual's subjective intellectual self-consciousness, the *cogito*, as the basis for certainty in relation to the self and one's existence and in relation to external objects. The empirical tradition, as in Locke's work as considered a moment ago, somewhat similarly employs consciousness of private sense-experience as the basis for belief in relation to external objects and states. On such views, the notion of a unique and private language could be thought possible, since, as Locke thinks, it can be thought that personal linguistic meaning can be established by the individual through his own ostensive definitions of terms and senses. Our unique linguistic subject could denote personal and private sensations by signs or images that were logically distinct from any other language. Wittgenstein, of course, opposes this view since he thinks it incoherent, and one could add that it is misleading, giving rise to scepticism and pure relativism through its view of the primacy of the subject.

In countering the temptations of a private language theory Wittgenstein is not, it should be understood, arguing that it is impossible for an individual to elaborate a private code that differs from a conventional language. Such a code is

---

[124] See Descartes (1977), especially pp. 53-60 'The Fourth Discourse.'

possible, and it could be and could remain secret, private and personal. What Wittgenstein opposes is the further notion of such a code being a logically distinct and separate language. His reason is that all language is social and rule-following in origin. Thought, and thus language, are generated out of interaction with others. Language arises from, and is conditioned through, the dynamic and public context of life, and therefore no private language can be predicated save upon the basis of an awareness of rule-following – which is a social affair. Thus, he argues that a private act of rule-following is impossible since in such a context there could be no difference between following a rule and merely thinking that a rule was being followed:

'"following a rule" is a practice. And to *think* one is following a rule is not to follow a rule. And that's why it's not possible to follow a rule "privately"; otherwise thinking one was following a rule would be the same thing as following it.' (PI I 202)

Wittgenstein's view, as with the quotation from *Philosophical Investigations* 23 cited earlier, is that to use a language is to participate in 'a form of life'. So, to use a language is a social affair – participation is grounded in the social learning process. Privacy is based on and relative to this – to the public domain. Language-use, Wittgenstein suggests, is socially developed and culturally grounded. It is a plastic and dynamic medium evolved as a development of and substitute for natural and pre-linguistic expressions: we say 'I am in pain', rather than moaning and crying. Children, of course, do moan and cry, but over time and through interactions with adults, children learn the sense and meaning of sensations and experiences, and the language-game that is attached to them, which then gradually replace primitive natural expressions with patterns of speech. (c.f. PI I 244)

v. Criticism of Wittgenstein's Later Philosophy

As we have seen, Wittgenstein did not train as a philosopher through a conventional programme of study. His interest in philosophical problems arose through the combination of his questioning nature, his extreme capacity for concentrated work and, initially, from problems he met as a student of engineering. He disliked the academic life, apart from the teaching duties which he took seriously and used constructively in the development of his thinking, and he did not write in the conventional fashion of the philosophers of his age. Further, he submits a perspective through his later philosophy that is antagonistic to the central assumptions of the approach within modern philosophy. Accordingly, it is no great surprise that some in the philosophical community have found cause to react against Wittgenstein's later philosophy. Here we can examine three lines of criticism: one to do with Wittgenstein's view of the cause of philosophical problems, one on his treatment of the problems of truth and knowledge, and one on his attitude to theoretical systems.

Wittgenstein's diagnosis of the cause of philosophical problems has not met with universal approval – rather obviously, since there would be no philosophers at work in any school, college or university if his view had been completely accepted! Wittgenstein contends that philosophy fails to solve its problems through our 'urge' to abuse language. He means that we are inclined to fall under the spell of language induced by the view that through language we can achieve analysis and explanation of the matters of concern to us. Thus, we seek to penetrate phenomena in search of the true essence or nature of the things in question, whereas we should resolve our problems if we conducted a descriptive review of what lay before us, open to view in the language-games and forms of life that are 'given'. As one of Wittgenstein's comments in *Culture and Value* puts it:

'God grant the philosopher insight into what lies in front of everyone's eyes.' (CV p. 72)

Also:

'How hard it is for me to see what is *right in front of my eyes.*' (CV p. 39)

Against this is the view that actually, philosophical problems are not simply linguistic. Philosophy is not simply an activity of unravelling problems of intelligible language use. Instead, it is rather obviously the case that there are many causes of concern that promote philosophical investigation that do not arise through linguistic abuse nor through the wanton inclination to analyse phenomena without just cause. In relation to ethics, and particularly contemporary bio-ethics, such as in debates over gene editing of the human embryo to eradicate serious inherited conditions such as cystic fibrosis or Pick's disease, as well as in political philosophy and epistemology, there is just cause for the view that simply 'describing' what lies open to view will not resolve the difficulty. Cogent analysis of the issues and rigorous arguments to tease out the options, and arguments to reasoned conclusions remain a core part of philosophy. Perhaps this point does no more than to clarify matters procedurally: Wittgenstein's view is not mutually exclusive in relation to more overtly interrogative forms of analysis. However, it would be unfair to lose sight of the fact that his diagnosis of the nature of philosophical perplexity is a part of his radical re-orientation of the emphasis in modern philosophy on the first person – and so on the perils of subjective certainty. Wittgenstein's interest in the descriptive approach is that it serves as a prelude to the confrontation with a situational and contextualist sense of meaning, which is dynamic, relational and social in character. Making sense of writing this letter *this* way, and that letter *that* way, or of cooking a meal *this* way rather than *that*. Or making sense of any acts or 'forms of life', is, Wittgenstein's view implies, achieved through seeing the situation whole not through pulling it apart first through criteria drawn from the illusory self – illusory, since the self is capable only of being as such by employing public criteria.

Consider another remark from *Culture and Value:*

'People who are constantly asking "why?" are like tourists, who stand in front of a building, reading Baedeker, & through reading about the history of the buildings construction, etc. etc., are prevented from *seeing* the building.' (CV p. 46)[125]

If Wittgenstein was with us today, he would find no consolation. Baedeker guides will not be in evidence perhaps, but tourists will be using mobile devices to record or photograph what they will, thereby, be prevented from seeing.

In his intellectual autobiography[126], Wittgenstein's former associate, Russell, is particularly sharp in rejecting the approach of *Philosophical Investigations* which he finds to advance doctrines that are unfounded, trivial and uninteresting and to exhibit an attitude that abandons serious thinking in relation to the philosophical concern to work out a view of what may be regarded as knowledge as opposed to unfounded opinion. Russell does not think that

---

[125] Baedeker guides were popular travel guides produced from the 1830s, remaining in regular use to the mid-twentieth century.
[126] See Russell (1959) p. 160ff

we need Wittgenstein's *Philosophical Investigations* and its adherents to inform us of the obviously diverse nature of forms of expression: that there are interrogative (questioning), imperative (commanding) and optative (wishing) as well as indicative (fact-stating) expressions. The fundamental problem remains of having concern for the status of these various claims in relation to the state or condition of the world and our judgments over what is and what is not the case. But Russell suggests that the implication of *Philosophical Investigations*, although he allows that this is 'perhaps an overstatement', is that 'all sentences can count as true except those uttered by philosophers.'

This contentious aspect of Wittgenstein's later philosophy arises from his perspective on the question of truth. The *Tractatus*, of which Russell generally approves, offers a strict correspondence theory of language and reality and provides a definite method by means of which the truth-value of particular expressions can be determined. But the later philosophy envisages language as relating to activities and practices rather than to reality or, as is rather the case, in Wittgenstein's view, to selective criteria from certain domains of meaning. Thus, whilst the *Tractatus* offers firm and sharp criteria for meaning and truth, the later philosophy places meaning and truth relative to language-games and the forms of life, with a methodology that subordinates meaning and sense to use and function, and truth to meaning and sense. Truth is thus set out in contextual rather than in absolutist terms. To put the matter in extreme terms, the use of language in the later philosophy is evaluated relative to our adherence to the agreements within our group, rather than in relation to so-called 'objective' truth.

Wittgenstein works up this position consciously and anticipates the sort of criticism voiced by Russell through a consideration of whether his view amounts to saying that 'human agreement decides what is true and what is false?' (PI I 241)

He then makes the following comment:

'What is true or false is what human beings *say*; and it is in their *language* that human beings agree. This is agreement not in opinions, but in form of life.'

The term 'form of life' which we meet here again, is a key notion in *Philosophical Investigations*:

'What has to be accepted, the given, is - one might say - *forms of life*.' (PI PPF 345)

Typically, Wittgenstein does not pin down specifically the sense of the term. It signifies at one level the general perspective or mind-set of a specific linguistic group – the values, attitudes, assumptions, beliefs, traditions, and customs within a group as the context-forming matrix within which the group's language-use is set. But the context of a form of life can be much narrower within this matrix – for example, Wittgenstein suggests (PI II p. 174) that hoping is a 'form of life' and thus the term runs together with 'language-games', as we find in the passage from the *Philosophical Investigations* which we can cite again:

'the word "language-*game*" is used here to emphasize the fact that the *speaking* of a language is part of an activity, or of a form of life.' (PI I 23)

Wittgenstein's point, again, is that the functioning of language as a mode of communication is possible only through agreements and conventions over definitions and judgments. These agreements are set within socio-cultural communities which represent the context for life in its varying forms. All this is illustrative of Wittgenstein's considered opposition to the view that criteria for meaning and truth cannot be theoretical or private – they are public, practical and social. But the question Russell raises is whether this view entails an abandonment of evaluative or discriminatory criteria. The problem seen is that of the absence of criteria by means of which objective or progressive criticism of erroneous views can be advanced. Doesn't Wittgenstein's view preclude, for example, criticism of extremes of political and religious belief – aren't such extremes consecrated as forms of life or as language-games? Is Wittgenstein's proposal one that amounts to a defence of a form of socio-cultural relativism? And if all meaning comes through use, and as a 'form of life', does this not subordinate reasoning to use, to 'form of life' and to the socio-cultural relativity in question?

The point of this criticism is clear, but it does not seem at all clear that in practical terms Wittgenstein's position involves an absence of the ability to judge and discriminate. It is very clearly true that Wittgenstein does not advance an absolutist notion of truth, nor one via an orientation to a fixed criterion of truth – but he does operate with a dynamic and contextualist notion of truth dependent on meaning and use. We recall his notion of 'family resemblances' and the image of the 'thread' that derives strength from the overlapping of many 'fibres'. The point is that it is just an error to think that Wittgenstein envisages forms of life and language-games as separate and autonomous. Knowledge, views of the truth and legitimacy of particular views are thus determined progressively and dynamically. Such an approach entails an inability to establish cut and dried solutions to questions – such as those of the virtues of fundamentalism in religion or of abstraction in art. On the other hand, the view that Wittgenstein presents with the dynamic nature of the later philosophy is in line with the assault on objectivity and determinism in the sub-atomic physics of the last century or so.

Another problem in Wittgenstein's later philosophy arises through the unsystematic nature of his use of terminology, of language-games and forms of life, and of meaning as use. The lack of system here is, of course, indicative of the view of *Philosophical Investigations* that no general theory of the essence and nature of language is possible. But this rejection of general theory is dogmatic and prescriptive and at the very least doubly ironic. On the one hand, the *Tractatus* had advanced a general theory, one that Wittgenstein comes to think mistaken – and this fuels his rejection of all attempts to frame a general theory; but on the other hand, his later analysis together with the description of language that he sets out, does provide, a theory of the character and form of language. Wittgenstein rejects this, of course, (c.f. PI I 67); he likes to suggest that general theory is anathema, and that his approach is a simple, non-theoretical and descriptive exercise in therapy for the puzzles and confusions we create for ourselves through our misuse of language. But operationally, this does sound rather like a theory.

In no small part, Wittgenstein's positive achievements focus around this attitude. His critique of ostensive definition and promotion of a social and dynamic theory of meaning and his assault on the dualism of the Cartesian outlook without moving into either behaviourism or materialism, for example, as well as his attack on the role of reason. In *On Certainty* (287) he considers somewhat playfully whether squirrels store nuts each winter because they have solved Hume's problem of induction? Obviously, they haven't – they act out of instinctive senses in relation to the context of the environment. Similarly,

Wittgenstein thinks, we don't walk into fires or into other extreme situations because we have a rationale that confounds Hume's logic – but because our judgments are grounded in the logic of experience and it is this, rather than some theory, that we employ in what we do.

This is not at all incoherent, but the crucial point is that it is still *a theory*, and a very radical and anti-theoretical one, and it is understandable that there is frustration that it isn't clearer. It is perhaps rather hard to complain over the latter point since *Philosophical Investigations* and the other texts in which the later philosophy is found are posthumous, but the former point is correct: Wittgenstein's description amounts to a theory of the style and character of language, and there is thus scope for further analysis. For example, to review and describe the range of possible/actual modes of expression, like asking, ordering, questioning, evading, and so on.

Here we should note the view that, as per the theory of the *Tractatus*, representation is and remains central to the operations of language. Wittgenstein was perhaps more importantly right in his remark that 'no language is conceivable which does not represent the world' (PR 47), at least, we might say, in *some way represent* the world. It can be argued that whilst the operative range of representative functions within language are diverse, they can nevertheless be quantified in more specific senses than Wittgenstein appears to allow. It is as if Wittgenstein's lack of regard for theory encourages him to avoid this development and to rest with the impression that the complex of language-games and forms of life constitute an open diversity of possible meaning and usage. But representing states of affairs is central to the language-games we play, and since representation remains at the heart of language, an account, and analysis of the range of functions evident is more possible then Wittgenstein allows. To take again the example of how, in English, one might say 'Yes', the following usages can be suggested:

'Yes.'
'Yes!'
'YES!!'
'Yes...'
'Yeeeeees...'

These five usages can be said to be five language-games grounded in five forms of life: but we could imagine giving each an account, description and analysis. We don't just have to 'look' and 'describe'. And our ability to know how 'Yes!' and 'Yes' differ is based on our own participation in such 'language-games', such 'forms of life'. Our engagement and experience with those 'forms of life' and 'language-games' generates and empowers use-based meaning that is operative through being shared.

Despite the impact of Wittgenstein's work, his ideas simply have not revolutionised the activity of philosophy as a disciple of study, nor of philosophers in general. Courses on Wittgenstein's philosophy are commonly taught amongst other courses, but philosophers, in general, do not seem themselves as, to paraphrase Wittgenstein, therapists dealing with the bewitchment of the intelligence by language. As of old, concerns are with what we can know and with what degree of certainty, what we should do to act rightly in personal or in political life, what it is that good, beautiful, just and so on. It is probably true to say that Wittgenstein would consider the ongoing professionalism of philosophy as an unmitigated disaster, leading to work that is intellectually derivative, incestuous and sterile. He would think that too few people were prepared to think about the real nature of philosophical problems. What he meant by this could be a topic for a long study, but, in brief, one significant benefit of reading and studying Wittgenstein is that he is, like Kant and Nietzsche, to name but two, a thinker who provokes the reader to re-thinking problems and issues that had seemed resolved. There is an invaluable bonus to reading Wittgenstein in that regard.

A good line of thought to illustrate this comes in *Zettel*. Wittgenstein says that 'disquiet in philosophy' comes about from 'looking at philosophy wrongly', meaning the problems and questions the philosopher is investigating. Thus, things might be seen as 'being divided into (infinite) longitudinal strips instead of into (finite) cross strips' (Z 447). Wittgenstein explains that is the most difficult of things to change our thinking here. The key idea he has is that if philosophers try to solve infinite problems, the snag is that they cannot find viable or persuasive solutions. But if we look at things differently, so look at cross strips, not at longitudinal lines, then 'wild conjectures; and be replaced by the 'quiet weighing of linguistic facts.' Whatever other influences Wittgenstein has or has not had, his view that language is an expression of an 'activity' or a 'form of life' (see PI I. 23) is significant and has fed into a range of disciplines, including anthropology, and theological hermeneutics[127]. This view entails the key argument that it is wrong to think that insight into the meaning of language is a consequence of thought alone. The view developed in *Philosophical Investigations*, is, as we have seen, that language is an experience of activity, and in *Zettel,* we have a good example of how Wittgenstein sees things:

'Let us imagine someone doing work that involves comparison, trial, choice. Say he is constructing an appliance out of various bits of stuff with a given set of tools. Every now and again there is the problem "Should I use this bit?" – the bit is rejected, another is tried. Bits are

---

[127] See Thiselton (1980) for abundant examples of this.

tentatively put together, then dismantled; he looks for one that fits etc., etc. I now imagine that this whole procedure is filmed. The worker perhaps also produces sound-effects like "hm" or "ha!" As it were sounds of hesitation, sudden finding, decision, satisfaction, dissatisfaction. But he does not utter a single word. Those sound effects may be included in the film. I have the film shewn me, and now I invent a soliloquy for the worker, things that fit his manner of work, his rhythm, his play of expression, his gestures and spontaneous noises; they all correspond to this. So I sometimes make him say "No, that bit is too long, perhaps another'll fit better." – Or "What am I to do now?" – "Got it!" – Or, "That's not bad" etc.' (Z 100)

Wittgenstein's idea here is that the person doing the job of construction had thoughts and feelings as he worked, but the descriptions and words given by Wittgenstein could be an acceptable expression of the work in progress. Words, as Wittgenstein has said, work and matter to us as deeds.

6. Applications of Wittgenstein's Perspective

In this chapter, the focus is on two lines of thought in which the ideas of Wittgenstein's later philosophy were applied to issues and problems arising over considerations of the validity of religious language. This will provide us with some case-studies in how Wittgenstein's ideas might be developed and allow some more reflection on the questions we have raised about the way in which Wittgenstein's perspective might inform an ethical view that would have relevance to us.

One of two lines of thought we will examine comes from the work of R. B. Braithwaite, who knew Wittgenstein at Cambridge from the early 1930s. He specialised in mathematics, game theory and the philosophy of science, spending his career on these areas of study at Cambridge where he became a professor. He developed a response to the problem of religious language in a lecture, 'An Empiricist's View of the Nature of Religious Belief', given in 1955, two years after the publication of *Philosophical Investigations*, the earlier ideas of which he would have known from the mid-1930s. His lecture shows the appropriation of Wittgenstein's ideas of meaning being prior to truth, and of meaning being given through use. The lecture was published and has subsequently been widely anthologised.

The other line of thought comes from D.Z. Phillips (1934-2006), who studied at Swansea and Oxford, and later taught at the University College of North Wales, before moving to Swansea University where he late became a professor. He was also the Danforth Professor of Philosophy of Religion at the Claremont Graduate University in California. Phillips wrote extensively on

Wittgenstein's later philosophy, applying the language game theory to Christian understanding in particular.

We will review Braithwaite first. In his lecture, he explores the nature of religious belief by putting the focus on language as the medium by means of which beliefs come to expression and then applying the ideas of Wittgenstein on meaning via use from a consideration of the role of intention. He approaches the issue of religious language by affirming that he does not intend to consider ethical or religious language as language to be categorised as cognitivist, or as language to be analysed on a framework of literal or factual truth. Nor is he keen to agree with the logical positivists that ethical language is purely emotive, that is simply an expression of raw feeling. Rather, Braithwaite proposes a non-cognitivist view where the question of truth is thus subordinate to the question of meaning, and, following the later Wittgenstein, the view presented is that the meaning of language is expressed via the user, and the usage determines the meaning.

Braithwaite states that 'the meaning of any statement... will be taken as being given by the way it is used.'[128] Braithwaite explains that his view is 'conative' not 'emotive'.[129] By 'conative' he means that his view will be related to the intentions expressed in the language – the intention, the will to act in a certain way, is the indicator of meaning. Whilst feeling is a key aspect of moral assertions and all that follows from them, Braithwaite does not think it is the most significant aspect. The key thing is the 'intention to perform the action.' Braithwaite then affirms that 'the primary use of a moral assertion is that of expressing the intention of the asserter to act in a particular sort of way specified by the action.'

---

[128] Braithwaite in Santoni (1968) p. 333
[129] Braithwaite in Santoni (1968) p. 334

As an illustration, following Braithwaite's exposition, if we consider a utilitarian's assertion of acting well to maximise happiness we know that what this means is that this utilitarian is intending to act so as to bring about the greatest happiness to the greater number. Considering the assertion in this way is, Braithwaite argues, helpful, as it gives us something that the emotivist could not provide, namely, a way of explaining how the user could think that he had reason to make the assertion – or that he has a reason for the action, thus it wasn't just emotive. The reason for the action to the user is that he intends to do it so as to maximise happiness, all other things being equal. Turning to religious language and to assertions made in that context, Braithwaite thinks that is clear from the vast literature that exists on religious and theological matters that religious language has to a good deal to do with emotion and feelings, such as the feeling of harmony between the self and the universe. But he thinks that for religious people the language of faith is about more than just feeling. It is a common feature of religious self-understanding that a person's commitment will be demonstrated through action. Therefore, Braithwaite says that 'the intention of a Christian to follow a Christian way of life is not only the criterion for the sincerity of his assertions of Christianity; it is the criterion for the meaningfulness of his assertions.'[130]

Braithwaite then considers an objection: if we take a moral assertion, such as the proposal that "I am going to act so as to tell the truth and not be a liar", the resolution to so act presupposes that I know what it is to lie and what it is to tell the truth. It is not problematic to set out the empirical facts concerning these alternative modes of action. But what about religious assertions? How are we to know the worth of the policies specified by the religions to which

---

[130] Braithwaite in Santoni (1968) p. 336

we affirm allegiance? This is an issue, of course, for example, for the logical positivists who consider that the legitimacy of both metaphysical and theological utterances has been wholly eroded. Braithwaite's solution to this difficulty is in effect to promote a coherence view of truth: he thinks that the assertions of a distinctive religion are a part of a larger body of assertions that collectively constitutes the religious system in question. The particular assertions are therefore to be 'taken by the asserter as implicitly specifying a particular way of life.' Braithwaite thinks that the matter is analogous to what happens in science:

'We understand scientific hypotheses, and the terms that occur in them, by virtue of the relation of the whole system of hypotheses to empirically observable facts; and it is the whole system of hypotheses, not one hypothesis in isolation, that is tested for its truth value against experience. So there are good precedents, in the empirical way of thinking, for considering a system of religious assertions as a whole, and for examining the way in which the whole system is used.'[131]

Braithwaite then puts focus on the sense in which religious assertions have a moral function – as in 'specifying a particular way of life'. To deny this, he argues, would require the mediation of a moral assertion between the assertion of the religious view and the intention to follow the policy of action in question. However, the intention-to-act concept of moral and religious assertions requires no other reason to explain why a religious person acts morally. This view of religious assertions 'is the only view which connects them to ways of life without requiring an additional premiss.'

Braithwaite thinks it is clear that within Christianity the assertion that 'God is love' – *agape*, as in I John 4: 7 – is

---

[131] Braithwaite in Santoni (1968) p. 337

the epitome of Christian assertions and that it connects directly to the intention 'to follow an agapeistic way of life.' Braithwaite then explains how empirical testing can be applied to interrogate the asserter of such a view to see whether other consistent and coherent principles are expressing the systematic view of the religion as typically understood. And we would observe the actions of the asserter to examine the extent to which they were consistent with the assertions made as statements of intent. Here again the maxim of 'actions speaking louder than words' fits the case.

We thus come to the most commonly cited passage from Braithwaite:

'the primary use of religious assertions is to announce allegiance to a set of moral principles: without such allegiance there is no "true religion".'[132]

Braithwaite adds that the religious commitment is a 'state of the will' – emphasising the conative nature of his view as mentioned earlier. Braithwaite anticipates the criticism that he has reduced religious to moral assertions, and he is keen to argue that this is not his purpose. He suggests that there are distinctive empirical features of religious as opposed to moral assertions; religious assertions are a part of a system – moral assertions might not be; religious assertions are not abstract – they are related to concrete examples, such as Christian teachings, parables and so on in the case of the assertion of Christian commitment. And religious assertions imply an implicit as well as an explicit aspect; there is a concern for the inner life of the asserter, for reflection, as well as for the active side:

'The conversion involved in accepting a religion is a conversion, not only of the will, but of the heart.

---

[132] Braithwaite in Santoni (1968) p. p. 338

Christianity requires not only that you should behave towards your neighbour as if you loved him as yourself; it requires that you should love him as yourself. And though I have no doubt that the Christian concept of agape refers partly to external behaviour - the agapeistic behaviour for which there are external criteria - yet being filled with agape includes more than behaving agapeistically externally: it also includes an agapeistic frame of mind.'[133]

Braithwaite thus thinks we can empirically distinguish religious from moral assertions. But this raises another question: *How do we distinguish particular religions?*

Braithwaite thinks that each religious system is characterised by its own particular stories or sets of stories, and he says that for the Christian the intention to follow the agapeistic way of life is associated with thinking of particular sets of stories. In this sense, we might say, the assertions of the Christian are a form of the 'imitation of Christ.' Braithwaite thinks that there will be variations of types of Christian assertion, but that they will all be empirically testable. By the same methods, we can identify and measure other religious traditions. Braithwaite's Wittgensteinian allegiances come through again when he argues that on the view he has developed it is not necessary 'for the asserter of a religious view to believe in the truth of the story involved in the assertion; what is necessary is that the story should be entertained in thought, i.e. that the statement of the story should be understood as having a meaning.'[134] The meaning is more vital than the truth and what Braithwaite sees is that religious stories have a psychological and inspirational force that can shape and direct action:

---

[133] Braithwaite in Santoni (1968) p. 339
[134] Braithwaite in Santoni (1968) p. 342

'A religious assertion... is the assertion of an intention to carry out a certain behaviour policy, subsumable under a sufficiently general principle to be a moral one, together with the implicit or explicit statements but not the assertion, of certain stories.'[135]

One major question is raised against Braithwaite: is it accurate and is it legitimate to cast 'religious assertions' into the role of *intentional states of mind and then statements* of an ethical character? Linking the ethical and religious dimensions of life is, of course, consistent with the approach shown by Wittgenstein. A problem is that as a rule, religious people are not only making ethical statements when they express, in devotional or theological terms, statements of faith. Some statements may be referential, relating to the nature of reality, the divine (however conceived) or to the self as a means to the end of obtaining a clearer insight. Braithwaite's reference to the 'implicit' meaning of religious language is his acknowledgment of this aspect – but is it sufficient? A Christian might say that she uses theological and religious language in prayer and other devotions to express faith in God (who is eternal), reality (regarded as Creation) and life (seen as a gift of grace). Our Christian might say that all this language has meaning, but that it has meaning because in or through faith, it is expressing the truth. Braithwaite argues that his is a non-cognitivist view, and here he is being a faithful interpreter of Wittgenstein's somewhat relativistic theories of language-games and forms of life in *Philosophical Investigations*. But if we stick with the case of Christian faith, our Christian might say that Jesus' characteristic teaching was not, as a matter of historical fact, just of an 'agape ethic': it is a lot to do with the tensions between of living with and for, or without and against God. John Hick writes on this that:

---

[135] Braithwaite in Santoni (1968) p. 345

'Jesus was a realist; he pointed to the life in which the neighbour is valued equally with the self as being indicated by the actual nature of the universe. He urged people to live in terms of reality... Whereas the ethic of egoism is ultimately atheistic, Jesus' ethic was radically and consistently theistic. It sets forth the way of life that is appropriate when God, as depicted by Jesus, is wholeheartedly believed to be real.'[136]

If Christian faith assertions make in effect factual claims about reality, it is not adequate to reduce them to non-cognitive terms as Braithwaite does. Another criticism of Braithwaite concerns his assumption that an ethical assertion signals the intention to act in an ethical way. This sounds good in theory, but it can be argued that we do not always find that ethical assertions are universally consistently applied. What people say when they assert ethical intentions is one thing, what they actually do is another, and whether it is ethical and consistent with the intention would surely be a third matter for consideration. This suggests that Braithwaite's application of Wittgenstein lacks precision: by putting a focus on intention rather than on what is expressed in the practical setting of life he may be warping the insights that he has from Wittgenstein for whom the deed, the act, the practice of life, was of the greatest worth.

If we now turn to D. Z. Phillips, he was, in his own view, not as vulnerable to the drift to relativism that some saw as a feature of the later Wittgenstein. Phillips thought that what he termed the 'cool place' of philosophy was attainable. He meant by this that, in the Wittgensteinian sense, philosophy is an activity, of reflective enquiry into ways in which humans respond to, and have discourse over, issues of meaning, purpose, and value in life. This is the primary reality for investigation, and the elucidations

---

[136] Hick (1990) pp. 95-96

of the situations and styles of human life and speech goes a step further than purely Wittgensteinian problem-solving over issues of meaning in language. Phillips' view was that philosophical reflection had an abiding concern with basic questions about reality. Phillips thus asks rhetorically how philosophy can:

'give an account of reality which shows that it is necessary to go beyond simply noting differences between various modes of discourse, without invoking a common measure of "the real" or assuming that all modes of discourse have a common subject, namely, Reality?'[137]

One of Phillip's most famous studies considers the tensions in Christian faith between immortality and eternal life, *Death and Immortality* (1971). A key point is that it is a common view within orthodox Christianity that immortality is the promise the faithful have as the mode of life after death. There is no doubt at all that this view is, as a matter of fact, a Christian belief and teaching. There is, arising from such beliefs, a mass of philosophical debate about the nature of the soul, the meaning of immortality and the cognitive status of such propositions on every side of the debate. Phillips, applying Wittgenstein, thinks such debates are mistaking the rules of the real language game that is truly relevant to the issues. The problem is that these terms are used if they denoted something substantive, something essentially real and true. Phillips does not think religious concepts have that kind of status anyway. If we look at the mode of discourse in the key narratives in the New Testament, Phillip's point is that debate about the immortality of the soul is not a topic we find in the characteristic teachings of Jesus. What we find there is a focus on 'eternal life' as a way of living within what we might call 'this life'.

---

[137] Phillips (1999) *Philosophy's Cool Place* Ithaca: Cornell University Press, 11.

We can consider examples of this. In Luke 10: 25[138] a lawyer is portrayed as asking what he must do 'to inherit eternal life?' In Mark 10: 17 a rich man asks the same question of Jesus. If we look hard at the answers the gospel writers present Jesus as giving, we find that to the lawyer, Jesus affirms that he must follow the teaching of the law; in summary 'You shall love the Lord your God with all your heart, and with all your soul, and with all your strength and with all your mind; and your neighbour as yourself.' In Luke's narrative, the lawyer asks a supplementary question, "Who is my neighbour?", and this gives Luke the opportunity to unleash the parable of the Good Samaritan (Luke 10: 25-37). When that is told, Jesus asks the lawyer (who has asked, 'What must I do to inherit eternal life?' and 'Who is my neighbour?'), 'Who was neighbour to the man who fell into the hands of the robbers?', he turns the lawyer's question around: this re-orientates the direction of enquiry. The lawyer replies 'The one who showed him mercy.' According to Luke, Jesus' reply is 'Go and do likewise.' Note, 'Go and *do* likewise.' The ethical and religious perspective here is very much akin to the approach taken by Wittgenstein; it is a mode of practice. And the point is that this is the answer to both of the lawyer's questions: 'eternal life' is living a certain way towards others now and for the future. The meaning of the faith is action, or, we may say, deeds, of a particular kind.

The answer to the rich man in Mark 10 is strikingly similar. The man is told to keep the commandments. He says he has kept them '… since my youth.' (Mark 10: 20) Jesus then tells him the one thing he needs to do is to 'sell all that you own, and give the money to the poor.' (Mark 10: 21) The man will then 'have treasure in heaven' and can become a follower of Jesus. Again, the entailment of eternal life is living in a different and qualitatively distinct

---

[138] Biblical quotations come from the New Revised Standard Version.

way now and for the future. In relating this to the approach taken by Phillips, which takes account of modern trends in New Testament study, his insight into Wittgenstein gives rise to the view a language-game of one kind – soul theory and immortality – is mistaken and that another – living eternal life – is correct. Eternal life is not, in Phillips' view, something that comes into play for the faithful after death. Eternal life turns out to be the way the faithful could and should be living now and the language of eternal life is thus expressive of the affirmative commitment to that way of being where faith and hope are real aspects rather than belief in the immortality of souls.

An abiding issue for the use of Wittgenstein's views of 'forms of life', of meaning being prior to use, and of 'language-games', is that, despite what Wittgenstein says about family resemblance, it seems that each language game runs by its own rules and values. This suggests that there are criteria for a given language game or form of life; that of Phillip's view on eternal life, for example, that are distinct from the rules for the language-games (or 'forms of life') of orthodox Catholicism, or of sceptical determinism: each of these will have very distinct takes on souls, immortality and eternal life. The implication of arguing that truth is relative to meaning, and meaning relative to use, is that no overarching criteria for use, meaning or truth can be appealed to. Just as an emotivist in ethics, for whom evaluative statements are pseudo-propositions empty of cognitive content and so purely emotive, can give no cogent reasons for saying, for example, that "Nazi genocide is morally wrong" – they can only firmly announce that they don't like it, so, on the operating system of the later Wittgenstein, it is hard to say of, for example, the Nazi language game, that it was morally and intellectually wrong. Thus, a key problem with this entailment in the work of both Wittgenstein and Phillips is how to live with intellectual security with this degree of relativism. To counter this we need something else, something more secure. We noted that Phillips thinks that philosophy is in a 'cool place'; it is not at all obvious that it will be 'cool' if Wittgenstein's approach and Phillips' application cannot avoid loose relativism. But whether we can find something more secure in Wittgenstein is our next task.

7. Wittgenstein and the Imperatives of Philosophy, Religion, Faith, and Ethics

Having reflected on some applications of Wittgenstein's thought to matters to do with religious language, this chapter puts the focus back on Wittgenstein's own writings and what he has to say on the purpose and role or philosophy, as well as on the nature and role of ethics, and on matters of religion and faith. How these ideas merge and what they might, or might not amount to, is something we will develop over the next three chapters.

One way in which the ideas of Wittgenstein find illustration is through a consideration of his attitude to and comments on religion and on the nature of a commitment to a religious life. His biographer Ray Monk notes in his chapter on the end of Wittgenstein's life that his friend's decision to bury him according to the rites of the Roman Catholic Church was appropriate since Wittgenstein had, 'in a way that is centrally important but difficult to define... lived a devoutly religious life.'[139] In this chapter, we will look into this 'centrally important' but perhaps 'difficult to define' aspect of both Wittgenstein's life and thought.

As we have seen in the previous chapter, Wittgenstein's approach through the period of the later philosophy has a positive implication for religious understanding that has been the subject of development within Christian philosophy of religion. This is, in effect, in two ways. For some, a religion might constitute or involve 'forms of life', and Wittgenstein's perspective encourages the view that the religious dimension is or might be sufficiently well-

---

[139] Monk (1991) p. 580

attested to count as a verifiable context of perceived and shared meanings, within which the use and meaning and thus the validity and in this sense the truth of statements can be determined. This does not permit an uncritical rehabilitation of all modes of past religious understanding, for Wittgenstein's position does not suggest that the self-conscious sense of identity within a religious group can thereby guarantee the validity of the view of things generated by the group. In his understanding, the style of religious insight is, we may suggest, radically non-realist in character and so a distinct challenge to classical realist theology: the life of faith thus has a practical form, it is a way of life and an attitude within life as it is and can be. This approach also faces an acute problem from the perspectives within Wittgenstein's later philosophy, and which in brief is that if we take seriously the methodology of the philosophical approach of linguistic therapy advanced by Wittgenstein in his later work, then the 'religious' or 'Christian' or 'Islamic' or 'Buddhist' language-games or forms of life, will be subordinate to philosophical investigation. This is not something that sits at all well with Wittgenstein, whose view of the nature of religious belief and commitment remains unflinchingly austere, distinct from and a basis for other ways of being.

This is, however, leads to the other view of the religious life that emerges from Wittgenstein's writings and outlook, and can be seen as something that is in his writing and thought throughout his life. We can take an instance of it for the record of another conversation related by Maurice Drury, who writes that Wittgenstein said to him:

'If you and I are to live religious lives it must not just be that we talk a lot about religion, but that in some way our lives are different.'[140]

---

[140] 'Some Notes on Conversations', in Rhees (1984) p. 94

We know from our review of Wittgenstein's career that he considered a monastic vocation on a number of occasions, and it is also evident that he was in no way, shape or form an orthodox religious devotee. Yet for Wittgenstein, living in the right way and in a way that was good and pleasing to God, as he sometimes put it, was, for most his adult life, a vital matter.

Evidence of this concern comes from an early phase of Wittgenstein's career: his period of military service in the First World War. As we said earlier, during this period of life under the constant threat of death, Wittgenstein wrote up notes that in due course provided much of the published text of the *Tractatus*. The *Notebooks 1914-1916* are mostly concerned with the development of quite technical discussions of logical problems but, rather like the *Tractatus*, there are also some which include some poignant reflections on religion, the problem of the meaning of life, and ethics. These start with a question: 'What do I know about God and the purpose of life?' (N 72) It is notable that he links these points together, and his reasoning makes a further connection to the very fundamental question of the point or meaning of life. Wittgenstein then reasons that he cannot doubt that he exists in the world: 'I know that this world exists... I am placed in it like my eye in its visual field.' (N 73) Wittgenstein's point – which is a swift refutation of empirical scepticism, but also a move toward Wittgensteinian solipsism, is that the human subject 'is not a part of the world but a presupposition of its existence' (N 79).

Wittgenstein's thinking in the *Notebooks* is related to his thoughts about the methods by means of which particular factual and logical problems within the world can be solved. But he thinks that we can also raise the more general question of the meaning of life. Here, just as logic has a distinctive and independent character and 'must take care of itself', so in a neatly similar manner, for Wittgenstein, the meaning of the world 'does not lie within it but outside it' (N 73).

Wittgenstein makes some comments about the will which we can enumerate as follows:

i.   'my will penetrates the world'
ii.   'my will is good or evil'
iii. 'I cannot bend the happiness of the world to my will. I am completely powerless'
iv.   'I can only make myself independent of the world – and in a certain sense master it – by renouncing any influence on happenings'
v.   'The world is independent of my will' (N 73 – see also T 6.373).

Wittgenstein here offers an account of what for him was very clear. We might call it the human consciousness of the world, of reality, as being finite and indeterminate. Linked to this is Wittgenstein's sense that an attitude of a disciplined renunciation is the true means of living rightly. That reality is morally neutral is a part of this view, and that the will, the human will, can be 'good or evil' puts Wittgenstein's thinking into a type of ethical voluntarism: a version of the view that intentional human acts freely undertaken constitute the injection of values (positive or negative) into the world. Wittgenstein layers into these reflections more thoughts on the question of the meaning of life, again in relation to the question of God. His simple, direct comments are that 'good and evil are somehow connected to the meaning of the world' and that 'the meaning of life, i.e. the meaning of the world, we can call God.' Thus, 'To pray is to think about the meaning of life' (N 73). From this Wittgenstein sets out the following points:

'To believe in a God means to understand the question about the meaning of life.

To believe in a God means to see that the facts of the world are not the end of the matter.

To believe in God means to see that life has a meaning.' (N 74)

As reality is morally neutral, it means that in every reflective moment we are not actually willing, the will appears to us as 'alien'. But we are dependent on this will as by means of it 'good' (and 'evil') are 'connected to the meaning of the world' and this meaning, we recall, 'can be called God'. Thus 'we are, in a certain sense, dependent, and what we are dependent on we can call God.' We must also note that here Wittgenstein correlates belief or faith in God with the question of the point or meaning of life, and this, if we consider the later notions in his thought of meaning through use and forms of life, explains why Braithwaite, for example, thought that the ethical could be seen in the light of Wittgenstein's outlook, and be the expression of a religious perspective.

Wittgenstein himself is disarmingly self-critical in his writing and remarks that he is 'conscious of the complete unclarity of these sentences' (N 79). But consistent in his writing in this section of the *Notebooks* are the points he makes about the human will. First and foremost, he says, the will is 'the bearer of good and evil' (N 76) and to illustrate he offers an example that runs as follows: let us suppose that a person has lost the use of all of his limbs. He could not, in the usual sense, 'exercise his *will*'. But this person could still think and communicate, and thereby he could freely express his will to others, and so he could 'do good and evil' through others. Such a person is still, 'in the *ethical sense*... the bearer of a *will*' (N 76-77).

Wittgenstein still maintains that like logic, ethics 'must be a condition of the world'. This means that neither logic nor ethics 'treat of the world'. Ethics, as Wittgenstein puts it in the *Notebooks* and the *Tractatus*, 'is transcendental' (N 79 & T 6.421) and in both texts, Wittgenstein holds that ethics and aesthetics are 'as one' (N 77 & T 6.421).

Explaining this, Wittgenstein uses the evocative Latin phrase, *sub specie aeternitatis*, meaning from the standpoint of (or under the aspect of) eternity (N 83 and T 6.45). Thus, the value of a work of art, its aesthetic value, and the ethical worth of 'a good life', are connected by both being considered *sub specie aeternitatis*, which he explains as being 'seen... with the whole logical space' (N 83). It then follows that 'Ethics' as such, '*cannot* be expressed' (N 78). But what is ethical, the good will, has to do with what it is to have a happy, worthwhile and harmonious life. Such a life is describable, for although ethics and the good life are not objects in the world, they are to do with the life of the subject. It is in this sense that Wittgenstein sees ethics as 'transcendental' (N 79). Wittgenstein's approach to values comes with his view that the world as such is 'neither good nor evil', for good and evil can only enter the world 'through the *subject*' (N 79). To be, for Wittgenstein, is not be an object in the world, but to be as a subject and so 'a boundary of the world.'

The writings of Norman Malcolm are relevant to this aspect of Wittgenstein's outlook. As we saw earlier, after his studies Wittgenstein in the late 1930s, Malcolm returned to the USA where he later became a professor of philosophy at Cornell. Wittgenstein visited him the late

1940s and subsequently, Malcolm published a number of books on Wittgenstein's character and thought.[141]

Malcolm relates a story that Wittgenstein told him. In his youth, Wittgenstein said that he had rejected orthodox religious belief, the only kind he had experienced. But when he was about twenty-one (so in about 1911) he had been to the theatre in Vienna. He had seen a play within which a character who had had a very unhappy life and thought he was facing death, had then the thought that nothing in life could now harm him. He was 'independent of fate and circumstances.'[142] Wittgenstein apparently thought that this attitude, which is, we may say, a kind of transcendental immediacy, re-opened a sense of the possibility of living a truly religious life. It is related to the view Wittgenstein took in 1914 that serving in the army and so being confronted with the possibility of death, was good for clearing the mind for honest thought and work. This is a view he communicated to various friends at the time and later, and to be fair, the period of the war did prove an effective time for study, bringing the ideas into shape for what became the *Tractatus*.

Wittgenstein made a further advance in his thinking about religion from reading Tolstoy's *The Gospel In Brief*[143], a book he bought early in his period of military service in the First World War. Apparently, it was the only book remaining in a bookshop he visited, and he bought it on impulse. There is no doubt at all that Tolstoy's re-working of the gospels had a transformative effect on Wittgenstein, as indeed the book has had on many other readers. It seems clear that Wittgenstein read the work over and over and could thereafter quote from it from memory. It is

[141] See for example, Malcolm (1984) and (1997).
[142] Malcolm, (1984)p. 58
[143] Tolstoy (2011) Quotations are from the work's Preface.

worthwhile setting out what it was that Wittgenstein found to his taste in Tolstoy's work.

Tolstoy (1828-1910) had enjoyed enormous success in the 1860s and 1870s with his novels *War and Peace* and *Anna Karenina,* but then he had fallen into a serious personal and spiritual crisis and had rejected Orthodox Christian teaching. By 1879 he was immersed in a deeply scholarly study of the latest writings of New Testament scholarship in relation to the gospels and then produced a sizable draft he entitled 'A Synthesis and Translation of the Four Gospels'. This work included a personal account of Tolstoy's crisis of faith, an account of his studies and their findings, a critique of the false teaching of the Orthodox Church and then the synthesis of the gospels into one coherent view. As it turned out, only the synthesis was published, in 1883, as *The Gospels in Brief.*

In this reworking of the material, Tolstoy, who really had got to grips with the insights given by New Testament study, presented a lucid and humane view of the teaching of Jesus as that which can give 'meaning to life' and fuel a life of faith as 'the strictest, purest, fullest metaphysical and ethical teaching'. Key ideas in Tolstoy's presentation are that the teaching of Jesus entails the message that the kingdom of God is within each person's humanity, that the kingdom comes in and for the 'this day' of the present, and that the life of faith is not one of prayer and devotion, or doctrine, ritual or ecclesiology, but one of simple living in accordance with the will of God in a life of service to others. Wittgenstein was drawn to these ideas, and they would have fused ethical notions with the strictly apophatic view that he developed in the notes he was writing for what in due course became the *Tractatus.*

Another more philosophical influence on Wittgenstein's religious outlook came towards the end of 1914 when he picked up and read a collection of some of Nietzsche's writings that included *The Anti-Christ*[144]. If Wittgenstein read Nietzsche with the same care that he gave to Tolstoy, then he cannot have failed to see that in Nietzsche's work ideas of striking similarity came to expression. Friedrich Nietzsche (1844-1900) wrote *The Anti-Christ* in 1888, the last year before his cataclysmic descent into some kind of dementia which rapidly left him helpless, deranged and increasingly paralysed. The text, in numbered sections as is the norm with Nietzsche's works, (62, in this case) presents a sharp, richly allusive and sustained polemic against Christianity, against doctrine, against religiosity and the like. The work assumes, and to some degree draws on, the views Nietzsche developed in his works of 1886 and 1887 – *Beyond Good and Evil* and *On the Genealogy of Morals*. Amongst the ideas that Wittgenstein could have found support for in Nietzsche is the view that reality is morally neutral as well as for the claim that values come from acts of the will.

Like Tolstoy, in points of detail, Nietzsche affirms Jesus as an exemplary figure.

To illustrate: Nietzsche says that Christianity 'has been up to now man's greatest misfortune.'[145] In one sense this is because the elaboration of doctrines includes that of universal salvation which results in the, for Nietzsche, shattering error of the idea of '*equal* rights for all'.[146] The concept of God is, in Christian doctrine, a 'corruption' as the 'God of the sick' is 'degenerated to the *contradiction of life*, instead of being its transfiguration and eternal *Yes!*'[147] The developed religiosity, doctrine and culture of Christianity distorts a foundational view that Jesus' life

---

[144] See Monk (1991) pp. 121-123
[145] Nietzsche (1990) 51
[146] Nietzsche (1990) 43
[147] Nietzsche (1990) 18

'had been precisely the existence, the fulfilment, the *actuality*', of the 'kingdom'.[148] Nietzsche's highly-charged polemical view is crystalized in the oft-quoted remark that 'in reality there has been only one Christian, and he died on the Cross.'[149] This is, we would now say, an anachronistic remark, since the term 'Christ' is the later Greek variant for the Hebrew title 'Messiah', which meant 'anointed one'. Nietzsche's point thus needs to be revised: Jesus of Nazareth is, in the strongly consensual view of modern New Testament studies, someone who lived and died a Jew; the Greek term 'Christ' is certainly a part of a later developed view evolved in nascent Christianity; Nietzsche is keenly aware of this historical shift, and so he would be better off saying that Jesus, the prophet of the kingdom died on the Cross, and that the developed and arguably distorting figure of the Christ as the redeemer of the world and so on, emerges in the teaching of Paul, and in the gospels later in the first century. Nevertheless, what Nietzsche wanted to say would still apply. His argument was that to be a Christian was not a matter of 'belief', of 'holding something to be true', such as belief in the truth of redemption; it was rather a matter of 'instinct' and 'a doing, above all a *not*-doing of many things, a different *being*'. Jesus' life as a 'free spirit'[150] and as 'the Son of Man'[151] is, Nietzsche suggests, a symbol of an 'eternal' fact of the 'kingdom of God', where the notion of God the Father is not denoting an object or a person but a symbol of 'perfection and eternity', as 'a condition of the heart'. That links to the view, echoing Tolstoy, that it is 'through the *practice* of one's life' a person can feel 'divine' and 'blessed'[152] and the like.

---

[148] Nietzsche (1990) 40
[149] Nietzsche (1990) 39
[150] Nietzsche (1990) 32
[151] Nietzsche (1990) 34
[152] Nietzsche (1990) 33

From Tolstoy and Nietzsche, Wittgenstein seems to have derived the view that it was not a person's beliefs that mattered, but rather that person's outlook, disposition and will: a person's outlook had to do with inner feeling, will and resolve and in the doing of things well, in relation to the self and towards others. Nothing, for Wittgenstein, has more significance in life than this. Reading Tolstoy and Nietzsche would confirm Wittgenstein's rejection of formalised religiosity and of objectivism in theology. In light of this, we can make better sense of the ideas considered earlier on the mystical and the ethical that come towards the end of the *Tractatus*, and the ideas cited on the essence and existence of God. But there are more comments and ideas of a similar character that come in the notes collected and published as *Culture and Value*, where how a person acts is central to the meaning of their religious commitment.

In one of these, Wittgenstein says that as he understands it, 'Christianity says... that sound doctrines are useless.' What matters is that 'you have to change your *life* (Or the *direction* of your life) (CV p. 61). Doctrine is likened to the prescription you get from the doctor and which you then follow: that does not '*seize* you' but the 'passion' of faith has to seize you and turn you around. Wittgenstein seems here to be taking it as read that true Christianity is not grounded in church doctrine but on the ethical challenge in the teaching of Jesus. So right action, we might assume, will come from the right outlook, or faith. Wittgenstein does not, however, say all this in such a direct manner. What he does, is make a number of remarks where he juxtaposes wisdom and faith. Commenting on Kierkegaard, he says 'Wisdom is passionless. By contrast, Kierkegaard calls faith a *passion*' (CV p. 61). Then he says:

'Wisdom is something cold & to that extent foolish. (Faith, on the other hand, a passion)' (CV p. 64).

Wisdom '*conceals* life from you', it is 'like cold, grey ash covering the burning embers.'

In a famous remark Wittgenstein moves on to say this:

'It appears to me as though a religious belief could only be (something like) passionately committing oneself to a system of coordinates. Hence, although it's belief, it is really a way of living, or a way of judging life. Passionately taking up *this* interpretation. And so instructing in a religious belief would have to be portraying, describing that system of reference & at the same time appealing to the conscience. And these together would finally have to result in the one under instruction himself, of his own accord, passionately taking up that system of reference.' (CV p. 73)

In another comment he says:

'The honest religious thinker is like a tightrope walker. It almost looks as if he were walking on nothing but air. His support is the slenderest imaginable. Yet it really is possible to walk on it.' (CV p. 84)

A comment reflecting much of what we have just covered comes in the following passage:

'A proof of God's existence ought really to be something by means of which one could convince oneself that God exists. But I think that *believers* who offered such proofs wanted to analysis & make a case for their 'belief' with their intellect, although they themselves would never have arrived at belief by way of such proofs. "Convincing someone of God's existence" is something you might do

by means of a certain upbringing, shaping his life in such
& such a way.

Life can educate you to 'believing in God'. And
experiences too are what do this but not visions, or other
sense experiences, which show us the 'existence of this
being', but, e.g., sufferings of various sorts. And they do
not show us God as a sense experience does an object, nor
do they give rise to *conjectures* about him. Experiences,
thoughts, — life can force this concept on us.' (CV p. 97)

Here we have, in quite an explicit manner, the view that
our general beliefs are, as a rule, related to objects and
things the reality, nature or existence of which we can
check as through a review of everyday experience. The
classical so-called 'proofs' of the existence of God – such
as the first cause, cosmological, and design variants –
seem to operate in that way. But this suggests, falsely, that
God must be an object amongst the other objects. The
truth of the idea of God's essence guaranteeing his
existence, as in the writings of medieval thinkers like
Anselm and Aquinas, is that 'God' is unique in having
what can be termed 'aseity', that is, infinite self-existence
– which means he does not 'exist' in the material or
objective sense but rather in the sense that he exists and
cannot not-exist. Wittgenstein has the idea, as we have
seen, that 'God's essence is supposed to guarantee his
existence', and as he points out 'what this really means is
that what here is at issue is not the existence of something'
(CV p. 94). By 'something' here, Wittgenstein means
something objective in the world. His positive view is that
those who have faith in God do not, in fact, reach that
condition via such arguments. His idea is that the
experiences that matter in respect of the conviction of the
existence of God come through a certain mode of 'life', by
life being shaped 'in such and such a way'.

Norman Malcolm relates how he knew from conversations with Wittgenstein how much he distrusted the view that arguments could prove God's existence. Malcolm cites another comment from Kierkegaard: 'How can I doubt that Christ exists since I know that he has saved me'. Apparently, Wittgenstein then said 'You see! It isn't a question of proving anything.'[153]

Commenting on Christianity, Wittgenstein says it is 'not a doctrine, not, I mean, a theory about what has happened & will happen to the human soul, but a description of something that takes place in a human life' (CV p. 32). He cites 'recognition of sin' as an event within a person's life, 'despair' and then 'redemption through faith' – as noted above, faith is a mode of experience, a type of passionate commitment: Wittgenstein says that for him real redemption can come via '*certainty*'; not that of 'wisdom, dreams, speculations' but of 'faith'. And this faith is 'faith in what my heart, my soul, needs, not my speculative intellect' (CV p. 38).

These ideas and affirmations point to a religiously minimalistic but operative outlook that is deliberately far from orthodox, but nevertheless clearly religious in character. Wittgenstein is quite consistent through his life in writing along the lines we have been considering, but as Drury points out, his ideas 'changed and deepened'[154]. Drury gives an example, noting that once, near the end of Wittgenstein's life, he reminded him that early in their acquaintance, and this was in 1929-30, Wittgenstein had said 'there was no such subject as "theology"'. Wittgenstein's response was 'That is just the sort of stupid remark I would have made in those days.'

[153] Malcolm (1997) p.19
[154] 'Conversations with Wittgenstein', in Rhees (1984) p. 98

Wittgenstein's general outlook sees every problem, as he also said to Drury, 'from a religious point of view.'[155] This comment is prefaced by the observation, 'I am not a religious man', and in other remarks in conversations with Drury, the sense in which Wittgenstein was and was not 'religious' becomes clear. Wittgenstein rejects any way in which religious or Christian belief can be given 'philosophical justification' or 'proof'.[156] He reasons that the attempt in Catholic thought in particular, to prove God's existence through natural theology would make faith impossible: 'If I thought of God as another being like myself, outside myself, only infinitely more powerful, then I would regard it as my duty to defy him.'[157] Thinking ahead, Wittgenstein speculates about the future shape for religion: it will be 'without the consolation of belonging to a Church', it will be 'without priests and ministers',[158] and it will be 'ascetic', but, adds Wittgenstein, 'I don't mean just going without food and drink.' What we go without, is religion in the institutionalised sense. To live in this ascetic manner, going without organised worship and the like, means, as we found earlier, that 'our manner of life is different.'

---

[155] 'Some notes on Conversations', in Rhees (1984) p. 79
[156] 'Conversations with Wittgenstein', in Rhees (1984) p. 102
[157] 'Conversations with Wittgenstein', in Rhees (1984) p. 108
[158] 'Conversations with Wittgenstein', in Rhees (1984) p. 114

8. Wittgenstein and Philosophy

If we turn to Wittgenstein's actually rather consistent perspective on philosophy, it is worth considering how philosophy has been characterized by some other thinkers as a means to put into context Wittgenstein's views on the point and purpose of philosophy. In the context of this study, it is useful to contrast Wittgenstein with A. N. Whitehead, and with the American thinker Henry David Thoreau. But we can begin with Bertrand Russell.

Here we move back to the world of thought and activity that Wittgenstein joined when he went to Cambridge to meet Bertrand Russell in 1911. In the months before meeting Wittgenstein, Russell, who was also working on the proofs of *Principia Mathematica*, the work he had written with A. N. Whitehead, had taken some time out to write a new book, *The Problems of Philosophy*. This was to serve as an introduction to philosophy to be placed in a new series of books called the Home University Library. The book came out in 1912 and proved a great long-term success, remaining in print to the present as one of the best introductions to philosophy ever written. Priced initially at one shilling, Russell later referred to the book as his 'Shilling Shocker'[159]. Wittgenstein was very critical of the book, not least because he was very suspicious of any attempt to produce a popular introduction to philosophy. Nevertheless, in the book Russell articulates some abiding perspectives that offer memorable characterizations of philosophy.

At the start of the book, for example, he asks rhetorically:

---

[159] See Monk (1997) p. 239

'Is there any knowledge in the world which is so certain that no reasonable man could doubt it?'[160]

This puts the focus of enquiry very firmly into the area of epistemology, the problem and theory of knowledge, which is very much a main interest in the background tradition of British philosophy. Russell then answers his question in a manner that defines the point and purpose of philosophy:

'This question, which at first sight might not seem difficult, is really one of the most difficult that can be asked. When we have realized the obstacles in the way of a straightforward and confident answer, we shall be well launched on the study of philosophy - for philosophy is merely the attempt to answer such ultimate questions, not carelessly or dogmatically, as we do in ordinary life and even in the sciences, but critically, after exploring all that makes such questions puzzling, and after realizing all the vagueness and confusion that underlies our ordinary ideas.'

Here we find philosophy working to sort our puzzles and confusions, particularly those which arise in our more casual, everyday thinking. Towards the end of the book, Russell writes a peroration on the value of philosophy and says that its value lies 'in its very uncertainty'[161], this in contrast to the non-philosophical outlook that goes through life trapped in the certainties of prejudice, common-sense and habit. By opening our minds to questioning, the value of philosophy comes as it enlarges 'our conception of what is possible'[162], enriches 'our intellectual imagination' and reduces the grip of 'dogmatic assurance'.

---

[160] Russell (1998) p. 1
[161] Russell (1998) p. 91
[162] Russell (1998) p. 93

Here Russell articulates a view of philosophy as a method of questioning with the value of fostering an open, imaginative and intellectually curious outlook. By stressing that philosophy is 'uncertain' Russell wants to contrast the point and value of philosophy with both everyday uncritical thinking and with the relative certainties of other academic studies. For all the matters of fine argument between Russell and Wittgenstein, and they certainly had some extreme disagreements in matters of logic, there is a resonance between them in the presentations they make about the character and value of philosophical reflection. We can see this if we look again at some of Wittgenstein's highly characteristic comments on the point, scope, and purpose of philosophy.

As we saw, central to his concern is that the puzzles the philosopher faces arise in connection with language. As a reminder, in the *Tractatus* we have the following:

'Most of the propositions and questions to be found in philosophical works are not false but nonsensical... Most of the propositions and questions of philosophers arise from our failure to understand the logic of our language.' (T 4.003)

And:

'All philosophy is a "critique of language"...' (T 40031)

And again:

'Philosophy aims at the logical clarification of thoughts.

Philosophy is not a body of doctrine but an activity.

A philosophical work consists essentially of elucidations.

Philosophy does not result in "philosophical propositions", but rather in the clarification of propositions.

Without philosophy thoughts are, as it were, cloudy and indistinct; its task is to make them clear and give them sharp boundaries.' (T 4.112)

Here we have remarks orientated around the view to do philosophy and to be a philosopher is above all an *activity* centred on a task of *clarification* of what is expressed in and through language. What we think and what we say, what express or elucidate in propositional form is, via the activity of philosophy, brought into sharper focus. In this mode of understanding, philosophy is not about creating first-order readings of reality or of the nature of things; it about getting things clear, straight and logical.

Since in Wittgenstein's view philosophy is an activity, it is very helpful that in his writings there are many instances of illustration from everyday life of the sort of activity it is. In *The Big Typescript,* there is a sustained section of notes on philosophy. Within this the wrong, and then the preferred approach in philosophy is characterized by the example of someone who is chaotically looking for something in a drawer, messing everything around and of course finding nothing. This how 'most people… engage in philosophical investigation'. Wittgenstein's view is that the right way is to be methodical, examining everything with care and 'in complete peace' (BT 92). That philosophy is an activity that rejects 'false arguments' (BT 87) is never in doubt, but it is still an activity that means that it 'may in no way infringe upon what is really said; in the end it can only describe it' (BT 89). In a phrase reminiscent of the *Tractatus* Wittgenstein observes that 'Philosophy simply sets everything out, and neither explains or deduces anything.'

This descriptive approach, at one remove from 'what is really said', as by, for example, science, sociology or history, is not at all far removed from the characterization we saw in Russell, but both thinkers can be seen as operating very differently from A. N. Whitehead. From 1880 until 1910 Whitehead was based in Cambridge, at Trinity College, where he worked closely with Russell on mathematical philosophy. After a period as a professor at Imperial College, London, in later life, from the mid-1920s, Whitehead was a professor of philosophy at Harvard, and he produced a systematic metaphysical view in his book *Process and Reality*. This book, based on the Gifford Lectures for 1927-28 delivered at the University of Edinburgh, was first published in 1929, the year, it will be recalled, that Wittgenstein returned to Cambridge to resume his own philosophical endeavours.

Whitehead sets out his perspective at the start of his book with his definition of his enterprise as a form of 'speculative philosophy':

'Speculative Philosophy is the endeavour to frame a coherent, logical, necessary system of general ideas in terms of which every element of our experience can be interpreted. By this notion of interpretation I mean that everything of which we are conscious, as enjoyed, perceived, willed, or thought, shall have the character of a particular instance of the general scheme. Thus the philosophical scheme should be coherent, logical, and in respect to its interpretation, applicable and adequate.'[163]

Note here that the aim is a holistic interpretation whereby 'everything of which we are conscious' is seen as 'a particular instance of the general scheme.' The whole enterprise displays confidence that such a general account of reality as a whole is possible. The criteria for success

[163] Whitehead, (1979) p. 3

are that the 'scheme' proves 'coherent', and 'logical' and that its interpretation is 'applicable and adequate'. As the title of the work implies, Whitehead's argument is that *reality* is actually best conceived as a *process*, and by a process, he means one interactive and relational process. Another term he uses for this outlook is the 'Philosophy of Organism'[164], the key idea being that the various elements 'of our experience' can be seen 'in a consistent relation to each other'.

This is, quite obviously, a wholly different orientation for philosophy than that endorsed and exemplified by Wittgenstein. Whereas Wittgenstein sees the philosopher as engaging in a tidying critique of language, Whitehead sets out a 'cosmology'[165] in which 'all particular topics find their interconnections'. In contrast to the tradition that can be traced back to Aristotle, that aims to define things by their substance and qualities, Whitehead prefers, as a more accurate view, the dynamic notion of 'relatedness'[166]. In his estimate, a grave error in the intellectual tradition has been to think that 'being', what is the case, is of greater significance than 'becoming'. For Whitehead, 'the actual world is a process, and... the process is the becoming of actual entities.'[167] Every explanation that tries to characterize reality as static, fixed or distinct is an artificial mode of reductionism that Whitehead dismisses as a form of the 'fallacy of misplaced concreteness.'[168] To counter this in his own work as well as in that of others Whitehead says that, 'in philosophical discussion, the merest hint of dogmatic certainty as to finality of statement is an exhibition of folly.'[169] Although Whitehead makes no

---

[164] Whitehead (1979) p. xi
[165] Whitehead (1979) p. xii
[166] Whitehead (1979) p. xiii
[167] Whitehead (1979) p. 22
[168] Whitehead (1979) p. 7
[169] Whitehead (1979) p. xiv

specific reference to the philosophic outlook of Wittgenstein in his book, he makes an assault on the approach that Wittgenstein took as in the *Tractatus*, arguing that philosophy has been 'misled by the example of mathematics'[170] meaning that the reductive use of logical analysis and the method of calibrating propositions as either true or false in terms of their factual status, is 'largely irrelevant for the pursuit of knowledge.'[171]

All of this a considerable contrast to the more pragmatic approach to philosophical work set out by Wittgenstein. Here we can reflect on a conversation he had with his friend Drury in 1930, when Wittgenstein likens doing philosophy the way he tries to do it, to being business-like:

'My father was a business man, and I am a business man. I want my philosophy to be businesslike, to get something done, to get something settled.'[172]

Wittgenstein says this because Drury had suggested that in his work at that point Wittgenstein had reached 'a resting place.' Rather wonderfully, Drury adds in a footnote that many years later, Wittgenstein recalled this conversation, and then said it was wrong, because he could never stop doing philosophy.[173]

Wittgenstein is fond of down-to-earth descriptions of philosophical activity, particularly when differentiating good from bad philosophy:

'A philosopher who is not taking part in discussion is like a boxer who never goes into the ring'[174]

[170] Whitehead (1979) p. 7
[171] Whitehead (1979) p. 11
[172] 'Conversations with Wittgenstein', in Rhees (1984) p.110
[173] Rhees (1984) p. 219, n.7
[174] 'Conversations with Wittgenstein', in Rhees (1984) p. 117

And:

'A bad philosopher is like a slum landlord. It is my job to put him out of business.'

As a more definite contrast with Whitehead, whose enterprise is, by economic analogy, 'macro', Wittgenstein goes on to centre the philosophic business on the 'micro' problem of language. We recall how in *Philosophical Investigations* Wittgenstein has the luminous remark that:

'Philosophy is a struggle against the bewitchment of our understanding by the resources of our language.' (PI I 109)

In a tighter sense the business of philosophy is characterised as a locational question:

'A philosophical problem has the form: "I don't know my way about."' (PI I 123)[175]

And we also keep in mind this rhetorical question and the answer that comes to it:

'What is your aim in philosophy? - To show the fly the way out of the fly-bottle.' (PI I 309)

In an earlier phase of writing Wittgenstein observes that the philosopher 'strives to find the word that delivers us – that is, the one that finally permits us to grasp what until then had constantly and intangibly weighed on our consciousness' (BT 87). He uses a railway analogy to make the point – 'The railway carriage must be placed on

---

[175] In BT this phrase appears as 'A philosophical problem always has the form: " I simply don't know my way about"' (BT 89)

the tracks exactly, so that it can keep on rolling as it is supposed to.'

Wittgenstein moves on to use a social example to describe philosophical activity: the philosopher does work that consists of 'assembling reminders for a particular purpose' (BT 89) and:

'A philosophical question is similar to one about the constitution of a particular society. – And it's as if a group of people came together without clearly written rules, but with a need for them; indeed also with an instinct that caused them to observe certain rules at their meetings; but this is made difficult by the fact that nothing has been clearly articulated about this, and no arrangement has been made which brings the rules out clearly!'

Wittgenstein then imagines that this society has assumed that one of their number is their president – but this individual has no capacity to lead them. Thus 'we come along and create a clear order: we seat the president at a clearly identifiable spot, seat his secretary next to him a little table of his own, and set the other full members in two rows on both sides of the table'.

Thus, the activity of philosophy is likened to a process of finding order and in getting rules established for effective operations. If we ask what philosophy is for, we are in effect 'asking for a rule'. It will be, to anticipate the notions of meaning being relative to use and so prior to truth, 'a rule according to which I have decided to play'.

Wittgenstein then says that the contrast between philosophical unease and its resolution can be illustrated with another example:

'... it is like the suffering of an ascetic who stands there lifting a heavy ball over his head, amid groans, whom someone sets free by telling him: "Drop it"'.

Philosophical activity, Wittgenstein means, frees us from operating under a 'false system' to which we become committed and for which we suffer and, he thinks, through which we will fail, unless we give it up. Again, the positive activity of the philosopher 'can be compared to opening locks on safes, which are opened by dialling a certain word or number, so that no force can open the door until just this word has been found, and once it has been found, any child can open it.'

In his focus on the language problem Wittgenstein certainly justifies the tribute on his memorial tablet, that his 'new way of philosophizing' aimed to free reason from 'the shackles of language.'[176] This 'micro' task is in stark contrast to Whitehead's bolder 'macro' vision of what can term organic philosophy's speculative project, and it is clearly the case that the philosophic firmament is generous enough to embrace both approaches.

However, it would be a mistake to think that Wittgenstein's notion of philosophy is simply a narrow, technical linguistic one. As we saw in considering the ideas in *Philosophical Investigations*, Wittgenstein sees his approach to philosophy as having a resemblance to anthropology, to the study of the natural history of humans. His writing on philosophy in *The Big Typescript* introduces this line of thought. Humanity is, Wittgenstein remarks 'deeply embedded in philosophical, i.e. grammatical, confusions' (BT 90). But language has developed 'because humans had – and have – the tendency to think in *this way*'. Philosophical activity has to work to 'extricate' and 'regroup' the various associations of

---

[176] See the 'Introduction', above.

language with its attendant 'grammatical confusions' but philosophy can only work with and for those who 'live in an instinctive state of dissatisfaction with language', not with those who following rather different instincts, 'live within *the very* herd that has created this language as its proper expression.' We have an echo of Nietzsche here, with the reference to the herd.

In another illustration of philosophical activity, Wittgenstein likens it to the situation where two people have agreed on a contract which contains a form of words that are easily misunderstood, although there are clear explanations for this form of words. As one of the people has a poor memory and quickly gets confused, he 'runs into difficulties.' But the other person can explain everything clearly and so 'remove the difficulty.' This person is akin to the philosopher.

We can see that in his varied comments and characterisations of philosophy Wittgenstein holds certain strands as central to his view. One is that philosophy is an activity of diagnostic clarification with focus on what, via language, we express as what we think we know, believe and understand and as a corollary of this, it is clear philosophy is not, in contrast to Whitehead, a system-building discipline. This leads to a view that places philosophical activity at a 'meta' or second-order level in relation to other disciplines and in relation to life. This leads on to a second theme which is that this diagnostic activity has a therapeutic benefit: philosophical clarification can solve problems and confusions and so make our life smoother. There is a realism and an anti-perfectionism here, for Wittgenstein does not suggest that philosophy can lead to a life wholly free from anxiety or concern. But the philosopher, if he operates in the modes suggested by Wittgenstein, is like someone, who, coming to a garden that is wild and overgrown, works steadily to cut the grass, trim the hedge, prune back the overgrown plants and remove the weeds. The garden is restored – but how we use it – and how we go on living our lives, is another matter.

Wittgenstein has this analogy in *Culture and Value*:

'… along with the roses a gardener has manure & *sweepings* & *straw* in his garden, but they are distinguished not only by value but above all too by function in the garden.' (CV 67)

Note here that the rose is distinguished by 'value' as well as 'function'. This suggests that we might think Wittgenstein is moving into a mode of naturalism, and that this is a theme we can pursue in connection with his thinking on ethics.

Before we do, however, there is some merit in contrasting Wittgenstein's approach with that of the American transcendentalist, Henry David Thoreau (1817-1862), whose most famous work is *Walden*.

Thoreau spent most of his life in and around the small town of Concord in Massachusetts where his family had a business manufacturing pencils. At various times Thoreau helped with the family firm, worked as a surveyor, ran a school, was an abolitionist, a writer, and lecturer. He studied at Harvard (1833-1837) and worked on a much wider range of courses than was needed for his degree. He studied classical and modern languages as well as courses in history, philosophy, literature, and science. He was a friend of Ralph Waldo Emerson (1803-1882), the key thinker in the movement of thought that became known as American Transcendentalism. Throughout his adult life, Thoreau walked in and around the area of Concord, and he maintained a journal, and so much was written into this in terms of philosophic reflections as well as accounts of the various things he did, that now the collected edition of his journal runs to fourteen volumes.[177] It was from the entries made in the journal that Thoreau abstracted the material for his books, and as mentioned, *Walden* is the most famous of these. The book is named after a lake on the edge of Concord called Walden Pond. Emerson owned a part of the shoreline of the lake and in 1845 he gave Thoreau permission to build a cabin to live in by the lake, in return for which Thoreau was to clear out the overgrown areas thereabouts. Thoreau spent just over two years living at Walden, and whilst he was there he cultivated food and lived in a simple but effective manner, doing his writing and putting together his first book, an account of a river trip he had taken with his brother in 1839. Thoreau began writing *Walden* in 1846 when he still resided by the lake, but he did not complete the text for publication until 1854. The book enjoyed good sales and gradually assumed the status of a classic of American literature and thought.

In *Walden* Thoreau offers the following thoughts on what it is to be a true philosopher:

'To be a philosopher is not merely to have subtle thoughts, nor even to have found a school, but so to love wisdom as to live according to its dictates, a life of simplicity, independence, magnanimity, and trust. It is to solve some of the problems of life, not only theoretically but practically.'[178]

The ideals here have a very close affinity with Wittgenstein's perspectives on philosophy and on the point

---

[177] There is an excellent one-volume edition of Thoreau's Journal: Henry David Thoreau, (2009) *The Journal 1837-1861*, Edited by D Searls, New York Review Books, New York.
[178] Thoreau (2008) p. 15

and purpose of life. Like Wittgenstein, but without anything like the same degree of tension or angst, Thoreau eschews the academic life and follows an independent path. He is focussed on being and doing, on living with passionate engagement, but without a commitment to an ideology or institution. Thoreau is enacting the sort of advice that Wittgenstein gave his students, that they should not move from the study of philosophy into professional or academic philosophy, but rather find an occupation or job within some other sphere of life. Wittgenstein had a nomadic tendency and at times of his life, such as in the 1920s and again after 1945, he lived in a manner akin to Thoreau. But all-round, any study of Thoreau's life and work would suggest that he has acquired a sense of what Wittgenstein later termed 'a system of coordinates' (CV p. 73) that gave a 'way of living… a way of judging life', a way of passionately 'taking up *this* interpretation.' Of course, in contrast with Thoreau, Wittgenstein has a temperament given to an intensity of focus, and to what we termed a 'micro' focus on, at times, quite technical problems, and to insights and innovations that mark out his work as of real distinction. But the point of this comparison with Thoreau is to point to the possibility of an exemplification of an ethical life that is philosophically informed: that is an instance of what Wittgenstein's core teaching is about. And this is, in turn, linked to the idea that the point and value of philosophy is not what is done in the narrow specialisms of academic life: it is to do with how the philosophical imagination percolates through a person's life, disposition and outlook; it is to do with how a person wills and lives – with the deeds a person performs.

9. Perspectives on Ethics

The key issue that we need to put some focus on next is really the approach to ethics that runs through Wittgenstein's work. But to do this without first setting out some sort of context for the discussion of ethics would be to risk reviewing Wittgenstein's ideas in something of a vacuum. To put Wittgenstein's approach to ethics, and what might be made of it, into context, it is as well to move into a reflection on the background pattern of ethical thought, and to cover the main trends that envelope his work in the twentieth century. This will give this study another dimension as providing a kind of introduction to moral philosophy. What we need to look at is the shape of ethical thought that lies behind the traditions into which Wittgenstein moved. His thoughts on ethics emerge in writings that came to bear in the period from 1922, (when the *Tractatus* was published), and then onwards up to the present, as his many posthumous works are still spreading their influence through contemporary thought. Before we consider Wittgenstein's ideas, the broader historical perspective is illuminating and worthy of attention. A further reason for this is that when we come to look in a little more detail at what Wittgenstein says, or implies, about ethics, we may well feel that what he is appealing to, is, in some senses, assuming, aspects of the classical or traditional mode of moral thought.

The background story of the ethical tradition in the West is one with some quite emphatic changes, such as the shift in mind-set from the medieval period, through the Reformation of the sixteenth century and the Enlightenment of the seventeenth and eighteenth centuries, to the perspective of the so-called 'post-modern' world. We will characterise the shift from what can be termed 'moral realism', and explain the key development of thinking from Hume, G. E. Moore and A. J. Ayer, that gives rise to a major trend identified in the twentieth century as a form of pluralistic relativism. This we will see to have been given a significant analysis by the Canadian philosopher Charles Taylor. As a whole, this perspective will provide the intellectual framework against which to explore Wittgenstein's ethical thinking.

To begin with, the background shift we have just mentioned involves a move from a broadly singular, homogeneous culture with a clear religious ethos and a formal authority structure, to a culture rich in diversity and pluralism, with a more relativist secular character, as well as some clear trends towards a revival of religious fundamentalism. The shift entails a change from a commonly held and institutionalised pattern of thought having definitive moral and legal status to a situation of no-less definitive complex interaction and active but often unresolvable debate.

According to the precepts of classical realism and orthodox Christian theology, reality is dualist or two-fold in character, in the sense that the finite, mundane, contingent and particular is informed by, expressive of and essentially dependent upon an infinite, necessary, eternal and sacred domain or being. Reality is seen to have a basis in an objective (though mysterious) ground that provides a structure of authority and command related to values and obligations within the everyday. Here the assumption relating to the authority and purpose of objective value entails that the essential value-structure is absolute and pre-existent. Such values address man in his true, essential or created nature and direct him towards an immortal aspiration, in contrast with the constraints and vicissitudes of finite life.

Such an outlook can be termed 'moral realism', because the view is that there is an objective moral reality that can be known, so some things and some actions are morally good and so 'right'. This is also a form of moral cognitivism, that is to say, it is assumed that it provides knowable moral truths.

Many traditional styles in ethics operate on the basis of some assumed hierarchy or structure that in some way or other is seen as being expressive of a system or domain of values. Classical realism posits a transcendent conceptual realm, which embodies the rule for every instance, the form for all matter, the universals for all particulars, and so on. The just and appropriate, the right and the good, all can be known and delivered in and through the structures of law and reason. Traditional theology embraces much of this in association with a rich mythology of a cosmic tension between good and evil.

In more modern debates, variant lines of ethical thought include deontological approaches in ethics, which place emphasis on obligation and motivation in relation to good acts. In contrast, teleological approaches put the focus on goals; virtue is achieved through the progression towards an inner purpose, ideal, goal or condition. In these systems some versions involve something external to man as the goal and point of morality and as that which determines ethical conduct. Others see the goal of ethical action as intrinsic to fulfilling what it is to be rational and human. But in traditional realist theories the immediate practical sphere of personal and social life is subjected to a theoretical realm accessed through obedience and learning, through obligations or projections in line with rules, policies or procedures. Thus, the operational assumption in the classical, and though much of the modern, intellectual tradition has been that the realm of ideas stands over and above the everyday; the theoretical and abstract is elevated above the practical and applied. In the philosophical tradition, a working assumption has thus been that reflection on theory, on general principles as opposed to practical and individual cases, is the means to the end of gaining true insight into the character of life.

In classical realism, this assumption reflects the view that there are fixed, eternal, universal truths to measure and evaluate contingent particulars. In morality, this is indicative of the general view that the point and purpose of good action are found through abstraction and rational investigation away from the praxis and immediacy of the dynamics of life. The sense of the contrast here can be felt in the connotations of tension between 'facts' and 'values', between 'is' and 'ought', 'appearance' and 'reality', 'existence' and 'essence', 'contingent' and 'necessary', 'particular' and 'universal'. With regard to the 'is/ought' and 'fact/values' distinctions, the implication is of a distinction between the actual and the ideal. The actual is thus less than the ideal that is to come or be attained, typically through some form of world-negating renunciation, and the ethical life is a programme of conversion to turn the 'is' into the 'ought', to affirm the 'ideal' over and against the 'actual'.

Within the traditional perspectives, the 'really real' facts are taken to be expressive of absolute value. Absolute value grounded either in the theoretical realm of pure essences or in the being and will of the creator God. Guided by reason, the truth-value of ethical judgements made in accordance with 'natural law' are not in doubt: real knowledge of ethical truth can be obtained through the prescribed patterns of obedience and training.

But within, and then against this tradition, critical and scientific thought comes into play. Initially, this is with the tradition from the later middle-ages of nominalism, the view which denied that universal terms like 'beauty' or 'truth' were simply names or terms and not words standing or actual entities. Later, it was greatly influenced by the rationalism coming from Descartes. These influences promoted the primacy of the subject as the basis for knowledge and virtue. This had several entailments: truth and virtue were seen to be relative to the evidence and the case as experienced by the subject, the knower; the place for value thus shifts, the implication is that reality is morally neutral and so values are not objective features of the world of experience; rather, they are expressive of individual preferences, personal feelings, and the like. The mediators of tradition no longer dispense truth. Instead, truth is held by within a progressive and critical community of scholarship, and in due course, the individual subject, empowered by the accumulative doctrine of human rights, becomes the arbiter of truth.

Thus, the breakdown of the classical world-view throws open fundamental questions for ethics, questions about the basis or source of value and of the truth-value of ethical judgements. The classical views, whether philosophical or theological, share in broad terms a view of value located in and validated through a transcendent realm or being of truth, meaning and virtue. But this solution falls into doubt as the classical view itself is discredited, as through the empirical and Kantian critiques of the scope of human knowledge and reason.

Here we should again consider specifically the contribution of the philosopher David Hume who, against the realist position in metaphysics and in a major contribution to the assault on the traditional theory of knowledge, makes a clear presentation of the view that factual or descriptive propositions differ in character from propositions in which moral assertions are made.

In his *Treatise of Human Nature* (1739) Hume has the following comment:

'Take any action allowed to be vicious: Wilful murder, for instance. Examine it in all lights and see if you can find that matter of fact, or real existence which you call vice. In which ever way you take it, you find only certain passions, motions, volitions and thoughts. There is no other matter of fact in the case.'[179]

Hume's idea here is that if we take an example of something we agree to be a 'vice', by which he means an aggressive crime that is identified in a system of law, and what he terms 'wilful murder' is his example, his point is that all examinations of the case will result in our simply enumerating a range of feelings; we can note 'passions' and 'volitions' and infer 'thoughts', but all are expressive of the feelings of the speaker: 'tis the object of feeling, not of reason'[180]. There is, Hume thinks, 'no other matter of fact in the case'[181]. He continues to argue that in our language we are used to the 'usual copulations of propositions, *is*, and *is not*', but we are then confused into errors of thought when we find propositions connected by '*ought* or... *ought not*', we are being tricked – for it is not possible 'that this new relation can be a deduction from others, which are entirely different from it.'[182]

The implication noticed by Hume, and reaffirmed throughout the subsequent empiricist tradition, is that although everyday linguistic usages tend to embrace moral claims within the same formulations as are employed in relation to empirical claims, and although such moral claims are presented as having a clear logical relationship

[179] Hume (1978) p. 468
[180] Hume (1978) p. 469
[181] Hume (1978) p. 468
[182] Hume (1978) p. 469

underlying the grammar, it is impossible to derive a particular moral truth with logical necessity from an empirical or factual judgement; and neither can the moral judgement be derived through the type of empirical deduction that might attend a purely empirical judgement. Thus, it is said that 'you can't get an ought from an is': particular moral judgements do not follow of necessity from specific empirical propositions; and moral judgements are, following Hume, simply expressions of feeling, and not rational judgements of any kind.   A classic example would be to say, as a matter of fact, that wars kill innocent people. It is a general fact in legal and ethical systems that killing innocent people is a crime, and something considered wrong. But from these facts, it does not follow with logical necessity that wars are wrong.

We now meet up again with some of the ideas we discussed at the outset of this study. Hume's thinking comes back in a slightly modified way in the twentieth-century formulation of the principle of verification with the logical positivists. Thus, all meaningful statements are those where the degree of truth or error entailed can be known: these fall into one of two basic categories. Either the statement expresses what Hume calls 'relations of ideas'[183], an analytic truth as later writers term it, where something that is true by definition in virtue of the terms employed, but not concerned with any material or empirical state, matter or condition.   'If p then q; q therefore p' would an example of such a truth.   Or, the statement must express 'matters of fact', truths of experience or synthetic empirical claims, arising from experiment and observation. 'There are nineteen lions and four tigers at Longleat' is a statement of this type.

From the logical point of view, an important consequence of this twofold division of meaningful propositions is that

---

[183] See Hume (1975) p. 24f and p. 165

the former type, analytic propositions, express meaning and truth that is legitimately termed necessary. In contrast, the feature of all synthetic propositions is that the meaning and truth is contingent, it can never be more than probable. Here the sense and the truth of a proposition is determined through verification by sense experience, relative to certain and thus limited conditions, and the truth-claim cannot be extended or universalised.

This twofold approach to meaning and truth creates a particular difficulty for traditional ethical claims, for ethical rules are clearly not logical determinations to use specific symbols in a certain way. Ethical reason was traditionally termed 'Practical Philosophy' because of the orientation of morality to the practice of human life. But moral ideas have, as in classical realism, been presented as absolute, necessary and as universal, not as contingent as in the sense of the truths arising from empirical observation and experiment.

We can look at one of the most famous applications of verificationism to ethics in a moment. But as we move towards this, and so as to keep a degree of historical progression to this part of our study, we need to look at another significant input to philosophical reflection on ethics that came in 1903 when, as we noted early on in this study, G. E. Moore published *Principia Ethica*. In many respects, this text modelled the analysis of ethical theories that is now classified as the job of 'meta-ethics'[184]. The book, and the ideas it was seen as promoting, had an abiding influence of the so-called 'Bloomsbury Group' of writers, artists, and intellectuals: it was also a text that thereby contributed to a moral landscape that Wittgenstein

---

[184] To clarify, 'meta-ethics' is the term used in moral philosophy for the philosophical analysis of normative ethical theories (such as natural law or utilitarianism) and the aim is to explore, define and assess the principles and value-terms used within the theory in question.

found uncongenial. It was also a text that Wittgenstein read during his first period of study at Cambridge: he did not like the work, writing to Russell that he disagreed 'with most of it' and that the many bits that were unclear did not get clearer 'by being repeated.'[185]

Moore's arguments in *Principia Ethica* can be characterised as being in part critical and deconstructive, and then, and in the light of the critique, positive. The critical deconstruction comes as Moore develops his now famous revelation of what he calls the 'naturalistic fallacy' found, he thought, in many ethical approaches. Moore says that the aim of his enquiry is to answer the question 'what is good?'[186] In answering this question, Moore suggests that most developed moral theories fail, since they involve the attempt to base moral claims on theological, metaphysical, scientific, or humanitarian theories of reality. Such views may rest on speculation or on more secure factual or experimental premises, but in Moore's view, such premises cannot serve as legitimate grounds for the assertion of a moral view.

Moore is against what we have termed earlier 'moral realism' but he is equally opposed to what he sees as 'naturalism', the view that the good can be known and proved as a part of the world of general experience. The error, the 'naturalistic fallacy'[187], as he sees it, is of defining moral terms like 'good' in non-moral terms, in terms of something arising from the descriptive or speculative theory in question that is said to manifest the good. The classic example would the phenomenon of happiness, as in the teleologically orientated utilitarian approach to define the good as that which produces the

---

[185] Letter to Russell in June 1912, quoted in McGuiness (1988) p. 109
[186] Moore (1965) p. 3
[187] See Moore (1965) p.10ff

'greatest happiness to the greatest number'[188]. The fallacy occurs as we identify 'happiness' as 'good'. Moore's point is that we can't, in our usual discourse, just replace 'good' with 'happy' or 'goodness' with 'happiness'; we simply don't think that 'good' and 'happy' are synonyms. I can say 'it is good to make people happy', but if 'good' means the same as 'happiness', this amounts to saying that 'It is good to make people good' means the same as 'It is happy to make people happy'. Moore would not be alone in thinking this is obviously wrong, yet those such as the utilitarians, with their commitment to the view that, for example, the greatest good is the greatest happiness of the greatest number, commit the 'naturalistic fallacy'!

Moore's argument is sometimes termed the 'open question argument'. He means that if pleasure or happiness *was* good, it would make no sense to ask on a specific occasion whether this or that pleasure or happiness was good. But of course, that is precisely what we do: we do ask, in given circumstances, whether this or that pleasure or happiness *is* good. The implication is that happiness may be good or bad: in reality, whether it is 'good' or 'bad' is an open question, and again, to assume the identity of happiness and good is to commit the naturalistic fallacy.

Any definitive perspective of the nature or form of the good is said to fall into this error. But Moore, as mentioned, does not just offer a critique, he also has a positive theory to offer. For Moore, the good remains distinctive as a unique and distinctive but 'non-natural' quality: the good is a simple, unanalysable property that cannot be defined. We might think this close to some of the ideas expressed about ethics by Wittgenstein in the *Tractatus*, that it is 'transcendental' and that is something that can be 'shown' but not 'said'. So, what is Moore's line of thought here?

---

[188] This is the classic formulation used within utilitarianism.

Moore's first point is that the definition of 'good' cannot be thought of as a 'verbal' definition: we can't, he thinks, truly define 'good' by expressing meanings via other words or terms. Of course, we might often do this often in everyday life, committing various forms of the naturalistic fallacy as we do; but Moore thinks we need to be a lot more stringent when conducting a philosophical investigation. Moore then says that:

'If I am asked "What is good?" my answer is that good is good, and that is the end of it. Or if I am asked, "How is good to be defined?" my answer is that it cannot be defined, and that is all I have to say about it.'[189]

Moore then argues that 'propositions about the good are all... synthetic and never analytic'[190] He means that we cannot predefine by reason alone what is 'good': we will find and know what is 'good' in and through our experience. Explaining how this works, Moore says that 'good' is 'a simple notion'. His point is that it is a simple notion' just as 'yellow' is. He means that 'yellow' is a clear, direct and simple notion; it means what it means, and either you know what 'yellow' means or you do not. Moore thinks colour sensations are intuitively known to be natural notions, they are known in a simple and direct manner. 'Good' is similarly a simple notion. As a contrast, 'horse' is a 'complex notion': if we define 'horse' we do so via a number and range of other qualities and attributes; each of these attributes can be reduced, ultimately, to simple notions that cannot be further reduced. However, 'Good' (and 'yellow') just are simple notions.

---

[189] Moore (1965) p. 6
[190] Moore (1965) p. 7

Moore's major idea then is that when we say that something is 'good', we meant by 'good' a quality that we assert to belong to a thing, that is incapable of any further definition, 'in the most important sense of that word… in which a definition states what are the parts which invariably comes a certain whole; and in this sense "good" has no definition because it is simple and has no parts.' [191]

The oddest aspect of what Moore proposes is his view that 'good' must be seen as a non-natural property, a simple and indefinable property. As we saw, Moore likens 'good' to 'yellow'. But 'yellow' is a natural property and of course, Moore thinks it a fallacy to consider 'good' a natural property. Thus, his next move is the claim that we discern or judge the good as a non-natural property via our capacity of moral intuition[192]: 'good' is simple, non-natural and indefinable; by intuition, we are able to discern the good directly, but not in a manner that allows identity with a natural phenomenon. Pleasure, for example, can be something alongside other things where we find goodness; but, against the naturalistic fallacy, pleasure cannot be the sole good. Moore considers that the highest good we can 'know or imagine' are the states of consciousness that we have when, in art or through nature, we consider beauty, or aesthetic value; and equally the values we find in personal relations: so the enjoyment of beautiful things and of personal relationships with our closest and dearest friends are, for Moore, intrinsic goods, goods that we consider to be worth having for their own sake.[193] And from this Moore certainly thinks we can have cognitive truths in our statements about the good.

Moore's approach perhaps seems appealing as it appears to offer a liberal and humane solution to the problem of

---

[191] Moore (1965) p. 9
[192] See for example, Moore (1965) p. 59 & p. 77
[193] See Moore, (1965) pp.188f

defining the good. Suggesting that 'good' is simple, non-natural, indefinable and discerned directly by intuition sounds clean and handy. The implication is that the good will be self-evident and known via intuition. But there is at least one large problem with all appeals to intuition. If the good (a non-natural property) is discerned by moral intuition, akin to the way that we might agree that a wall was blue (a natural property) and not in the least bit red, then it is reasonable to assume that we would find easy agreement about where and what the good was, and where and what it wasn't? The snag is that one person's intuition of 'good' is whatever it is, and there is no guarantee that it will correspond to any, let alone a few, other intuitions. Intuitional views are potentially highly individual and personal, and the danger is that this can lead to a retreat to pure subjectivism. And if individual intuitions are the criteria for discerning the good, what happens when there is disagreement about the good? If my 'intuition' and yours are different, which is right? We are back to an open question without the solution that Moore thought viable. In any case, if Moore thinks that we intuitionally find 'the good' in certain works of art, or in certain patterns of friendship, is he not, with those works or art and those friends, committing another variant of 'the naturalistic fallacy'?

There is also a problem with the idea of the good as a simple, non-natural and indefinable property, and with Moore's so-called open-question argument. Moore wants to say that it always makes sense to ask 'Is this or that happiness good?', or 'Is this or that pleasure good?' This suggests that whilst happiness and pleasure are natural parts of the world of common experience and open to investigation in the same way as natural phenomena are generally, the good is different, and the question of whether a given phenomenon is good is an open question.

This argument is considered invalid. Scruton, for example,[194] argues that questions are 'open' reasonably enough at a preliminary stage of the investigation. When we start to investigate 'Is *this* happiness good?' we are open about whether it is or not, just as we are open about the answer to a complicated mathematical problem at the start of our attempt to solve it. But happiness is linked to human welfare and well-being and so goodness and happiness are linked concepts and phenomena. Moore seeks to push the good into an abstract non-natural domain which, paradoxically, contradicts his other claim that some things or states have intrinsic value.

Moore can also be criticised for failing to distinguish ideas of things, or concepts, from the attributes, predicates or properties a thing may be said to have. To illustrate this, we can consider the concept H2O, and the phenomenon of water. We might ask if water is H2O, which means that the nature of being water cannot be identical to the property of being H2O, or we would be asking 'Is H2O H2O?' The key point is that 'water' and 'H2O' are both concepts that can be used to denote a liquid that is a natural property in the world as we experience it.

Applied to Moore's theory, this argument says that 'goodness', 'happiness', 'beauty' and so on are different concepts we might use for perhaps identical or perhaps different phenomena in the world of natural experience. It would be an error to see them as synonyms, and Moore is right to this extent, but some phenomena are good and beautiful, some are good because they make us happy, and so on. Against Moore, there are open questions, and ones we answer without a retreat to intuition.

Finally, Moore's view would be criticised by modern as well as by classical virtue theorists. Virtue theory, in

Scruton (1994) p. 272f

classical and modern forms[195], suggests that as socio-cultural persons, we acquire the ethical sense to know how to act virtuously, by reflection on experience and reasoning about our circumstances, our relationships, and our feelings: then, as we become more mature ethical operators, the virtue approach says that we acquire stronger ability to have an intuitive sense of whether and how to act ethically. The virtue approach embraces intuition, but it also puts a high tariff on reason, and it is not an approach that favours the view that the good is a non-natural property. All in all, Moore's positive theory does not achieve well.

Following on from Moore, and recalling much that was in Hume, A. J. Ayer's *Language, Truth and Logic*[196] brought a number of matters to a head. Ayer (1910-1989), develops a version of the 'principle of verification', using in particular ideas derived from the philosophers in the so-called 'Vienna Circle' of the 1920s and 30s, with whom Ayer had studied in the early 1930s. We have explained the ideas of this group earlier on, and so here we can focus on how Ayer applied the method of verification to ethics.

With the principle of verification in mind, Ayer suggests that the concepts used in moral judgement are 'pseudo-concepts'. That is to say, he thought that they conveyed nothing that could be calibrated in terms of truth or falsity. It followed that moral propositions were basically emotive, they simply operated as expressions of feeling, and as feelings are what they are, they can't be right, wrong, good or bad. Thus, Ayer maintains that moral propositions are emotive in character and non-cognitive.

---

[195] Modern versions that are worth exploring include those of McIntyre (1981) and Foot (2003)
[196] Ayer (1990) See pp. 171-185 & pp. 104-119

Ayer denies that value statements are controlled by any species of 'absolutism', by which he means some kind of 'intellectual intuition' rather than by empirical observation. This is an attack on Moore, of course. He reasons that value judgements are non-analytic, and that therefore their sense and status should be determined empirically. But when he addresses the question as to whether ethical experience can be verified through sense-experience, he concludes that this cannot be achieved. He shows this in part through a critique of two approaches which seek to translate ethical experience into propositions which can be verified synthetically, namely, subjectivism and utilitarianism.

The subjectivist argues that assertions of value or quality express degrees and states of approval. Thus, I might say that education to the age of eighteen as a working norm is 'good' because I strongly approve of educating everyone to at least the age of eighteen. I approve of it so thus it is a good I affirm, and if a lot of other people similarly affirm that they approve of it then it acquires a greater force as a general good. But Ayer denies that it can mean the same to assert that 'x is good' is equivalent to 'x is approved of', for it is possible that x might be approved of although 'x is wrong' is a possible non-contradictory assertion. A case to contradict the idea that education is good is not, it seems a self-contradiction!

Similarly, utilitarianism (the view that x is good, if it tends to increase the general happiness or pleasure of those concerned), is invalid since it is not contradictory to hold that it is wrong to pursue the actions that would bring about, say, the greatest happiness for the greatest number for the case to hand.

Ayer presses on to his 'emotive' theory of ethics. Moral expressions literally express the instinctive feelings, positive or negative, that the individual has in respect of the thing in question. 'Good' or any positive sounding moral term is a linguistic form of a feel-good sensation. And how you feel is just how you feel: so, as we have said, it is what it is, so it cannot be 'right' or 'wrong', 'true' or 'false'. This why Ayer thinks that ethical propositions are non-cognitive, and thus are ethical concepts 'pseudo-concepts'. Following Hume, Ayer argues that the predication employed in value judgements is actually spurious since no real empirical predicates are actually being defined or denoted in the subject in question:

'The presence of an ethical symbol in a proposition adds nothing to its factual content. Thus if I say to someone, "You acted wrongly in stealing that money," I am not stating anything more than if I had simply said, "You stole that money." In adding that this action is wrong I am not making any further statement about it. I am simply evincing my moral disapproval of it. It is as if I had said, "You stole that money," in a peculiar tone of horror, or written it with the addition of some special exclamation marks. The tone, or the exclamation marks, adds nothing to the literal meaning of the sentence. It merely serves to show that the expression of it is attended by certain feelings in the speaker.' [197]

Ayer does not share Moore's solution, a form of intuitionism, but in much the same way as Moore, he confronts attempts to give definitive true definitions of the good. For all such definitions, Ayer thinks, the question 'Is x good?' could be raised to the end of showing that the definition could be denied without contradiction. Thus, the so-called moral content in a proposition adds nothing to the empirical sense of the proposition. If nothing is said in a given proposition other than 'x is wrong,' then really all that has been said is that 'x is,' for nothing is said

[197] Ayer (1990) p.110

above that, that can be examined for its truth or falsity: the evaluative claims are no more than expressions of approval or disapproval, and for Ayer it thus follows that the role and nature of moral judgements is that they are expressive of our feelings. Thus, there can be no ethical dispute or argument, for there can be no issues of truth or falsity over the expressions of feeling.

Ayer writes with the distinction between normative and descriptive ethical terms in mind. Ethical terms may be used relative to a social code, or to a set of rules or conventions. In this context the use-value of ethical terms or symbols is descriptive and the sense of an ethical or moral judgement can be defined relative to the sociological context or situation. Ayer accepts this, and he affirms that ethical language can function to the end of arousing feelings and stimulating action in the social sphere, and sees that it thus has a persuasive and extensive role. However, Ayer does not think that the descriptive use provides the basic instances of 'normative' ethical language, ethical language that prescribes 'correct' rules for conduct. On Ayer's view, what passes for normative ethical language occurs as individuals express their feelings in the sense of the emotivist theory. In such a mode there may be conventions of use over the terminology, but the terms used denote feelings, thus nothing is defined or described, and the question of ethical truth cannot arise.

On this reading of ethical judgements, the so-called ethical dimension of experience is characterised as either a domain of feeling, of instinctive preference that expresses choice as a matter of bare fact – it simply is what it is – though it may stand as a token of what the subject in question might commend to others – or as a preference that may be registered by reference to its place within the sociologically determined structures of life within which it

215

appears.   But Ayer denies that these characterisations allow scope for a rational ethical philosophy.

Emotivism was, for all the problems that might be raised against it, a very influential trend in the period from the late 1940s onwards. In the UK, as well as in the USA, the link between the emotivist view, and that of liberalism with the development of claims as to what was entailed by the so-called doctrine of human rights, gave rise to a distinctive perspective on life. Within the prevalent outlook that emerged, merit was placed on such themes as being true to oneself, on the view that every person was entitled to their own preferences on how to live and on what to put significance; freedom of thought, speech, and action, subject to not harming or inhibiting the equal right of everyone else to the same equalities, seemed the right way for all. And with this came the value of each and every individual subject to be the arbiter of what was best for that individual.   This, due to the deep influence of emotivism, gave rise to an equalised relativism that meant that no coherent preference for any particular perspective in ethics could easily be given. The upshot was the development of what has been termed by Charles Taylor, the 'malaise of modernity'.[198] In a presentation first given as a series of radio lectures in Canada, the three aspects of this 'malaise' were said to be individualism, instrumental reason, and the loss of freedom. This analysis is worth exploring.

By *individualism,* Taylor means the view that to be genuine in human terms, and wholly fulfilled, one must be a sovereign individual, a person who operates sufficient unto themselves. He takes the view that in modernity we have a much-enhanced defence of individual human rights, of liberal values that support individual freedom of

---

[198] This phrase was used as the title for the first edition of the book *The Ethics of Authenticity* by Charles Taylor.

thought and expression, and freedom of conscience and action, with the legal defence of the autonomy of the individual against the past, traditional view that the good life would be one of obedience to a controlling power, whether political or sacred.

Taylor argues that problems can be identified with individualism: our sense of meaning and value in the wider sense truly comes, he suggests, via our participation in the social orders of life, with reference to values and norms that have cultural and historical depth. In contrast, individualism involves a dislocation from a structured and determined life, but by the same token, this means a dislocation from the world of values that such participation gives. There is a double loss here. Taylor argues that 'the rituals and norms of society had more than merely instrumental significance.'[199] He means those rituals and norms were not simply a means to the end of individualism What has been lost, he says, is the 'heroic dimension' of life, meaning the sense of a higher point and purpose to life that makes life worth living and dying for.

The problem of the modern focus on individualism is that it promotes a heightened disposition for individual self-absorption, so that our lives become, and here Taylor deploys a favourite image, 'flattened and narrowed'[200] in that they are 'poorer in meaning, and less concerned with others or society.' This he says, perhaps having seen *Star Wars*, is the 'dark side' of individualism.

Taylor next considers what he calls the 'primacy of instrumental reason'[201] in the modern setting, meaning by 'primacy' that it is something of massive influence, and by 'instrumental reason' he means 'the kind of rationality we

---

[199] Taylor (1991) p. 3
[200] Taylor (1991) p. 4
[201] Taylor (1991) p. 5

draw on when we calculate the most economic application of the means to a given end.' If we operate on the assumption that the most cost-effective solution to a problem is good, then we are using instrumental reason. This kind of approach might often be identified with the utilitarian style in ethics, which is instrumental, consequentialist and so subordinates the means to the end. Taylor argues that for the developing secular mind-set of modernity, the influence of instrumental reason means that there is a loss of the sense of obligation to higher orders; the test of the worth of actions becomes ends that are self-related, personal and achieved by the most cost-effective means. Within economic activity, maximising ends via the minimal means is the recipe for success. But Taylor suggests that we now all know that this attitude gives rise to an exploitative attitude to both labour and to the environment – both of which become means to the end of the product or project. Thus, whereas reason ought to allow humanity to rise above narrow outlooks or prejudices, as in the ideal of the rational enlightenment, the instrumental form of reason sets up a prejudice to the efficient.

The culture of instrumental reason also entails a fixation with the development of the 'new' or 'better' – here the concept of planned obsolescence lurks in the background. In modern times the scale and pace of technological innovation has been very rapid, and since Taylor wrote in the early 1990s the '.com' generation has seen dramatic instances of change on this model, up to and including the Android vs iPhone conflicts of 2014. But innovative change becomes an end in itself and this leads, in medicine, for example, to the neglect of care for the patient as a whole, as a person in their own right; instead, the patient is seen as 'the locus of a technical problem.'[202] Taylor thinks that the dominant role of technology in our

---

[202] Taylor (1991) p. 6

lives contributes to the 'narrowing and flattening' of life, noted earlier as a feature of individualism. An example is how, in modern industrial production, the commodities produced for sale are, in general, not made to last: this can be compared with the traditional model of artisanship, where products were crafted and had lasting value. Another example Taylor gives concerns the various technologies that make heating the home a matter of flicking a switch, as opposed to the traditional activity of pioneer times (a haunting allusion for a Canadian) where the whole family would be engaged in the business of collecting firewood, cutting and stacking it, and in building and maintaining fires. The ideas that Taylor favours include those which, against planned obsolescence, sees human life encompassed by things that endure far longer than the time that was taken to produce them. His argument is that instrumental reason in developed societies gives rise to a cult of management, where decisions are taken for impersonal reasons and for ends dictated by economic motives of profit. Does this mean, as could be argued, that humanity has become subservient to the forces of the market and to the control of the state? If so, the image of 'the iron cage' is perhaps right as the way to characterise the fate of modernity, captive to instrumental and technological operations.[203] (p.7)

As it happens, Taylor thinks these views too pessimistic: we are not, he says, incapable of freely considering 'what ought to be our ends'.[204] He says that our 'degrees of freedom are not zero', meaning that the reality of freedom we have is not an absolute liberality. We can note that here Taylor has a mildly Kantian moment as he links 'freedom' to ends shaped by 'obligation'. What Taylor

[203] Taylor (1991) p. 7. Taylor takes the image of the iron cage from the writings of Max Weber.
[204] Taylor (1991) p. 8

also argues is that a considerable job needs to be done to argue for a reorientation in how we prioritise our actions and values. However, there is still the third 'malaise of modernity', which is termed the *loss* of freedom. This arises from the trends of individualism and instrumental reason. Taylor thinks that the one (individualism) atomises us – it treats humans as individual components thus eroding notions of civic order and social duty – whilst the other (instrumental reason) ensures that are prone to be governed by impersonal forces. This leads to a kind of retreat into inaction. Taylor argues that we prefer separate private lives, to engagement in social and cultural life: we become more and more reliant on central administration and global agencies to distribute and manage the means to the ends of our own satisfaction.

This gives rise to what Taylor calls 'soft despotism'[205], where an 'immense tutelary power' holds sway over all of our affairs and further constrains our motives for action. With individualism atomising life, we are being disabled from the necessary counter, which is to engage via voluntary action in the social, intellectual and cultural affairs of the day. This is a powerful issue of immediate concern, Taylor thinks, for the present and for what he sees as the generation ahead. Twenty or more years on from when Taylor wrote the very low levels of participation in national elections in the UK is perhaps one compelling example of the sort of problem he is concerned with.

The problem, Taylor suggests[206], is that the situation constitutes a form of alienation, a state where humanity is in some respects detached from its true nature or potential. Political liberty as a mode of life and thought by which individuals can achieve control of their own development,

---

[205] Taylor (1991) p. 9
[206] See Taylor (1991) p. 10

is threatened with being overwhelmed by the impersonal forces of instrumentalism and by the misguided ethos of individualism when taken as an end in itself.

In summary, Taylor thinks that individualism, the development of self-discovery as against a background of oppression, has paradoxically led to a loss of meaning, to what can be termed a 'culture of narcissism'; instrumental reason has brought the benefit of advanced science and technology, so criticism of it can seem reactionary and anachronistic, but there is emergent problem of an 'eclipse of ends' and together these two trends bring about a *loss of freedom*.

What we have traced in this chapter is a characterisation of some key features in the development of thinking about ethics from classical realism, to the development of subjectivism and emotivism, via the deconstructive critique offered by G E Moore that came to the problematic suggestion that the good was known by intuition. We have rounded this off with a review of the diagnostic check offered by Charles Taylor, whose proposal is to try to retrieve what he terms an 'ethic of authenticity', by which he means a life, dialogical in character, set within transcending and inescapable horizons of meaning. It is worth setting out what he means here before we return to Wittgenstein.

Taylor's project centres on the idea that humans actually have an aspiration for 'self-fulfilment' and self-development, that involves the principle of being 'true to oneself'.[207] Taylor terms this principle the ideal of 'authenticity'[208], his meaning being that it evokes an ideal of 'what a better or higher mode of life would be'. This amounts to the view that the 'ethic of authenticity' denotes

---

[207] Taylor (1991) p. 15
[208] Taylor (1991) p. 16

the moral ideal of being true to oneself to the end of self-fulfilment. However, if we ask what setting is required for this ideal to be developed, his answer is that we need to appreciate and support the fundamental character of the human condition, which is that is that he considers essential: this is what he terms the '*dialogical* '[209] character of human life.

What Taylor means has echoes of what we have seen in the development of Wittgenstein's more anthropological view of language in *Philosophical Investigations*. What Taylor argues is that humans are born into and grow within a rich and expressive language of art, love, gesture, and culture; we acquire 'languages of expression' by a process of induction through dialogue with others who are prior. It is via 'exchanges with others' that individuals gain the means to be self-developers, and this reveals that there is always a backdrop and point of reference (or 'horizon') of meaning and value for that individualisation, and for the capacity to reason rationally. Taylor's view is that we continue to operate in the tension of dialogue with others, to express, explain, justify and orientation our self-perspectives. Thus, our self-development, our authentication properly understood is always *dialogical*.

Taylor has another line of thinking to develop his emerging view: he maintains that we cannot defend the ethical ideal of authenticity by collapsing 'horizons of significance'. The key reason for this is that the sense of life having value, meaning and worth comes from its having been chosen. And here the implication is that it is chosen from and in relation to what is set by the 'horizon of significance'. This is the core truth of what we mean by self-defining freedom. This freedom 'depends on the understanding that independent of my will, there is

---

[209] Taylor (1991) p. 33

something noble, courageous, and hence significant, in giving shape to my own life.'[210]

Here, with reference to 'something noble, courageous, and... significant', we have a clear substratum of *realism* in Taylor's view, which here resonates with a rather neo-Platonic tone. This is something to bear in mind in considering Taylor's overall position. This 'noble' tradition resonates, as the voice of Western philosophy, not least through the age in which the 'courage to use your own reason' came to the fore, the Enlightenment. This raises an important question as to whether the ethic of authenticity is only viable for those who have moved through such an intellectual and cultural epoch. In other words, can be an ethic of authenticity for the developing world?

What is clear is that Taylor wants to hold to the notion that there are valid 'horizons of significance' which are the true and legitimate means of correlation for the drive for self-creation. Without that backdrop of meaning, the ideal of authenticity is distorted.

In his discussion, Taylor makes a passing reference to J. S. Mill's argument on this theme in *On Liberty* (1859), to Mill's case for individuals to choose for themselves their mode of life. Taylor wants to reaffirm that such choosing is trivial and incoherent if it is validated merely by the act of choice. The ethical ideal of authenticity is again affirmed as deriving its validity from the fact that some choices are better than others, that choices are made from a background horizon of meaning, and that self-defining freedom as an ethical ideal has to be more than a subjective preference; there has to be engagement with others, and this returns us to the dialogical or relational view as outlined earlier. Taylor then has another passing

---

[210] Taylor (1991) p. 39

reference, this time to Nietzsche's project of re-writing the 'table of values'[211] – what Nietzsche termed the business of 'revaluing all values'. This is a valid project in principle, but only, Taylor thinks, if the focus is on redefining values concerning 'important questions'. A purely arbitrary self-creation via choice is of no more worth than choosing what to wear or what to select from the menu at McDonald's! Warming to his theme, Taylor says that self-creation cannot exclude 'history' or 'the bonds of solidarity' – another version of the 'ties of others'. Arbitrary self-choosing is again characterised as that which 'flattens and narrows' the self. Against this, the conditions of significance for authentic selfhood lie beyond the self in a 'background of things that matter.'

Taylor sums up his view:

'Only if I exist in a world in which history, or the demands of nature, or the duties of citizenship, or the needs of my fellow human beings, or the call of God, or something else of this order *matters* crucially, can I define an identity for myself that is not trivial. Authenticity is not the enemy of demands that emanate from beyond the self; it supposes such demands.'[212]

The deeper problem in the emergence of emotivism is what lies behind Taylor's concerns over the rise of subjective relativism, and this worries him as to the viability of retrieving the dialogical authenticity he advocates. The snag that we see here is how a trend can have influence, despite having no credible intellectual value. Emotivism is especially fine in this respect as a mighty endeavour of smoke and mirrors. Emotivism is grounded in the logical positivist's view that a proposition is meaningful if, but only if, it can be verified analytically

[211] Taylor (1991) p. 40
[212] Taylor (1991) pp. 40-41

or empirically. However, it has been widely accepted that the proposition 'a proposition is meaningful if, but only if, it can be verified analytically or empirically' is itself impossible to verify by the principle of verification. The proposition 'a proposition is meaningful if, but only if, it can be verified analytically or empirically' is not true by definition, and if it is empirically true we would establish that through an examination of the totality of propositions. It begs the question to assume the meaningfulness and validity of the principle of verification prior to doing that. In consequence, it is arguable that the emotivist theory of Ayer should be rejected as it is based on a questionable if not meaningless principle of verification. In any case, there is a clear operational problem with emotivism: if two people have different estimates over how they feel about a film or a meal, we may say their difference of feeling trumps anything else in the matter as an explanation of their difference. But in cases of murder, or of genocide, or of the neglect of children, differences of view do not seem to work if a person's sense that these acts are 'wrong' simply is an expression of a feeling of disapproval.

It will be recalled that Wittgenstein did not relish the view of his work in the *Tractatus* taken by the logical positivists of the Vienna Circle, and that one reason for this was their dismissive view of the sections of the *Tractatus* that dealt with ethics and other matters that were 'mystical'. His own comments and thoughts in ethical matters do not ever seem to aligned to emotivism either. In most respects, he seems to favour positions that hark back to something like moral realism, with a few other ingredients mixed in. Now, in the light of the review we have made of themes in the general development of ethics, we need to return to consider in more detail Wittgenstein's ideas on ethics.

10. Wittgenstein and Ethics

In this chapter, we turn back to looking at the question of ethics, in respect of Wittgenstein's thought. When we gave this some attention earlier in this book, we reached the view that Wittgenstein did not really elaborate as much as perhaps his view on ethics would allow. Ethics was something that might be 'shown', but not much, it seemed could be 'said'. This view, from the *Tractatus*, was not in any way akin to the ways in which either Moore or Ayer portrayed morality. From the later philosophy, one might think viable an ethical 'form of life' and 'language game'. But there were strictures against this that seemed inbuilt to Wittgenstein's perspective. Now is the time to see if any style of legitimate elaboration is possible or appropriate. The problems with this include those arising from the limitations that Wittgenstein places on ethics. But in making this study we are noting and following up on something Russell said in the 'Introduction' he wrote for Wittgenstein's *Tractatus*. There he appreciates that Wittgenstein's work places ethics into the domain of the inexpressible and mystical. This is that upon which we should not be able to say anything, according to the *Tractatus*. Yet, says Russell, Wittgenstein still manages 'to say a good deal about what cannot be said', and he is certainly 'capable of conveying his ethical opinions'.[213] What might we say to build on this?

With regard to the *Tractatus*, the ethical sphere is, of course, in one sense what the book is about, but ethics is also amongst those things about which nothing can be said. In the later thought, as the notions of 'forms of life', 'family resemblance' and 'language-games' evolve, scope

---

[213] B Russell, 'Introduction' to *Tractatus Logico-Philosophicus*, T p. xxi

is arguably opened to articulate ways in which an ethical 'form of life' might be framed, with the problem that thereby such 'forms of life' are subordinate to philosophical investigation. In both lines of thought we have some components of an ethical perspective, yet in neither do we an ethical theory. One explanation for this that although Wittgenstein wrote a great deal on a wide range of topics, apart from a 1929 *Lecture on Ethics*, his writings on ethics are mainly condensed and brief remarks, such as are found within the collection *Culture and Value*. As well, we should recall that in his life and in his outlook, Wittgenstein maintained an approach akin to that we discussed in the section concerning his view of religion: the important thing ethically is the way you live, the outlook you have, the focus you have on being true in your dealings with others and with yourself: these are the practical imperatives of Wittgenstein's ethical perspective.

But here we hit another problem. What Wittgenstein often does is write procedurally about the status of ethical propositions, concluding in a lot of his work that nothing can be said. When he does this, he is not writing or providing a substantive ethic but operating more as a meta-ethicist. On the other hand, Wittgenstein often does articulate a moral concern that has an imperative character: his emergent view is that you can do what is good and right, but you can't talk about it or have a theory of it. Or can you?

To explore this, we can turn to the *Lecture on Ethics*[214], which is the single most extended piece that Wittgenstein produced on the topic of ethics. The lecture was given on 17th November 1929 to the Heretics Society at Cambridge, at the invitation of C. K. Ogden to whom Wittgenstein (who hated giving lectures of this sort) perhaps felt a debt

---

[214] *The Lecture on Ethics* is reproduced in PO pp. 36-44. Quotations are from this source.

of gratitude for his work on the *Tractatus*. The argument that the lecture develops shows a considerable allegiance to the ideas of the *Tractatus*, but the sustained focus leaves us in no doubt as to the signal importance of ethics for Wittgenstein. The lecture is not that well known, so we will attend firstly to the line of argument it presents.

Wittgenstein begins by affirming that ethics is 'of general importance' (PO p. 37) and he cites an idea from Moore's *Principia Ethica* to the effect that ethics 'is the general enquiry into what is good' (PO p. 38). Wittgenstein says he will extend this to include notions that would usually be included under the heading of 'Aesthetics' – and here is he also in effect following Moore's thinking in *Principia Ethica* – as earlier in the *Tractatus* – 'Ethics and aesthetics are one and the same' (T 6.43), in that he considers that the enquiry into what we might say about what is 'good' could just as easily be an enquiry into what was 'valuable' or what was 'really important', into the 'meaning of life', into 'what makes life living' or 'the right way of living'. This sounds as if it is a prelude to a 'meaning relative to use' line of thinking, and as we shall see, it is, although Wittgenstein is not yet at the more open stage of his thinking that developed by the time of the *Philosophical Investigations*.

Wittgenstein's next move in the *Lecture* is to point out that from the examples he has given we can see that value terms as such are identical to terms that can be used in other everyday ways. Nevertheless, he thinks that we should see that the use in ethics is distinct from the way that the terms might be used in everyday life. We can, for example, use the term 'good' in relation to this as opposed to that chair, as to a given person's ability in tennis, or to this rather than that cup of tea. Such uses here are factual and so relative to the fact or facts in question. Now Wittgenstein states that these 'relative' uses are in sharp contrast to what is meant when we make an expression of value, for then the uses are 'absolute'.

The differences are shown with firstly, the example of a tennis player who is playing badly but who says, when challenged about it, 'I don't want to play any better' (PO p. 39). That is perhaps understandable but if, we are to imagine, that someone told a lie, and then he was challenged over it, if he then said, 'I don't want to behave any better' this just would not do: one would say of such a person that he '*ought* to want to behave better.' With this emphasis on the term 'ought', which Wittgenstein says expresses 'an absolute judgment of value', we are clearly in the framework of what in moral philosophy generally would be termed a deontological mind-set. That is, a moral theory where obligation in a presupposed inter-personal, social and communal setting is given imperative value so that those acts which are right and good are done for their own sake.

Wittgenstein does not link his remarks in the *Lecture* to this theory, but within the spectrum of ethical theory, we can orientate the view he is developing to one with a deontological entailment. As a mode of deontology, as Wittgenstein expresses it, we also have the sense that judgements of value and obligation are grounded in dynamic states of affairs – in the example given, with a person with whom we are in dialogue.

What Wittgenstein does next in the *Lecture* is to juxtapose the notion of obligation as an 'absolute' judgment of value with the earlier judgments over the chair or the game of tennis, where the judgments of what was 'good' were all 'relative'. Here Wittgenstein means that all 'relative' judgments of value relate of necessity to facts. A 'good' runner is 'good' because for a given distance he is quicker than average for that distance. But 'absolute' judgments of value are by default not 'relative', so they cannot be factual in the sense of 'relative' judgments. Wittgenstein asserts that 'no statement of fact can ever be, or imply, a judgment of absolute value' (PO p. 39).

Here Wittgenstein seems to be making a brief, allusive reference to the facts-values argument in moral philosophy. As we saw in the preceding chapter, this has a history going back to Hume. The gist of the matter is that statements of fact and statements of value appear to work in the same, subject-predicate way: 'This is a heavy book' looks and seems to work in the same way as 'This is a good book'. But Hume's idea was that whereas a statement of fact could be checked and tested by 'experimental reasoning', the value term in a statement like 'This is a good book' is not capable of being shown to be factual. In Hume's view, the term 'good' is no more than an expression of subjective feeling or sentiment. Wittgenstein does not enter into discussion with this problem, but he offers a novel take on it. His argument is that if 'absolute judgments of value' were factual, they would, of course, be 'relative' in the way he has defined it. Thus, they would be equal to all other judgments of fact – all such judgments being equal since all are 'relative' to the factual matters or states of affair in question. Taking the view that is in the *Tractatus*, that '… it is impossible for there to be propositions of ethics' and 'Propositions can express nothing which is higher' (T 6.42). Wittgenstein says in the *Lecture* that all such factual and relative propositions about the world 'stand on the same level' (PO p. 39). Wittgenstein similarly rejects the possibility that 'good and bad' can be subjectively defined as attributes of the mind or of feelings or positive or negative sensation, since any account or description of a state of mind will also be 'a fact which we can describe' and so it as such cannot be either good or bad. Here Wittgenstein is rejecting subjectivism, emotivism, and as we have said, siding much more with the deontological mode in ethics.

Wittgenstein thus comes to the view that harks back to some of the comments about ethics at the start of the *Lecture*. Ethics has reference to a subject matter that is 'intrinsically sublime and above all other subject matters' (PO p. 40). The snag is that our words have ordinary meaning, sense and focus within and for the everyday natural world – whereas ethics (and so ethical propositions) has to do with that which, in the *Lecture*, is 'supernatural' – as in the *Tractatus*, it was 'transcendental':

'It is clear that ethics cannot be put into words.

Ethics is transcendental' (T 6.43).

To emphasise his view on the limitations of the factual and relative domain, Wittgenstein takes as an example the idea of 'the right road'. The idea is that in and for a given route, 'the right road' will be *the* 'right road' for some 'arbitrarily predetermined end.' It will be 'the right road' in relation to and so relative to that end. But what if we had the idea of such and such a road being 'the absolutely right road': this would be the road that all would of necessity have to take – or 'be ashamed for not going.' In the same way, the 'absolute good' would, if it were a matter of fact or a 'describable state of affairs', be that which everyone, regardless of taste or inclination, would feel guilty if they did not bring it about. But such a notion is an illusion, a 'chimera'. 'No state of affairs has, in itself... the coercive power of an absolute judge' (PO p. 40). Wittgenstein means that no factual or describable state constitutes the 'absolute good' – a deliberate challenge to Moore, of course. He then argues (see PO p. 41) there is yet a sense in which the terms used in ethics (and aesthetics) have an expressive value.

He takes two examples to illustrate this. First, the general metaphysical question as in our wondering 'at the existence of the world' and secondly, the sense in which we can feel 'absolutely safe' – a notion we have encountered earlier in considering Wittgenstein's notion of the possibility of religious faith. In the factual and relative sense, both of these phrases are verbal nonsense. The point is, we can rightly wonder at the existence of something if, but only if, we can imagine it not being the case. A dog or a house would be fine in this respect. And being 'absolutely safe' – well I can be absolutely safe from being run over by a car if I am in my study on the first floor. But to be 'absolutely safe whatever...' or to '*wonder at the existence of the world whatever it is*' seems, as a verbal expression, nonsense.

Wittgenstein then makes an apophatic move: he says that this misuse of language 'runs through *all* ethical and religious expressions' (PO p. 42)[215]. On the face of it, such expressions often seem to work as similes. Thus, if we say that a certain person is good or of value we mean it in a way analogous to saying that a given cup of tea was good or that a certain book was of value. Ethical and religious language *seems* to work in this way; but Wittgenstein's argument is that actually, it does not, since there are no 'facts' behind the simile. This means that the statements are literally nonsensical: yet they reflect the 'paradox' that a fact, an experience, 'would seem to have supernatural value' (PO p. 43).

To explain this, Wittgenstein moves from wondering at the existence of the world to considering the concept of miracle. He suggests that we all know that by a miracle we

---

[215] Again, Wittgenstein correlates the religious and ethical.

mean, 'something we have never seen the like of', and suggests, as an example, it would be a miracle in this sense of one of his audience grew the head of a Lion and roared. This would provoke shock and then, all other things being equal, a medical examination. This examination would, of course, give us the facts of the case, and at a stroke, we would lose the sense of miracle. Wittgenstein, against the tradition from Hume that says a miracle is something contrary to the law of nature, where laws of nature allow no exceptions, thinks that this proves that 'the scientific way of looking at a fact is not the way to look at a miracle.' The 'absolute' sense of miracle is akin to the 'absolute' sense of value. Then Wittgenstein says that he wonders 'at the experience of seeing the world as miracle'. This works, he argues, because he is 'shifting the expression of the miraculous from an expression by means of language to the expression by the existence of language' (PO p. 44). This is why we cannot have literal sense, factual and relative sense, for statements concerning absolute value. No descriptive or factual language would ever be adequate for 'what I mean by absolute value': such expressions as we make them are truly nonsensical, but valid as such, since 'their nonsensicality was their very essence.' For this reason, the language of ethics and religion 'runs against the boundaries of language'. Ethics, however, 'springs from the desire to say something about the ultimate meaning of life, the absolute good, the absolute valuable', but in no way can we have an 'ethical science.' We can't add to our knowledge via ethics, but ethics truly 'is a document of a tendency of the human mind which I personally cannot help respecting deeply and would not for my life ridicule it'. With the closing comment of the *Lecture*, Wittgenstein is almost certainly aiming a critique at the logical positivists of the Vienna Circle and at their reduction of morality to emotive feeling[216].

---

[216] See for example, Ayer (1970) pp. 102-114

In his later writings, as evidenced in the various books of collected sayings on certain themes – like *Culture and Value* and *On Certainty* – as well as in the *Philosophical Investigations*, Wittgenstein provides a range of ideas which give a slightly more developed sense of the shape of the ethical perspective that he favours. In *Philosophical Investigations*, as we have seen, the 'question of meaning' is 'prior to' the question of truth and to ask for the meaning, we have to 'ask for the use'. It should be clear that from this we can't have, on Wittgenstein's framework, a basis for a normative ethical theory, certainly not one that operates with some absolute mono-value as its determinative point of reference. But we have a starting point in the focus given on 'practice' when Wittgenstein writes on the right outlook towards religion. As we have seen, his idea of a religious life turns on how 'you change your life', or, he adds, 'the *direction* of your life' (CV p. 61). Faith has to seize you like a 'passion', so that you commit yourself to 'a system of coordinates' (CV p. 73), to 'a way of living, or a way of judging life.' Learning to live this religious and ethical life, this 'interpretation', comes from participation in it, through one's 'passionately taking up that system of reference.' When Wittgenstein considers the matter of how to convince someone 'of God's existence', he says that this 'is something you might do by means of a certain upbringing, shaping his life in such & such a way' (CV p. 97). This is because 'Life can educate you to "believing in God". And *experiences* too…' As to ethics, and for the ethical life, Wittgenstein similarly remarks that 'an ethical training' must precede the 'incomprehensible mystery' (CV p. 93) of an ethical doctrine.

It might be said by orthodox religious believers that Wittgenstein reduces the religious to the ethical. But his consistent view is more that he understands the ethical as the *form of the religious life*, and this consistency harks back to the *Tractatus'* diagnosis of ethics as 'transcendental', something to be *shown not said*, not something that can be 'put into words' (T 6.421). But to return the ideas in his later writings, when he writes on the themes of language-games and the like he has a similar view on *practice* insofar as he says that 'our *acting*, lies at the bottom of the language-game.' (OC 204). The language-game is, as we have seen, socially and culturally grounded: it is a system or network of activity and nuance through the web of 'family resemblance'. Language-games have an organic character, they 'change with time' (OC 256), and we can develop or evolve variant rules as we proceed (see PI 86). If we link this to the ideas just noted, that an upbringing can cultivate a life within an ethical 'system of reference', then if an ethical system of reference, as a mode or 'form of life', will be articulated within the 'form of life', or the 'system of coordinates in question'. The rules or conventions of the system in question will be learned through an 'upbringing', through the emulation of a given way of life. In and for such a life, and as Wittgenstein's own life seems to demonstrate, what is 'good' or 'right' is shown as having a relational meaning relative to the use-setting, the context, of life where, in practice, an outlook or perspective of a certain kind is shown. In the practice of the ethical life what counts is whether, and then how we act and in the sense outlined of cultivating a true sense of the ethical, the reference-range of what is, say, 'good' or 'right', is developed by our life being shaped 'in such & such a way' (CV 97).

Norman Malcolm relates an exchange that intrigued Wittgenstein and epitomised his sense of the ethical. He had been in Wales on a walking holiday (sometime in the 1930s) and was staying at a house, the home of the local preacher. When he first arrived, the hostess, the wife of the preacher, fussed over him, offering him various things – tea, and so on. Then her husband, the preacher, called from another room: 'Do not ask; *give*.' Wittgenstein liked that a lot.[217] Actions, deeds, not words, are what matter and what signify. As he writes 'Language – I want to say – is a refinement, "in the beginning was the deed"' (CV 36), and so it is wholly consistent to say words 'are also deeds' (PI I 546). Malcolm adds another insight, that it was Wittgenstein's habit to say, of anyone who had been kind, generous or honest, 'He is a *human being*.' Wittgenstein's remark that 'The human being is the best picture of the human soul' (CV 56e) is helpful here.

As we discovered earlier, Wittgenstein liked many of the ideas that came from the nineteenth-century Danish philosopher Soren Kierkegaard. Drury reports that Wittgenstein thought of Kierkegaard as a philosopher who introduced 'new categories' and Drury thought that there were a number of lines in *Concluding Unscientific Postscript* that illustrated Wittgenstein's ethical perspective. One of these was:

'Ethically, the highest pathos might be to renounce the brilliant poet-world without saying a word.'[218]

If this is pertinent, so might be another of Kierkegaard's points that recall the discussion we had of D. Z. Phillips and the language-game of 'eternal life':

'Only in the ethical is there immortality and an eternal life'.[219]

---

[217] Malcolm (1984) p. 52
[218] Kierkegaard (2009) pp. 327-328. See Drury, 'Some Notes on Conversations with Wittgenstein', in Rhees, (1984) pp. 88-89
[219] Kierkegaard (1990) p. 128

Drury tells another story of relevance. He told Wittgenstein that a Cambridge friend who had been working on a Ph.D. thesis for a year had given the work up as he had decided that 'he had nothing original to say.' Wittgenstein's reply was that 'For that action alone they should give him the Ph.D. degree.'[220] Resisting doing something that would not be sincere is for Wittgenstein a vital quality of good will.

Malcolm explains that another characteristic phrase used by Wittgenstein was 'Leave the *bloody* thing *alone*.' He used this phrase with mock seriousness whenever something was to his mind correct so that no further adjustment was needed. When staying with Malcolm in America the phrase was used when a button had been sewn back onto his jacket and needed, he thought, no further work. And then, when a toilet flush needed repair, Wittgenstein enjoyed the mechanics of the job to put things right. When it was done, and Malcolm proposed a further tweak, Wittgenstein said, 'Leave the *bloody* thing *alone*.'[221]

The remarks and anecdotes we have considered confirm that while Wittgenstein has no systematic rationale for a structured normative ethic, he has, as Russell thought, an outlook and disposition that is singularly ethical. Malcolm's broken toilet coveys a lot: it was fixed – so nothing more should be done. So, in life, certain actions in certain circumstances are right and good: then nothing else is to be said or done. There is anti-perfectionism here: 'What's ragged should be left ragged' (CV 51) he says. Yet to do the right and good thing is beyond all in worth and value – although that value cannot be said.

---

[220] 'Conversations with Wittgenstein', in Rhees, p. 109
[221] Malcolm, (1984) p. 69

The notion that ethics 'cannot be put into words' strikes a chord in an analogous sense as when, on occasions when musical performers or sportsmen or women are interviewed after a major success and asked how it feels to have achieved so well, they are more or less incapable of saying anything bar some kind of variation along lines of 'I don't have words to express how I feel.' And when, in a more obviously ethical sense, people have acted heroically to save someone from a fire, or car accident, or from some terrorist incident, and they are praised for what they have done, they are usually embarrassed and say something like, 'I just did what was needed', or 'I just did what anyone would have done.' That doing what is good and right is as a deed, beyond words, is perhaps a Wittgensteinian corollary of the maxim that 'words are also deeds' (PI I 546).

The distinctive view Wittgenstein has is that the truly ethical is an act of irreducible significance, just as an unethical act would be of utter and irreducible worthlessness. His notions of what is right, good, decent and honest seem, to put them in a cultural setting, to be conditioned by and expressive of the values of the era of Wittgenstein's earliest phase of reflective maturity, and of the values and manners of everyday life in the various settings of the life he had thereafter. If we factor in the concept that meaning is relative to use (see PI 43), and that the question of meaning is thus prior to the question of truth, then the question remains as to whether we can squeeze into action a sense of the ethical as a 'form of life'. Just as we might learn the use of language, and thereby grasp its meaning and so gauge its truth, so might we learn the rules of use for moral decision-making, for ethical judgement. That the use, meaning, and truth of values, ethical and aesthetic, are acquired as and through practice seems to be the view Wittgenstein consistently suggests. This idea is reminiscent of the virtue approach advocated by Aristotle and also, interestingly, by Wittgenstein's pupil Anscombe,[222] as well as by other notably modern philosophers such as Philippa Foot[223]. But what lies at the heart of Wittgenstein's ethical project is akin to something the writer and philosopher Iris Murdoch once said, that in art, in literature as an example, 'There is always something moral which goes down further than the ideas'[224]. Her point recalls all that Wittgenstein says about the 'transcendental' or 'absolute' nature of ethical value. Such value is, on this view, that which we live toward, but that which lies beyond capture or reduction. And the point that emerges from all that Wittgenstein writes on this, is that if we place the values at the core of ethical dimension of life into any other form or mode, then it is relativized and thereby misrepresented, distorted and diminished. The unfashionable conclusion on this aspect of Wittgenstein's thought is that 'what is important is not the *words* you use or what you think while saying them, so much as the difference they make at different points in your life... *Practice* give words their sense' (CV p. 97).

---

[222] See her 'Modern Moral Philosophy' in *Human Life, Action and Ethics*, (2005) Essays by G E M Anscombe, edited by M Geach and L Gormally, Imprint Academic, pp. 169-194
[223] See Foot (2003)
[224] Iris Murdoch and B. Magee, 'Philosophy and Literature', in Magee (1978) p. 277

11. Conclusions

In the light of all that we have considered a question that we can address here is that of the extent to which an ethic of passionate commitment, as Wittgenstein favours, can be framed in a coherent manner, without drifting into descriptive relativism? In a comment on whether it would be possible to train someone to be ethical, Wittgenstein suggests that you could only teach a doctrine or theory of ethics on the basis of a training in the *activity* of ethics. (See CV p. 93) His developed view, in general, is that the 'question of truth' is left behind in favour of the search for 'sense' (CV p. 3). Given that Wittgenstein consistently places the ethical and the sense of the purpose to life in the domain of the unsayable, it is no surprise that he can say that 'What is Good is Divine too' – and this, he then says, 'sums up my ethics' (CV p. 5). Some parameters emerge to allow a characterisation of this ethic, but perhaps instructively the ideas come from cultural and aesthetic examples:

'… the difference between a good & a poor architect consists in the fact that the poor architect succumbs to every temptation while the good one resists it.'

Here we can assume that, in parallel to the architectural model, ethical goodness involves resisting temptation: and we recall Wittgenstein's lifelong concern with integrity, honesty, and with being true to oneself. In other remarks, Wittgenstein, perhaps reflecting on his experiences of getting his hut built in Norway and building a house for his sister, trades more on links to design and architecture: a thinker, he says, 'is very similar to a draughtsman' who 'wants to represent all the interconnections' (CV 14). Working as a philosopher is said to be like 'work in architecture in many respects' (CV 24). The likeness comes as in both there is a process of 'work on oneself', on one's 'own conception. On how one sees things. (And what one expects of them.)'

Works of art enable us to see 'life itself', to see things 'in the right perspective', meaning as a whole, as 'God's work of art' (CV 6-7). Culture is seen as the expression of 'human value' (CV 9), but of course, cultures change, and given cultures can disappear. This does not mean that values disappear, but that they will be differently expressed. We might say the form of values can alter, but that the content does not. As Wittgenstein sees it, what is expressed is, if it is true value, resistant of temptation and engaged with integrity in and for human life.

Aesthetic considerations again overlap with ethical concerns here, as in the *Lecture on Ethics*. Wittgenstein's writings include many observations on intellectual and artistic life in general, perhaps unsurprising given his Viennese upbringing. In *Culture and Value* there is a remark from 1939 that makes an assault on one modern trend:

'People nowadays think, scientists are there to instruct them, poets, musicians etc. to entertain them. *That the latter have something to teach them*; that never occurs to them. (CV 42)

That poets and musicians might teach us something about the point and purpose of life is Wittgenstein's thought. Drury writes of how Wittgenstein came to see him in his rooms in Cambridge in 1930. Wittgenstein seemed upset, and Drury asked him what was wrong. Wittgenstein said that he had been walking through Cambridge, and had 'passed a bookshop, and in the window were portraits of Russell, Freud and Einstein. A little further on, in a music shop, I saw portraits of Beethoven, Schubert and Chopin. Comparing these portraits I felt intensely the terrible degeneration that had come over the human spirit in only a hundred years.'[225]

Wittgenstein was being characteristically honest when he places composers such as Beethoven, Schubert, and Chopin as instructors with 'something to teach' us. The more modern focus on science and on mathematical thinking as represented by Russell, Frege, and Einstein is, Wittgenstein thinks, a sign of a moral degeneration via a focus on the purely scientific. Here the teaching of the *Tractatus*, that 'event when all possible scientific questions have been answered, the problems of life remain untouched' (T 6.52) may be recalled.

Elsewhere Wittgenstein wrote that all great art 'has primitive human drives as its ground bass', and that all such art contains a 'WILD animal: tamed' (CV 43). Thinking about the house he (mostly) designed for his sister he says it was 'the product of a decidedly sensitive ear, good manners, the expression of great understanding'. A theme, as in within music 'no less than a face, wears an expression' (CV 59) and can communicate new insight. In keeping with these points, Wittgenstein has a remark on philosophy:

'I believe that I summed up where I stand in relation to philosophy when I said: really one should write philosophy only as one *writes a poem.*' (CV p. 28)

He explains that he means by this to convey the temporal nature of philosophical writing, which follows from one not quite being able to do as one wants, just as the poet must sometimes follow his muse.

---

[225] 'Conversations with Wittgenstein' in Rhees (1984) p. 112

We have seen that Wittgenstein's notion is that through language, meaning is derived from use, and use is developed in and through practice, as in the development of the mastery of a technique: we considered briefly the link with the idea in virtue ethics that the acquisition of virtue is something a person develops over time and through the processes of upbringing and relationship with others.

The virtue approach assumes that a process of educative activity, of ethical training, is the way to develop good character, to develop what a good person must have – mastery of the technique of acting as a person of good character or virtue, say. This is based, whether in classical or modern versions of the virtue approach, on the view that for a plant, an insect or a human, there are a range of factors including events, conditions, and activities, that are intrinsically good for the plant or creature in question. There are other factors, including events, conditions, and activities, that are intrinsically bad for the plant or creature. If an acorn is planted in good soil and regularly irrigated, if it is kept free from weeds and grazing animals as it grows, then over time, it will develop to realise its potency to become an oak tree. An acorn planted in rough ground amidst plentiful weeds and with herds of goats close by has little chance of good development. For humans too, the options for nurture, growth, and development could as easily be contrasted. The 'interconnections' and the 'process' of working towards what one expects which is true in art or architecture are, fundamentally, truths about the processes of the art of life.

Wittgenstein's ideas all point to an affinity with this view, but it looks clear that the main reason that Wittgenstein has for not making this link explicit is that he wants to hang on to the notions of the *Tractatus* and the *Lecture on Ethics* that maintain that ethics is 'transcendental' and not a part of the factual world where everything is 'relative'.

Virtue ethics, whether in classical or modern forms, is clearly a form of ethical naturalism. At first glance, this will not appeal to the Wittgenstein of the *Tractatus*. But, as we know from the later writings, Wittgenstein notes that he is dealing with the 'natural history of human beings' (PI I 415). The trouble is, the variety and diversity of language-games and 'forms of life' and the rejection of any general theory leaves the later Wittgenstein open to two problems: one is that the development of his later thought seems to entail an approach that fails to protect the 'transcendental' aspect of ethics; the other is that the descriptive method of the later thought risks a fall into some form of relativism. The suggestion here is that these problems could be countered if Wittgenstein's ethical thinking had a more fruitful integration with virtue ethics.

This would come at some cost to Wittgenstein.

The first modification to Wittgenstein's thought on ethics is over his view that ethical and aesthetic value is 'absolute'. We need to tweak this with the point that, as a matter of fact, ethical judgments (as distinct from *values*) are not abstract or theoretical: they do not happen in a vacuum or in a setting abstracted from that of the 'natural history of human beings.' It is a part of the 'natural history', the personal and social experience of humans, to have experiences of moral dilemmas, and to seek and adopt ethical solutions. If individuals, as a matter of fact, do this, and it is a part of the activity and practice of being human to do this, then it is a part of our 'natural history' and a part of the relative factuality of existence. Here the relativity is to do with setting, circumstance, and judgement, *not* with the *core content* of the *values*. This relativity so-called, is really better termed the particularity of the specific instances and occasions of our lives. The values that we might on this or that given occasion express, invoke or create, are considered contextually; they arise in relations of use. But if we take such matters as telling the truth, keeping a promise, being honest, being true to oneself and avoiding self-deceit – these ethical matters are also trans-situational principles we can learn, practice, adapt and develop 'in a complete lifetime', as Aristotle[226] put it.

Another modification is the sense in which Wittgenstein wanted to hold ethical value to be 'transcendental' and to be irreducible, inexpressible and so on. These latter points are valid, in the sense that the truth of an ethical proposition is not propositional but practical: we might say that it is 'good to tell the truth', or that it is 'right to pay one's dues', but the truths of these propositions is not to be defined out via the logical or empirical status of the propositions. The propositions signal the value of certain actions, certain ways of being, as matters both of existential fact and ongoing principle. This is not so far removed from the idea Wittgenstein suggests of ethics being something you train someone in, which is itself akin to the approach in the virtue tradition. It also means that the motif of 'words' being truly 'deeds' has some weight in this regard, or again to put it in a more colloquial phrase, it is always the case that actions speak louder than words.

However, it is from Nietzsche that another line of modification could be drawn. Like Wittgenstein, Nietzsche had a considerable influence from reading Schopenhauer. Nietzsche's variant on Schopenhauer's theory of the will, was to see the human will as possessing the creative force, the will to affirm, and through that affirmation re-create values. Nothing could be more natural than this, thought Nietzsche, yet insofar as thereby a person goes beyond herself, this value-affirmation offers a form of development and so transcendence for the 'what is' to the

---

[226] Aristotle, (2009) 1098a,

'what might be' that is arguably more plausible than that mooted by Wittgenstein, although as he also uses the notion of goodwill to express key elements in his ethical view, the affinity and development here is not, perhaps, so hard to imagine.

As a final line of thought to bring some redemption to the style of thinking Wittgenstein provides and which does, despite his unwillingness to elaborate it, make a consistent position that fits more with the virtue style as we suggested above. We can recall his view of the religious life having to do with how 'you change your life'; he adds the point that this means 'the *direction* of your life' (CV 61). To this Wittgenstein adds points that a person's faith has to grip them as a 'passion', so that a person is committed to 'a system of coordinates' (CV 73). Wittgenstein means by this commitment to 'a way of living, or a way of judging life.' Learning to live this religious and ethical life, this 'interpretation', comes from participation in it, through one's 'passionately taking up that system of reference.' This commitment to a system or approach to living is markedly ethical in character, as we have seen. It is a way of being and one that makes a difference in the sense of being in contrast to how one might otherwise be, as well as making a qualitative difference to how a person is in relation to others.

A good example of this comes from an incident recorded by Norman Malcolm. He recalls a walk with Wittgenstein by the river in Cambridge. It was the autumn of 1939 and just before the outbreak of war. A newspaper seller's sign had a headline saying something to the effect that the German government had accused the British of attempting to assassinate Hitler. Wittgenstein commented that he would not be surprised 'if it were all true.'[227] Malcolm explains how he disagreed with this view, on the grounds

---

[227] Malcolm (1984) p. 30

that it was against the 'national character' of the British to undertake such a thing as a political assassination. Wittgenstein was very angry at this response. He thought it stupid, and explained that it showed that Malcolm had learned nothing from coming to learn philosophy from Wittgenstein. Malcolm would not accept that he was being stupid, so he and Wittgenstein parted company in tense disagreement. For some time after this Wittgenstein avoided Malcolm and it was only due to learning from another student that Malcolm was ill that they met again and were, to some degree, reconciled. However, when Wittgenstein was in Cambridge in 1944, and Malcolm was back in America, Wittgenstein wrote to him and again took up the matter of the 1939 disagreement. He says that what was on his mind when he referred to learning philosophy was that such study was rather pointless if all it does is 'enable you to talk with some plausibility about some abstruse questions of logic, etc.'. What is better is if the study of philosophy can improve 'your thinking about the important questions of everyday life, if it does not make you more conscientious than any… journalist in the use of DANGEROUS phrases that people use for their own ends.'[228] Wittgenstein concedes that it is very hard to think properly about such notions as 'probability', 'certainty' and 'perception', but then he says that 'it is, if possible, still more difficult to think, or *try* to think, really honestly about your life & other people's lives.'

From this and from the earlier comments on the limits and potential in Wittgenstein's thought for a more developed theory of ethics, it is fair to Wittgenstein to conclude that his aversion to what we are suggesting rests most of all in his aversion to theory. His *Tractatus* aimed at a totalistic theory for language and for thought and thereby all philosophical problems were solved; the *Philosophical Investigations*, and so much of the rest of his later work,

---

[228] Malcolm (1984) p. 35

demonstrates a forceful and consistent rejection of the significance or worth of theory – where 'theory' means a model or explanation for the phenomena in question. However, that Wittgenstein offers reasons for this perspectivism suggests that rational development of what that perspectivism then entails, is not an impractical option. What remains as a more practical but ever more challenging alternative is, as we have just seen, 'to think, or *try* to think, really honestly about your life & other people's lives.'

Finally, we should reflect on the character of Wittgenstein, the person whose thought we have considered in this book. A common view of Wittgenstein emerging from those who knew him at every part of his life is of a person with great intensity of focus and drive. Wittgenstein had a remarkable capacity to work hard on detailed points that emerged only through a singular level of effort. He was argumentative and forceful to the point of dogmatism[229], but often he was gripped by thoughts that were intuitive and certain but as yet undeveloped. He was severe on his friends and students, but equally as hard in reprimanding himself. Throughout his life, Wittgenstein was driven by a passionate concern for what he variously, but repeatedly, called honesty, decency, and truth. He wrote and spoke about these virtues a good deal in his correspondence and in his dealings with friends and students. His intellectual progress and his method of work graphically illustrate his drive and integrity. He worked with great concentration and purity of thought as in the composition of the *Tractatus* – casting it in a formal, logical style as if in deference to rigour and purity. Regarding the *Tractatus* as the solution to the problems of philosophy, Wittgenstein altered the pattern of his life accordingly. He lived free

---

[229] As in the famous incident of Wittgenstein's apparently heated argument with Popper at the Moral Sciences Club in October 1946. See Monk (1991) pp. 494-495

from formal philosophy for a period, its problems having all been solved. But he kept thinking, and later, when doubts arose as to the adequacy of the *Tractatus'* doctrine – it appeared limited and limiting, and a more liberal and humane view of meaning seemed necessary – he fearlessly sought a new approach, one that led to a radical assault on some of the key assumptions of modern philosophy.

Wittgenstein formed close and intense relationships which were characterised by fierce loyalty and honesty. Wittgenstein could be a difficult companion, as he subjected others to the same rigorous standards as he imposed on his own life. He despised superficiality and complacency, regarding such attitudes as sinful, and he could be aggressive and dogmatic in argument and appear to be intolerant and rude. He was also courageous physically and intellectually, kind and sensitive, and through the vicissitudes of his life and times and in consequence of his own nature he experienced considerable anxiety and stress as he sought purity and honesty.

As noted, several times Wittgenstein contemplated a monastic life. In the event, he lived rather more like a wandering friar, living (once he had given away his inheritance) with few possessions, but with a passion and commitment that was religious in character. He exercised considerable influence over some of his students; he had little respect for the nature of academic life and thus he discouraged a number of his students from pursuing such a career, preferring them to work in a shop or factory. Despite this, he created a strong and committed band of disciples and interpreters who edited and translated and published volume after volume of his writings. *Philosophical Investigations* was but the first of these. When it appeared, the contrast with the *Tractatus* seemed stark and the differences between the two texts led to much intellectual debate. As the other works gradually appeared, these, in their turn fuelled an ongoing critical debate within philosophy, and in other disciplines where the later philosophy of Wittgenstein continues to have influence.

Bibliography

Ambrose, A. Ed., (2001) *Wittgenstein's Lectures Cambridge 1932-1935*, Prometheus, New York

Anscombe, G. E. M. (2005) *Human Life, Action and Ethics, Essays by G E M Anscombe*, edited by P. Geach and L. Gormally, Imprint Academic.

Aristotle. (2009) *Nicomachean Ethics*, Oxford World Classics.

Ayer, A. J. (1990) *Language, Logic and Truth*, Penguin, London.

Bacon, F. *The New Organon* pdf from http://www.earlymoderntexts.com/assets/pdfs/bacon1620.pdf

Bouwsma, O. K. (1986) *Wittgenstein: Conversations 1949-51,* edited by J. L. Craft and R. E. Hustwit, Hackett, Indianapolis.

Cater, J. and Lemco, I. (2009) 'Wittgenstein's Combustion Chamber' by J. Cater and I. Lemco, Notes and Records of the Royal Society, (2009) 63 5-104, published online 06/01/09 - rsnr.royalsocietypublishing.org/content/63/1/95

Edwards, J. (1985) *Ethics without Philosophy, Wittgenstein and the Moral Life*, USF, Florida.

Engelmann, P., (1967) *Letters from Ludwig Wittgenstein, with a Memoir*, Translated by F. Furtmüller; edited by B. F. McGuinness, Blackwell, Oxford.

Finch, Le Roy, H. (1982) *Wittgenstein – The Early Philosophy, An Exposition of the 'Tractatus'*, Humanities Press, NJ.

Flowers, F. A. and Ground, I. (2018) *Portraits of Wittgenstein*, Bloomsbury Academic, London.

Foot, P. (2003) *Natural Goodness*, Oxford University Press, Oxford.

Heidegger, M. (1973) *Being and Time*, (Translated by J Macquarrie and E Robinson), Blackwell, Oxford.

Hick, J. (1990) *The Philosophy of Religion*, (*Fourth Edition*), Prentice-Hall, Engelwood Cliffs, NJ.

Honderich, T. (20015) ed., *The Oxford Companion to Philosophy*, Oxford University Press, Oxford.

Hume, D.:

(1975) *Enquiries concerning Human Understanding and the Principles of Morals*, Third Edition; Introduction and analytical index by L. A. Selby-Bigge; revised and with notes by P. H. Nidditch, Clarendon Press, Oxford

(1978) *A Treatise of Human Nature*, Second Edition: Analytical Index by L. A. Selby-Bigge; revised and with notes by P. H. Nidditch Clarendon Press, Oxford.

Janik, A. and Toulmin. S., (1996) *Wittgenstein's Vienna*, Elephant Paperbacks, Chicago.

Kant, Immanuel:

(1907) *Fundamental Principles of the Metaphysic of Ethics*, Translated by T. K. Abbott, Longmans, Green & Co., London.

(1978) *Critique of Pure Reason*, Translated N. Kemp Smith, Macmillan, London.

Kenny, A. (2006) *Wittgenstein*, Revised Edition, Blackwell, Oxford.

Kierkegaard, S. (2009) *Concluding Unscientific Postscript*, Edited and Translated by E Hannay, CUP.

Kimball, R. (2002) 'G. C. Lichtenberg: a "spy on humanity" in The New Criterion, May 2002, online at www.newcriterion.com/issues/2002/5/g-c-lichtenberg-a-ldquospy-on-humanityrdquo

Lee, D. Ed., (1980) *Wittgenstein's Lectures, Cambridge 1930-1932*, Blackwell, Oxford.

Locke, J. (2004) *An Essay Concerning Human Understanding*, Penguin, London.

MacIntyre, A. (1981) *After Virtue*, Duckworth, London.

Magee, B. (1977) *Men of Ideas, Some Creators of Contemporary Philosophy*, BBC 1978

Malcolm, N.:

- (1984) *Ludwig Wittgenstein A Memoir with a biographical sketch by G H von Wright and with Wittgenstein's letters to Malcolm*, Oxford University Press, Oxford.

- (1997) *Wittgenstein: A Religious Point of View*, Edited with a response by P. Winch, Routledge, London.

McGuinness, B.:

- (1979) ed., *Ludwig Wittgenstein and the Vienna Circle: Conversations recorded by Fredrich Waismann*, Blackwell, Oxford.

- (1988) *Wittgenstein: A Life Young Ludwig* (1889-1921), Duckworth, London.

- (2012) ed., *Wittgenstein in Cambridge, Letters and Documents 1911-1951*, Wiley-Blackwell.

G. E. Moore:

(1965) *Principia Ethica*, Cambridge University Press, Cambridge.

(1959) *Philosophical Papers*, London: Allen and Unwin, London.

Nietzsche, F. (1990) *Twilight of the Idols and The Anti-Christ*, Translated by R. J. Hollingdale; introduction by M. Tanner, Penguin, London

Phillips, D. Z. (1999) *Philosophy's Cool Place* Ithaca: Cornell University Press.

Rhees, R. ed., (1984) *Recollections of Wittgenstein*, Oxford University Press.

Pinker, S.:

- (2003) *The Blank Slate*, Penguin, London.

- (2008) *The Stuff of Thought*, Penguin, London.

Popper, K. (1972) Conjectures and Refutations, (Fourth Edition) RKP, London

Russell, B.:

- (1921) *The Analysis of Mind*, Allen & Unwin, London.

- (1959) *My Philosophical Development*, Allen & Unwin, London.

- (1975a) *The Autobiography of Bertrand Russell*, Unwin, London.
- (1975b) *History of Western Philosophy*, Unwin, London.
- (2002a) *The Selected Letters of Bertrand Russell The Public years 1884-1914*, Edited by N. Griffin, Routledge, London.
- (2002b) *The Selected Letters of Bertrand Russell The Private Years 1914-1970*, Edited by N. Griffin, Routledge, London.
- (1992) *Theory of Knowledge The 1913 Manuscript*, Routledge, London.

Santoni, R. E. (Editor) (1968) *Religious Language and the Problem of Religious Knowledge*, Indiana University Press, Bloomington and London.

Scruton, R. (1994) *Modern Philosophy*, Sinclair Stevenson, London.

Stern, D. G. Rogers, B. and Citron, G. (2016) *Wittgenstein Lectures, Cambridge, 1930-1933, From the Notes of G E Moore*, CUP, Cambridge.

Thiselton, A. C. (1980) *The Two Horizons New Testament Hermeneutics and Philosophical Description with Special Reference to Heidegger, Bultmann, Gadamer, and Wittgenstein*, Paternoster Press, Exeter.

Thoreau, Henry David, (2008) *Walden*, Oxford World Classics, Oxford.

Tolstoy, L. (1983) *The Gospels in Brief*, Translated by D. Condren, Harper Collins.

Tillich, P. (1968) *Systematic Theology*, Combine Volume, Nisbet.

Quine, W. (1953) *From a Logical Point of View*, Cambridge, Massachusetts.

Wittgenstein, L.:
- (2003) *The Blue and the Brown Books, Preliminary Studies for the 'Philosophical Investigations*, Edited by R. Rhees, Blackwell, Oxford.

- (1994) *Culture and Value*, Revised Edition, Edited by G. H. von Wright and Heikki Nyman; translated by Peter Winch; text revised by A. Pilcher, Blackwell, Oxford.

- (2004) *Notebooks 1914-1916 2nd Edition* Edited by G. E. M. Anscombe and G. H. von Wright; translated by G. E. M. Anscombe, Blackwell, Oxford.

- (1972) *On Certainty* Edited by G. E. M. Anscombe and G. H. von Wright; translated by D. Paul and G. E. M. Anscombe, Harper and Row, N.Y.

- (1990) *Philosophical Grammar* Edited by R Rhees; translated by A. Kenny, Blackwell, Oxford.

- (1976) *Philosophical Investigations* (2nd edition) Translated by G. E. M. Anscombe, Blackwell, Oxford.

- (1993) *Philosophical Occasions 1912-1951*, Edited by J. Klagge and A. Nordmann, Hackett, Indianapolis.

- (1998) *Philosophical Remarks* Edited by R. Rhees; translated by R. Hargeaves and R. White, Blackwell, Oxford.

- (1971) *Prototractatus – An Early Version of Tractatus Logico-Philosophicus*, ed. B. F. McGuinness, T. Nyberg and G. H. von Wright, Routledge, London.

- (2013) *The Big Typescript: TS 213* Edited and translated by C. Grant Luckhardt and M. A. E. Aue, Wiley-Blackwell, Chichester.

- (1978) *Tractatus Logico-Philosophicus* Translated by D. F. Pears and B. F. McGuiness, RKP, London.

- (2007) *Zettel* Edited by G. E. M. Anscombe and G. H. von Wright; translated by G E M Anscombe, University of California Press, Berkley and L.A.

Whitehead, A. N. (1979) *Process and Reality*, The Free Press/Macmillan NY & London.

von Wright, G. H. (1982) *Wittgenstein*, Blackwell, Oxford.

Wood, A. (1957) *Bertrand Russell, The Passionate Sceptic*, Allen & Unwin, London.

Acknowledgements

I am very grateful for the work of all at New Generation Publishing for their help in getting this book into print. David Walshaw and Sam Rennie were extremely good to deal with and I much appreciate their help and advice. My thanks to Rachael Sergeant for her help with proofreading.

My family has given me great support and understanding over the weeks that I spent working on this book and so my thanks to them. But Moreblessing is the person to whom I owe everything, and so I dedicate this book to her in token of the love and the life we share.

Index

Words and Deeds

Lightning Source UK Ltd.
Milton Keynes UK
UKHW041253040319
338430UK00001B/46/P

9 781789 553727